THE
LONGEST SHOT

THE
LONGEST SHOT

*Jack Fleck, Ben Hogan, and Pro Golf's Greatest Upset
at the 1955 U.S. Open*

NEIL SAGEBIEL

THOMAS DUNNE BOOKS
ST. MARTIN'S PRESS
NEW YORK

THOMAS DUNNE BOOKS.

An imprint of St. Martin's Press.

THE LONGEST SHOT. Copyright © 2012 by Neil Sagebiel. All rights reserved.
Printed in the United States of America. For information, address St. Martin's Press,
175 Fifth Avenue, New York, N.Y. 10010.

www.thomasdunnebooks.com

www.stmartins.com

Cover design by Steve Snider
Cover photograph courtesy of Jack Fleck

Library of Congress Cataloging-in-Publication Data

Sagebiel, Neil.
    The longest shot : Jack Fleck, Ben Hogan, and pro golf's greatest
upset at the 1955 U.S. Open / Neil Sagebiel.
        p. cm.
    ISBN 978-0-312-66184-7 (hardback)
    ISBN 978-1-250-01240-1 (e-book)
    1. U.S. Open (Golf tournament) (1955 : San Francisco, Calif.)   2. Fleck,
Jack.   3. Hogan, Ben, 1912–1997.   4. Golfers—United States.   I. Title.
    GV970.3.U69S35 2012
    796.35266—dc23

                                                              2012007475

First Edition: May 2012

10   9   8   7   6   5   4   3   2   1

For underdogs

CONTENTS

THE
LONGEST SHOT

PROLOGUE

Word spread that there was still one man left out on the golf course who had an outside chance of catching Hogan—the unknown muni pro from Iowa. The longest shot in the field.

—James Dodson

Jack Fleck heard the distant roar of the 6,000 people surrounding the 18th green of the Olympic Club. The small, sloping green was set in a natural amphitheater, a new clubhouse decorated with red-white-and-blue bunting perched high above. The gallery cheered wildly for Ben Hogan, Fleck's idol and the era's greatest golfer, who had just completed his final round of the 1955 U.S. Open. Shooting an even-par 70—his best round of the tournament—Hogan was the tournament leader, 5 shots clear of Sam Snead and Tommy Bolt. By capturing his fifth U.S. Open title, Hogan would rewrite the record books, an exclamation point for an illustrious career.

1

"If I'm lucky enough to win here, I doubt if I will ever play in an important tournament again," said Hogan, who was two months shy of his forty-third birthday when he arrived in San Francisco. "It's just too hard."

Indeed it was. Every step Hogan took was a painful reminder of the near-fatal automobile accident six years earlier that had mangled his legs and permanently hampered his circulation. The Texan had summoned the courage and determination to return to championship golf when his doctors wondered if he would ever walk again. Hogan didn't just walk; he practiced, played, and won. In the five seasons following the accident, Hogan competed in no more than seven tournaments a year, capturing six major championships, more than anyone else.

The Texan's miraculous comeback was one of the greatest in the history of sports. Hogan won the admiration of fellow pros and was revered by fans everywhere. He was a national hero. Hollywood made a movie. In a *Sports Illustrated* feature story that preceded the 1955 U.S. Open, his accomplishments and place in the game were neatly summed up in a four-word title: "The Age of Hogan."

Playing in only his third U.S. Open, Fleck had comparatively modest ambitions. The thirty-three-year-old club pro from Davenport, Iowa, wanted to make it as a full-time player on the PGA Tour. No one knew much about Fleck, much less his ambitions. Although he had played the winter tour on and off since 1946, he entered the 1955 national championship as a virtual unknown. He had earned his spot in the field by squeezing through a U.S. Open sectional qualifier in Chicago. Fleck's best finish in two U.S. Open appearances was a tie for fifty-second at Oakmont in 1953, where Hogan won his record-tying fourth U.S. Open. Fleck won $150. In his first National Open in 1950, Hogan's miracle at Merion, he missed the cut.

On the 18th green at Olympic, a weary Hogan lifted his arms to quiet the crowd's prolonged cheers and applause so his playing partner, Chicago pro Bob Harris, could putt out. Moments later TV commentator Gene Sarazen rushed forward with microphone in hand to congratulate Hogan on winning his record fifth U.S. Open. It was only the third national golf telecast, and NBC had an hour of coverage.

"Ben, would you do everybody a favor and put up five fingers?" Sarazen asked. Hogan began to comply before he fully realized the implication.

"It's not over yet, Gene," he said, a comment Sarazen brushed aside.

Then Hogan turned to Joe Dey, the executive director of the United States Golf Association (USGA). "This is for Golf House," he said, handing Dey his golf ball for an exhibit at the USGA museum. Then he walked slowly up the steep slope toward the locker room.

Not long after, a little before 6:00 P.M. local time, NBC announcer Lindsey Nelson signed off from San Francisco, declaring Ben Hogan as the apparent 1955 U.S. Open champion. Nelson would catch a plane to New York, where he would accept an award the following evening on *The Ed Sullivan Show*. As NBC's coverage concluded at the Olympic Club late that Saturday afternoon, a national television audience believed the aging Hogan had done it again. Sunday's newspaper headlines would surely confirm the black-and-white images that had flickered across their television screens—Ben Hogan had rewritten the record books, surpassing four-time U.S. Open winners Willie Anderson and Bobby Jones. With East Coast deadlines looming, newspapermen scurried to their typewriters in the pressroom to write the Hogan coronation stories everyone expected to read.

However, as the NBC cameras switched off and sportswriters furiously pecked away, several players were still on the golf course. It didn't seem to matter. None of the remaining players had a mathematical chance to catch Hogan, save one. Jack Fleck, who trailed Hogan by 3 strokes as he began his final round, could do it. Maybe—but it was a long maybe.

One reporter calculated Fleck's odds of drawing even with Hogan as 8,000 to 1.

Although there were few leaderboards on the golf course, Fleck had learned of his position as he completed the 13th hole. George Tompkins, a roving marshal who had become a friendly acquaintance during the tournament, informed him that Hogan had completed play with a 287 total. The Iowan trailed by a single shot.

"All you have to do is play safe and get one more birdie," Tompkins said, loud enough for Fleck's playing partner, Gene Littler, to overhear.

"He'll need a few pars, too," added Littler.

Fleck approached the tee box of the par-4 14th hole. A swelling gallery pressed in from all sides. As far as anyone in America knew, including Fleck's wife, Lynn, who had listened to the radio broadcast in Davenport, Ben Hogan would be crowned the 1955 U.S. Open champion. Fleck had not given up, though. He still had 5 holes to play.

PART
I

—1—

MUNI PRO

In March 1955, after a week at home in Iowa to ready his two Davenport municipal courses for the upcoming golf season, Jack Fleck drove 1,300 miles southeast to rejoin the PGA Tour at the $12,500 St. Petersburg Open, the first event of the annual Florida swing.

For Fleck, sunny St. Petersburg wouldn't be just another routine stop on the tournament calendar. It would be a turning point, an unexpected detour in the career of a wannabe tour golf professional who was determined to lift his game as high as his hopes. A long cardboard box bound for Fort Worth, Texas, awaited him in Skip Alexander's pro shop at the Lakewood Country Club. The contents of that box would put his season and golf career on a surprising new path.

Fleck, now thirty-three with a wife and four-year-old son, needed any break he could get to achieve his dream of playing the PGA Tour full-time. Money was scarcer than birdies on the tournament trail, and he had family responsibilities. The pro golf tour was a young man's game—preferably those with a healthy bankroll. Fleck's youth was fading, and his twentieth-place finishes didn't earn him enough money or recognition to escape obscurity.

Fleck arrived on the palm tree–lined streets of St. Petersburg with his tour career riding on every drive, approach, chip, and putt. He needed to become a successful PGA Tour player, someone who could make an adequate living and support his family while playing the full circuit. The unfulfilling alternative was clear: He would return to Iowa for good and settle for the humble life of a hometown pro. The 1950s PGA Tour was unlike today's giant money grab; there was no financial security for marginal or middle-of-the-pack players, especially family men like Fleck.

Jack and Lynn Fleck had made their decision about his golf future before the 1955 season teed off in Los Angeles in January. Fleck would play full-time on the PGA Tour for two seasons while Lynn and Jack's assistant pro ran Davenport's two public golf courses. Not exactly a pact, the arrangement was one of those understandings between husbands and wives. This was Fleck's shot. With his two-year trial period, he would either make it on the tour, or, as Lynn said, "you will get it out of your system."

Maybe so—but it was hard to imagine that Fleck, a golf professional since the age of seventeen, would ever be cured of tournament golf.

·   ·   ·

A native Iowan, Jack Fleck was the head club professional of Davenport's Duck Creek Golf Course and Credit Island Golf Course, a post he had held since 1947. Iowa's third-largest city, Davenport was located 175 miles due west of Chicago on the Mississippi River, which formed the state's eastern border. Overseen by the Davenport Parks and Recreation Department, Duck Creek and Credit Island were Davenport's home of public golf. The greens fee for 18 holes was seventy-five cents, an affordable alternative to the private Davenport Country Club, the golfing playground of the privileged set.

Duck Creek opened in 1927 and was located in a residential neighborhood on Davenport's northeast side, not far from Jack and Lynn Fleck's home on East Street. It was a rolling, tree-lined layout of modest difficulty, playing under 6,000 yards and to a par of 70. There was no driving range. When Fleck gave lessons, he and his pupil would go to a nearby section of the city park. A caddie would tag along to shag the practice golf balls.

Several miles away, Credit Island was a small island in the Mississippi connected to the Iowa shoreline by a paved causeway. Also an 18-hole course, Credit Island featured a large clubhouse and practice field. The course had been invaded by the rising currents of the colossal river many times in its thirty-year history. In the spring of 1951, four years into Fleck's tenure, the course became submerged beneath fifteen feet of water. Credit Island was to flooding what California was to earthquakes.

Like many club pros of his day, Fleck earned his modest income from merchandise sales, golf lessons, and club repairs. The city of Davenport leased the two pro shops to Fleck for a dollar a year but paid him no salary. Similar to Iowa farmers, he lived off the land—his two golf courses. The length of his days at Duck Creek and Credit Island matched those of men toiling in nearby fields, lasting from first light to sundown.

The Davenport muni pro looked nothing like an Iowa farmer, though. While overalls and dungarees were the uniform of the farmer, creased trousers, cotton sweaters, polo shirts, and flat caps were the apparel of the postwar golf professional. One who set an immaculate standard for golf attire was Ben Hogan, the era's greatest golfer and Fleck's secret idol. Hogan looked the part of a golf god.

"The first thing that struck me about Hogan when I saw him the first time in person was his perfect clothes," Tom Weiskopf, a later-generation tour pro, told Hogan biographer James Dodson. "I'd never seen shirts that fit so beautifully on a human being before."

Hogan's "perfect clothes" came in conservative blues and grays. His apparel featured trousers with razor-sharp creases, cardigan sweaters, tailored shirts, and polished leather golf shoes, each shoe with an extra spike for better stability. Hogan's clothing was custom-made. He routinely removed labels, he said, to avoid offending anyone.

"I couldn't take my eyes off him. Nobody ever looked the way Hogan did," Weiskopf said.

Still, there were imitators. Hogan protégé Gardner Dickinson emulated the golf legend in almost every conceivable way, from clothing to golf swing to mannerisms, even puffing away on cigarettes. Hogan smoked Chesterfields, and no one would be a bit surprised if Dickinson did, too.

Fleck didn't smoke. He never had, despite two older brothers who smoked, and despite serving in the U.S. Navy, where cigarettes were as commonplace as salutes. Fleck epitomized wholesomeness. He shunned tobacco, alcohol, and vices in all forms. His mother once told him he would be just like his brothers, smoking and such—a form of reverse psychology, he surmised. Whatever his mother's motivation might have been, he turned out squeaky clean, a straight arrow who had no interest in straying from his heartland values.

Nor did Fleck have Hogan's perfect clothes, but he was blessed with good looks and a slender frame that helped off-the-rack golf shirts and pleated trousers look sharp on him. He stood 6'1½" tall and weighed 164 pounds, a weight he would maintain within a pound or two for the next half century. He favored his father, Louis Fleck, but had the gentle eyes of his mother, Elsie. His eyes were green. His thick brown hair was neatly parted, and his face featured dark, bushy eyebrows, a long nose, dimples, and a strong chin. It was a friendly, handsome face that, in photographs, sometimes had an aw-shucks grin and at other times a broad, gleaming smile. Lynn once gushed that her husband looked like matinee idol Tyrone Power, Hollywood's romantic lead in movies such as *The Mark of Zorro* and *The Black Swan.*

Fleck's movements matched his lanky frame. There was nothing abrupt or jerky about how he carried himself or approached golf. He had the easy, casual way of a man on an afternoon stroll. One golf writer wrote that Fleck "had a loose-jointed walk, his arms and legs flapping about as if with no plan." The Iowa pro remembered being called "slew foot" because his right foot turned out when he walked, the result of a broken leg at age seven when he and his older brothers were horsing around in an empty public swimming pool. Others described him as angular, straight, and Lincolnesque. Fleck possessed a long, fluid golf swing that wrapped around his lean body like a loose belt. He moved with unassuming ease.

Exhibiting social grace, on the other hand, was among Fleck's most enduring life challenges. He had been painfully shy since his schooldays. He would always choose to make a special project with his dependable hands rather than face the terror of an oral presentation to his classmates. "I would build guillotines or whatever illustrated the stories we were studying so I could get credit and not have to get up in front of people," he said.

In his early days as an assistant pro at the Des Moines Golf and Country Club, he preferred the solitude of the club room. He dreaded the encounters with customers in the pro shop. "At first, I was so bashful . . . that I had to talk myself into going into the front golf shop to wait on the members that wanted service."

His strongly held values, combined with his social unease, sometimes worked against him. Fleck was modest, serious, and, at times, stubborn. He was plainspoken and unflinchingly honest, which sometimes rankled others. Sugarcoating was not his style. He did not believe in undertaking special efforts to be popular or endear himself to others. He eschewed the art of politics that was so enmeshed in society.

Instead, Fleck sided with the unvarnished truth as he saw it, even if it occasionally hurt. Because there were few gray areas in his world, he tended to let fewer people in. In many ways, this made the solitary rhythms of life as a golf pro a perfect fit for Fleck, who was, at heart, a loner. He was adept with his hands, wielding a club, swinging it, and sending a golf ball toward a distant target. As in his days as a Davenport schoolboy, he would rather show you what he could do than talk about it.

•   •   •   •

Jack met Lynn when she walked into his pro shop in the summer of 1949. She wanted the pro to repair a golf club. The pro wanted a date. "I talked her into having dinner," he said. "We had many dates that summer and fall." The broken club later earned a permanent spot on the Flecks' mantel.

Originally from Chicago, Lynn Burnsdale was attractive and smart, a real brain, Fleck said. "She could read a book faster than anybody" and was good with numbers like her father, a bookkeeper for two large automobile agencies in Chicago and St. Louis. Fleck had fallen in love with someone who could manage a golf pro shop with great aplomb. Lynn's easy command of administrative tasks and her graceful people skills would later turn Duck Creek and Credit Island into well-honed golf operations.

By the time Fleck left home for the Miami Open in December 1949, he had received the blessing of Lynn's parents to ask for her hand in marriage. The couple married on January 5, 1950, in a Davenport church.

A honeymoon followed in California, which, not coincidentally, hosted events on the PGA winter tour.

Fleck had chased success on the winter tour since 1946. Starting in Florida and traversing the warm winter climes of California, Arizona, Texas, and Louisiana, the winter tour was where club pros tested their skills against the game's best players—Hogan, Sam Snead, Jimmy Demaret, Lloyd Mangrum, and others. If they were able to qualify and had the financial means, they could play in tournaments from December through March. Then they would return to their club pro duties at their home courses for the start of golf season, practicing and playing in local events when time allowed. If club pros played well on the winter tour, they dipped into the modest tournament purses and offset expenses. Most important, they discovered whether their game was ready for the big time, the full PGA Tour that staged events from early spring through Labor Day.

The newlyweds arrived in Lakewood near Long Beach, where Fleck shattered a light fixture while taking a full practice swing in the couple's motel room. "Glass flew everywhere," he said. He painstakingly picked the tiny shards of glass out of the carpet using wet paper towels. It was an omen of sorts.

Fleck's first tournament as a married man was a disappointment. He finished out of the money in the Long Beach Open. The honeymooners packed up and motored across the California desert to Arizona for the Phoenix Open.

Following along at the Phoenix Country Club, Lynn witnessed her husband's lofty tournament golf standards. Fleck shot a respectable 71 in the opening round, but despite sunny weather and solid play, things darkened for the golfer in the second round. He encountered his chief enemy on the golf course—himself.

Actually, Fleck was playing very well on the tight layout lined with tamarack trees and punctuated with elevated, well-bunkered greens. He drilled several laserlike iron shots, including a hole-out with a 9-iron, and was under par for his round as he played the second 9. Headed for another good score, the Iowa pro would be in contention at the tournament's halfway point. He had never won on the winter tour and had just one high finish in his career. It made what happened on the 14th green all the more confounding.

Fleck 3-putted. It was not unusual. It happened to Hogan, Snead, everybody. They missed putts due to a breakdown in technique, a misread, and, often in early tour days, bumpy, inconsistent putting surfaces. This created a certain injustice that has forever existed in the game of golf. A player can maneuver a small dimpled ball to a faraway green only to stab at and miss a 30-inch putt. It can induce rage. All too often, Fleck's putter failed him. The shortest club in the bag was the necessary evil of a difficult game. Its betrayal on the 14th green at the Phoenix Country Club shattered his fragile composure.

Lynn tried to encourage her husband. "You are doing well—don't let it bother you." Her soothing words did not calm Jack's simmering anger.

"If I 3-putt another green, we are going home!" he snapped.

On the 17th green, Fleck again took 3 putts to find the cup. He rallied with a birdie on the par-5 finishing hole to shoot 69, a 2-shot improvement on his opening round that placed him in the top ten with 36 holes to go. His highest finish and largest check were within reach.

It made no difference. When a few pro friends asked him how he did, Fleck said, "I'm leaving."

Not just to go to the motel, as his friends thought. After shooting rounds of 71 and 69—good tournament scores by almost anyone's standards—Fleck withdrew from the Phoenix Open and blew out of town. Three nights later he and his new bride rolled into snowy Davenport.

It was a disastrous winter tour season for Fleck: two tournaments without cashing a check, an abbreviated honeymoon, and hundreds of highway miles to wonder if he would ever master his emotions in tournament golf. He spent the rest of the cold Iowa winter at home chipping and putting on his carpet.

"I had to find a way to control my mental attitude," he said.

Phoenix would not be the last time Fleck would stomp off a golf course in the middle of a tournament. The temperamental pro had a history of blowups. The shy man with a friendly smile had erupted in sudden fits of anger dating back to his navy days during World War II. In a scuffle with a belligerent fellow sailor on the deck of a navy ship, he nearly tossed the man overboard.

One winter at Brackenridge Park Golf Course in San Antonio, Horton Smith, the winner of the inaugural Masters in 1934, advised Fleck to put his score on the board, whether an 89 or 69. The dapper Smith also counseled him to wear a sport coat on the pro circuit. We need to build the image of the tour pro, emphasized Smith, who went on to head the PGA of America for three years in the early 1950s.

Slipping into a sport coat—which Fleck would do for the rest of his career—was far easier than controlling his temper. He wanted to master his emotions, but golf had a way of lighting his fuse. On one near-career-ending occasion, the object of Fleck's fury was a person instead of his play.

The incident occurred at the 1954 Fort Wayne Open in northern Indiana. Heavy rains soaked the Elks Country Club the night before the first round, forcing the pros to play a course partially covered with standing water. The rules of golf allow competitors to take a free drop from standing or "casual" water, a situation that Fleck faced midway through his opening round.

On the par-5 9th hole, Fleck's second shot bounced left toward a greenside bunker filled with rainwater. Fortunately, his ball came to rest on the grass short of the bunker. Submerged in standing water beside the bunker, his ball was unplayable, a routine drop. He called over his playing partner for confirmation, took his free drop, and finished the hole. It was a normal occurrence in tournament competition, especially on a rain-saturated golf course.

Then things took an ugly turn.

"You know, it's a penalty to drop out of the bunker there," a PGA Tour supervisor said as Fleck walked by the clubhouse.

From his position, the tour supervisor could see most of the 9th-green area but hadn't seen where Fleck's ball came to rest. He'd made an erroneous assumption that rattled the Iowa pro.

"You tend to your job and I'll tend to mine," Fleck said.

A terse reply was understandable. The two men had an unpleasant history. A few years earlier Fleck had informed the same tour supervisor not to enter him in a Monday qualifying event. The tour supervisor said that was fine since Fleck had no chance of winning. The stinging comment motivated Fleck like nothing ever had before to succeed on tour.

In Fort Wayne, Fleck's fuse had once again been lit, a slow burn that would engulf him. The tour supervisor's false view could have been quickly corrected by Fleck's playing partner—if Fleck had called on him to clear up the misunderstanding. Instead, Fleck trudged to the 10th tee.

To his credit, Fleck completed his opening round in fine form, carding a 68. Combined with a 70 in the second round, he stood at 138, just 3 shots off the lead after two trips around the soggy course. With 36 holes to go, he was in excellent position to contend for the title. Even short of winning, he might record his best finish on tour and cash the largest check of his career.

Those career-changing possibilities abruptly ended the following day when Fleck's anger boiled over. Prior to teeing off in the third round, he learned from two fellow players that the tour supervisor had accused him of cheating. His game went to pieces. As he approached the 6th green several strokes over par for his round, there stood the tour supervisor, a huge smile plastered on his face.

"I'm going to go over there and punch him in his big fat belly for telling lies about me!" Fleck told his playing partner.

"Don't do it!" the pro exclaimed. "You will be barred for life!"

Instead, Fleck walked to the parking lot, got in his car, and drove home to Iowa.

Beginning with such promise, the Fort Wayne Open had ended as a disturbing failure. "You might as well not play tournament golf anymore," Lynn told her husband. "The supervisor knows how to upset you."

Fleck knew she was right. If he ever hoped to be a successful tour pro, he would have to find a way to maintain his composure.

•   •   •

Craig Harold Fleck, Jack and Lynn's only child, was born on December 5, 1950. Lynn would not agree to Jack's first name choice—Snead Hogan Fleck. The couple struck a compromise, and Lynn chose Craig Wood from a list of U.S. Open champions.

"Snead Hogan" would have been a peculiar name choice, but it made perfect sense if a father was intent on naming his son after the two best golfers of the age. Fleck was sandwiched between the two greats at the Richmond Invitational in 1946, a watershed year for Ben Hogan. The Texas pro won thirteen times, including his first major, the PGA Championship. Yet, as Fleck recalled at the time, Samuel Jackson Snead, the colorful hillbilly pro born in Ashwood, Virginia, was the biggest draw on tour. Snead had collected more than thirty titles with a swing Fleck and many others regarded as the best in golf. As much as he admired Snead, it was the hardworking Hogan that Fleck had idolized since his teens growing up in Bettendorf, Iowa, a factory town of 1,300 people on the banks of the Mississippi River.

Fleck was introduced to golf at age fifteen when he and a friend hitchhiked fifteen miles to the Davenport Country Club for the 1936 Western Open, considered a major championship in the days before the Masters gained prominence. The two hired on as forecaddies and saw Ralph Guldahl win with a course record–setting 64 in the final round. Over the next three years, Gudahl dominated golf with victories at the 1937 and 1938 Western Opens (making it three straight), the 1937 and 1938 U.S. Opens, and the 1939 Masters.

Fleck was hooked, becoming a regular caddie at the Davenport Country Club, where he had playing privileges on Mondays using a shared set of golf clubs. While waiting around the caddie yard for a bag to tote, he constantly swung his 7-iron and constantly took divots, earning the nickname "Gopher." His older brothers, Henry and Pete, were also caddies at the club. Fleck liked being a caddie, especially the money, forty-five cents a round, although he admitted the large leather golf bags got heavier as he lugged them over the hilly layout.

"He used to worry mother because he sometimes slept at the country club," said Fleck's younger sister, Shirley. "Jack would miss meals in order to caddie."

Within a year Fleck came under the tutelage of Dr. Paul Barton, a dentist and club member whom Fleck called his "father in golf." Dr. Barton was a fine player who once won the Iowa Amateur Championship and teed it up with tour stars such as Walter Hagen, Gene Sarazen, and Horton Smith in local exhibitions. Dr. Barton became Fleck's playing partner in tournaments throughout Iowa, Illinois, and Minnesota. The Davenport dentist encouraged Fleck's golf aspirations and would be a lifelong friend.

Although he was the number-one player on the golf team during his senior year at Davenport High School in 1939, Fleck did not consider himself to be an accomplished junior golfer. Yet there was a bit of early success. Fleck, along with friend Franklin "Whitey" Barnard, was part of a four-man team that won the Junior Eastern Golf Tournament in nearby Cedar Rapids. Davenport High golf coach Russ Bickford tried to talk his best player out of turning pro. He didn't think Fleck had the temperament. The young man was unswayed.

"I told myself I was going to be a professional golfer, if and when I got an apprentice golf pro position, and I was determined to do so!" Fleck said.

•   •   •

By the time Hogan emerged in the late 1930s on his long ascent to golf's summit, Fleck was a full-blown golf junkie who scoured the sports pages of the *Davenport Daily Times* and *Davenport Democrat* for every scrap of news about golf tournaments and the tour pros. "Who is Ben Hogan?" Fleck wondered as he watched Hogan's name creep upward in the tournament standings. Then something remarkable happened in March 1940 as the tour moved through North Carolina. Hogan got his first individual career win at the North and South Open at Pinehurst with a record score of 277, igniting a blazing run that produced three consecutive victories. He set another scoring record and bested the field by nine shots the next week at the Greater Greensboro Open. Seven days later at the Land of the Sky Open in Asheville, Hogan won again and took over the top spot on the money list from Jimmy Demaret. Fleck marveled at Hogan's torrid play. The Associated Press called Hogan's ten of twelve rounds in the 60s "the most sensational streak in the annals of the Professional Golfers' Association."

After years of toiling in the shadow of fellow Texan Byron Nelson, Hogan—who like Fleck turned pro at age seventeen—had finally won.

It was like salve for the hyperdriven pro. In the ensuing years, Ben Hogan would pile up wins faster than any other tour pro except Sam Snead.

Playing behind Hogan in the 1946 Richmond Invitational wasn't the first time Fleck trailed his hero. He followed Hogan during the 1940 winter tour, ducking in and out of the woods along the fairways to observe his idol's practice habits, concealing himself from the tour star. Fleck watched Hogan hit multiple shots into greens, memorizing club choice and noting the locations of trees, bunkers, and other landmarks. It was before the days of yardage markers.

"I copied him and actually did him one better," Fleck said. "I began pacing off yardage, which nobody else had done at that point."

Fleck perfected his method by measuring his stride in light snow in his yard at home in Davenport. He also determined the exact distance he hit each of his clubs. Amateur Gene Andrews was later credited as the first player to pace off yardage because he shared the method with Jack Nicklaus, but Fleck had preceded Andrews.

The young pro was looking for any advantage that would help him succeed in tournament golf. Fleck returned to the winter tour after World War II, which interrupted the tournament careers of virtually all pros. Chief Quartermaster Fleck served on a ship providing fire support in the Normandy invasion and was en route to Pearl Harbor when the Japanese surrendered. A few weeks later, he was back in San Diego, this time on the golf course rather than drilling at the Naval Training Center. Instead of drinking and telling war stories like other Bettendorf veterans, Fleck would use the few hundred dollars he had saved in the navy for another shot at the tournament circuit. His first round after a nearly four-year layoff was a rusty 93 at the San Diego Country Club alongside fellow Iowa pros Joe and Jim Brown.

"I played and practiced all day long," Fleck said about his return to golf. "That's all I did."

Occasionally, he qualified to play in tournaments such as the Richmond Invitational in northern California. He was seldom in the money. Tournament purses in the 1940s and 1950s could be measured in hundreds and thousands of dollars instead of the millions available on today's PGA Tour. A dozen to two dozen money places were the norm. A player could make the 36-hole cut and still need to beat most of the remaining players just to cash a check. Even so, the money was slim. For example, Fleck's twenty-fifth-place finish in the 1953 San Diego Open netted him $13.75, which fell short of his caddie fee of $21.50. Lynn once said the couple spent $8 for every dollar Jack won. Her husband was used to getting by on a shoestring.

.   .   .

The Great Depression came early for the Flecks. The middle child in a family of three boys and two girls, Jack Donald Fleck was born on November 8, 1921, on the northern outskirts of Bettendorf. When Jack was four-years-old, his parents lost their truck farm and moved to a rambling, eight-room house at 2002 Mississippi Blvd. on the edge of town. The home sat on a two-and-a-half-acre lot with two small abandoned houses on a hill.

Fleck and his older brothers did all types of chores and odd jobs to help his family endure the economic despair of the late 1920s and 1930s. "I had my first jobs in kindergarten," he said, "picking apples, topping onions, and catching cabbage butterflies. Every penny went to the family."

Piece by piece, including straightening all the nails, father and sons dismantled the two abandoned houses on the property for scrap. The boys chopped wood, raked leaves, and shoveled snow. Every spring they dug the three large gardens that supplied vegetables for the Fleck family. In the fall, mother and daughters canned the family's produce for winter consumption. Nothing was wasted. What wore out was repaired and re-used. Fleck's mother sewed patches over patches on his pants and put cardboard in his shoes when he wore holes in the soles.

As a young pro, Fleck traded the boyhood tools of shovels and rakes for those of irons and woods. Although he exchanged laboring in Betten-dorf fields for working in country club fairways, his existence on the tournament circuit was more uncertain than his family's survival during the Depression. Even in the worst of times the Fleck family could grow food for their table. Fleck would have to beat the country's best golf pro-fessionals to earn more than the paltry sums doled out for twenty-fifth-place finishes. The odds were long for every pro who dared to play tour golf.

"The tournament trail is a gaudy road lined with the best times a man can have—if he's on top," Jimmy Demaret wrote in *My Partner, Ben Hogan.* "But if he's just one of the crowd, putting in the pick-and-shovel work on this uncertain road to success, it is far and away the toughest haul in sports."

One of those on top, the man nicknamed "Sunny Jim" for his color-ful clothes and personality, defined the haves and have-nots. "The players themselves can be classified roughly into two groups—the attractions and the entry fees. This might seem a harsh way to describe the difference between those 10 or so top golfers who come away from the tour showing a profit and the other 140 or so who go home with indigestion and empty pockets. But it is, sadly, the truth."

"The money was really very scarce," said Fred Hawkins, a slender Illinois native who played on the PGA Tour from 1947 to 1965. Squeeze into the top ten, a good finish, and a player could expect a check of about $200. "We were really kind of foolish because we could have made more money doing something else," Hawkins said, "but we all loved to play and we liked the competition."

"It was tough," said Tommy Bolt, chuckling, a twelve-time winner in the 1950s and eventual Hall of Famer. "You had to win some money to get out of town. It was a lot of fun, but it was a lot of pressure."

Players didn't earn a dime for finishing beyond thirtieth, remembered Walker Inman Jr., a tour rookie in 1955. If a player made the cut, which was hard to do, he still had to beat half the guys to pocket $100.

As a result of the small purses, players knew how to stretch a dollar along the tournament trail. It was not a gaudy road for Inman, whose average weekly expenses amounted to $125. "So if I had $500," he said, "I could go a month—pay my caddie, eat, hopefully win a little money, and get to the next tournament."

For a struggling tour pro like Jack Fleck, the way to stretch small and uneven tournament earnings was to travel as cheaply as possible. In late 1946 he and fellow Iowa pro Bill McPartland pushed expense-saving measures to the limit as they embarked on a new winter tour season. They removed the backseat in McPartland's automobile and installed a mattress through the trunk so they could sleep in the car. They abandoned the bed on wheels after a couple of cold nights west of Iowa. Instead, they rented rooms in private homes, a common practice in the early days on tour.

There were few motels at the time—and they could be crowded. In town for the 1947 Tucson Open, Fleck was one of twenty-three pros who slept on cots on the balcony floor of the Pioneer Hotel. "We were glad to have the army cots," he said. Nor were the tour pros treated to the lavish buffets in plush country club dining rooms that are a mainstay of today's PGA Tour. Fleck recalled the roadside cafeterias and chuck wagons as good food at a good price.

It was the club pro job that enabled golfers to ride the financial roller coaster of tour life. Drawing a small salary and collecting earnings from merchandise sales and golf lessons provided a modest living for most club professionals. Even golf stars like Hogan, Snead, and Demaret held club pro jobs to augment their fluctuating incomes.

Landing a head pro job at the two Davenport municipal golf courses allowed Fleck to buy his first automobile at age twenty-five. Prior to that, as an assistant to Joe Brown at the Des Moines Golf and Country Club, he hitched rides and shared expenses with others on the winter circuit. It was the only way to make it across the hundreds of miles between tournaments in California, Arizona, and Texas.

The nomadic life began in January 1940 when the eighteen-year-old Fleck hitchhiked to San Antonio to intercept the winter tour at the Texas Open. In deep snow and icy cold, he caught a bus to Poplar Bluff, Missouri, then hitched three rides across Arkansas. Each driver offered the same greeting.

"Get in here, kid. Don't you know this is a chain-gang state?"

Fleck finally arrived in San Antonio, checked into the YMCA, and walked the streets and along the river downtown. The sunny winter weather and 89-degree heat amazed him.

"I never lived another full winter in Iowa," he said.

—2—

THE CLUBS

In the summer of 1954, a month after he stomped off the Elks Country Club course during the third round of the Fort Wayne Open, Jack Fleck entered the National Celebrities Open at Congressional Country Club in Bethesda, Maryland. He was determined not to let the tour supervisor get under his thin skin.

Opened in 1924 during the Calvin Coolidge administration, Congressional was a private golf haven for politicians and businessmen, a classic layout that demanded accurate tee and approach shots to its narrow fairways and small greens. It suited Fleck's game. He opened with rounds of 73 and 72, good enough to make the 36-hole cut.

Then, paired with veteran players Dutch Harrison and George Fazio, Fleck moved up the leaderboard with a 69. His playing partners took notice. As Fleck's long drives kept splitting the tight fairways, Fazio remarked, "Look where that damn kid hit it."

Fleck had one more score to put on the board, as Horton Smith might say. How would he finish? Would he finish? There was no quit in Fleck this time as he posted another splendid 69. His pair of 69s for 138 was the lowest final 36 holes in the tournament, and his tie for eighth was his best finish on the PGA Tour since a fourth at the 1949 Cedar Rapids Open. The accompanying check for $1,100 was his largest payday.

Fleck's golf game had improved as he gained tournament experience during the '54 season. After the walk-off at Fort Wayne and the soul searching that followed, the temperamental club pro had progressed at mastering his volatile emotions. He would need a firm grip on more than the golf club if he hoped to earn more $1,000 checks on the PGA Tour.

Fleck felt a quiet sense of urgency as the end of another tournament season approached. "I hope I can play championship golf before Hogan and Snead retire," he confided to Lynn.

The year 1954 ended on a disappointing note, a missed cut at the Miami Open. Fleck climbed into his automobile and drove cross-country to California to prepare for the 1955 season opener, the Los Angeles Open. After nearly a decade of nagging frustrations and slow improvement on the winter tour, Fleck would take his final shot. It would begin in Los Angeles, the sprawling metropolis to which so many restless souls flock to see if their dreams will live or die.

·   ·   ·

The clock on Jack's full-time tour run started ticking in January at the Inglewood Country Club, site of the Los Angeles Open. With a purse that had increased from $20,000 to $32,500, L.A. was one of the more lucrative stops on tour. Fleck was paired in the first two rounds with George Bayer, a bear of a man whose fame would spread as he launched drives in excess of 300 yards, an eye-popping distance in the days of persimmon woods and out-of-round golf balls. While up-and-comer Gene Littler won at Inglewood, Fleck tied for fifteenth and earned $386.25, a solid start for the Iowan.

Next up was the $15,000 San Diego Open, where Fleck's 1953 finish didn't net enough winnings to pay his caddie. This time he finished in a tie for twenty-seventh and collected a check for $85.72. Tommy Bolt, a three-time winner in 1954, bested the field.

The tour headed east for the $15,000 Phoenix Open at the Arizona Country Club. Five years earlier on his honeymoon Fleck quit midtournament and drove home to Davenport. This time he played all four rounds and finished in a tie for thirteenth, adding another $320 to his early-season winnings. Meanwhile, twenty-four-year-old phenom Littler won again.

Fleck was three for three: three cuts made and three finishes in the money, a decent beginning to the new season. As had been his habit, he skipped the Tucson and Texas Opens staged at El Rio and Brackenridge, respectively, two relatively short golf courses that favored good putting, often a weakness in his own game.

While Bolt won his second tournament of the year at Tucson and Mike Souchak humbled the Texas field with a record-setting performance, Fleck sped across the barren expanses of Arizona, New Mexico, and Texas to Houston. He spent two weeks practicing prior to the $30,000 Houston Open at Memorial Park Golf Course, a municipal facility.

Mike Krak, a young tour pro and frequent practice partner of Fleck's, called Memorial a great layout, although the golf course was a far cry from the first-rate venues of today's PGA Tour.

"You could count the blades of grass out there," Krak said in recent years, "and the clubhouse was just this little concrete pavilion. They didn't serve food or anything in it. It was just a place to go to the bathroom."

Grass-challenged courses and Spartan facilities were the norm for tour golf. While players competed on their share of private golf courses, public courses also served as regular venues on the 1950s PGA Tour. In either case, lush, manicured golf courses were mostly nonexistent.

Krak said he would never forget the time he took his new wife to a tournament at Beaumont, Texas. "She looked down and said, 'Do you putt on these greens?' I said, 'These are pretty good. Usually there's no grass on them at all.'"

As Krak recalled, except for the majors, the golf courses on tour were horrendous. There were no triplex mowers to cut the fairways. Rubber mats were used for tees at the Texas Open.

The primitive golf courses put a premium on shotmaking and finesse, the deft ability to strike, spin, and curve the golf ball out of a wide range of grasses and lies. The players never knew what kind of course conditions they would encounter.

"In those days," said Walker Inman, another of Fleck's practice partners, "you went from week to week and the golf courses were all different. The turf was different—it was never cut the same height—the greens were all different, and they had *Poa annua* greens everywhere, which are very inconsistent."

A few years earlier Fleck had become acquainted with Leon Thomas, an accomplished amateur and outstanding putter. Thomas routinely took his vacation during the Houston Open, and the pair played many rounds together.

"Mr. Thomas tried to help me with my putting in exchange for my trying to help him get more length on his tee shots," Fleck said.

The two weeks of extra practice paid off. Fleck cashed his largest check of the young season in Houston, a sixteenth-place finish worth $475. It was a Texas sweep for the red-hot Souchak, who won his second consecutive tournament.

The tour continued eastward to Louisiana for the $12,500 Baton Rouge

Open, where the Iowa pro recorded his highest finish of the season, a tenth-place tie that netted $288.75.

It was a satisfactory start. Fleck had missed no cuts and, except for his twenty-seventh place at San Diego, had consistent finishes from the West Coast to the bayou—a fifteenth, thirteenth, sixteenth, and tenth for total earnings of more than $1,500. He needed to crack the top ten to reach the next tier in money winnings—or win. Such a win—what every unproven player dreams of—would help Fleck break from the pack and earn the respect of his peers. One good tournament could change a career.

With an open week in the schedule after Baton Rouge, Fleck drove home to reunite with Lynn and Craig and ready his two Davenport courses for the golf season, which began on April 1. He returned to the highway a week later for the two-day drive to St. Petersburg—and the long cardboard box in Skip Alexander's pro shop that would send Fleck's season and career in a new direction.

•   •   •

Located on the Gulf Coast, St. Petersburg marked the beginning of the Florida swing and the run-up to the year's first major, the prestigious Masters Tournament at Augusta National in April.

The Lakewood Country Club, site of the $12,500 St. Petersburg Open, wove through a residential neighborhood called Lakewood Estates a few miles south of downtown St. Petersburg. Built during the land boom of the early 1920s, the development's serpentine streets wandered like the Spanish explorers for which they were named. The golf course was the centerpiece of Lakewood Estates and contained the abundant sand, water, Bermuda grasses, and palm trees that were the trademark of Florida golf courses.

Fleck's play at the year's first event in the Sunshine State picked up where he left off in Louisiana with a workmanlike tie for eighteenth, good for $155. While the Iowa pro found nothing new on the course, he did make a discovery in the pro shop. Packaged for shipment was a new set of golf clubs from a fledgling golf club manufacturer, the Ben Hogan Golf Company. Fleck had heard about the boxed set in Alexander's pro shop upon his arrival in St. Petersburg. He approached the Lakewood head pro with a special request.

"Skip, can I look at that box that you're sending back there?" he asked. "I'll seal it up and pay the postage. I just want to look at those clubs."

Stewart "Skip" Alexander was a former PGA Tour player who was the lone survivor of a 1950 plane crash in Evansville, Indiana, that burned 70 percent of his body. Alexander endured seventeen operations. Then he returned to tournament golf and helped the United States win the Ryder Cup in 1951 by upsetting Britain's best player in singles. On that March day in the Lakewood pro shop, Alexander responded graciously to the eager fellow pro. Sure, take a look. Don't worry about the postage.

Fleck carefully opened the box and examined the Hogan irons. He was smitten. "Gee, they looked good," he said of the shiny forged blades with straight hosels. It was long before the day of investment-cast offset irons with mammoth sweet spots.

He removed an iron or two from the box and waggled them. He liked the feel of the Hogan blades and how they were built. It also didn't hurt that the irons Fleck gripped in his hands were the workmanship of his idol.

"Boy, I'm going to write the Hogan company and see about getting a set of clubs made," Fleck said to Inman and Krak.

The two pros, both recently discharged from the U.S. Air Force, were fresh faces on tour who kept company with Fleck on the pro circuit. "We just kind of buddied around," remembered Inman. "We ended up playing a lot of golf together and working on each other's games together."

As for Fleck's plan to write Hogan, Inman and Krak reacted as if Fleck were dazed by the hot Florida sun. Hogan make clubs for Fleck? Forget it. The two young pros told him not to waste his time—Hogan would never approve it.

Fleck didn't listen to them. He posted a letter to the Ben Hogan Golf Company at 2912 West Pafford Street in Fort Worth, Texas. It was a long shot, but he took it. He wanted his own set of Ben Hogan golf clubs. There was no harm in asking.

3

THE HAWK

To say Ben Hogan was fussy about golf equipment was a colossal understatement. Whether it was golf clubs or golf balls, he was thoroughly obsessed, a perfectionist's perfectionist. One of his many nicknames, "the Hawk," was perhaps the most fitting and enduring, coined by his fellow pros because Hogan stalked the golf course like a bird of prey.

According to Hogan biographer Curt Sampson, the Hawk devised his own method for determining whether a golf ball was worthy of making it into his golf bag. Marking each golf ball with a pinprick or dot, he dumped a box of balls into a bathtub filled with water and Epsom salts. Then Hogan spun each ball in the buoyant water, discarding any ball that consistently had one side floating downward. The bathtub test revealed whether the rubber bands inside the ball were wound evenly. In addition, Hogan would inspect each golf ball under a magnifying glass to detect excess paint on the 280 dimples. He was also known to determine the compression of an unmarked golf ball by squeezing it between his thumb and forefinger. Ben Hogan was a quality assurance freak.

Actually, the Hawk had a good reason for his bizarre golf ball tests. Beginning in 1946, the MacGregor Tourney golf ball he was under contract to play was no longer outsourced to the Worthington Golf Ball Company. MacGregor manufactured the new Tourney ball at its Cincinnati plant. Hogan thought the new ball was inferior and made his feelings known. The golf ball problem put the relationship into a serious tailspin.

The Hogan-MacGregor affiliation had begun in 1937 when Hogan inked a $250 deal to play MacGregor golf clubs and golf balls. The customary arrangement was for players to receive free equipment, a salary, and bonuses based on tournament performance. It had been a good arrangement for Hogan, who was fond of MacGregor's custom club-making department. The feeling wasn't mutual. The guys in the company's custom shop respected Hogan as a golfer but dreaded his annual visits. He would spend days putting the top custom club grinder through the paces before leaving with a perfect set of MacGregors. While Byron Nelson would select an entire set and backups in an hour, Hogan would critique shafts, lies, swing weight—everything—for hours and days at a time.

The golf ball issue came to a head in June 1953 when Hogan was summoned to Cincinnati to meet with MacGregor president Henry Cowen. The company wanted to show Hogan how it was testing the MacGregor Tourney golf ball to ensure its quality and playability. Company personnel spent three days performing test after test while Hogan watched and listened in silence. The following week he won a record-tying fourth U.S. Open at Oakmont—using a Spalding Dot golf ball.

MacGregor wasn't alone when it came to ball-quality issues.

"The Dunlop ball used to go out of round in the showcase," said Larry Tomasino, a Michigan club pro who played the winter circuit in the 1950s.

"That's how bad it was back then." Like Hogan, Tomasino was on the MacGregor staff, but he played the Titleist golf ball. "Every time they came to check, I'd switch to the MacGregor ball," he said.

Hogan had been making plans to sever ties with MacGregor long before his Cincinnati trip and National Open victory.

"As soon as he could raise a couple hundred thousand dollars of investment capital and find the right financial partner who knew enough to stay the hell out of his way," wrote James Dodson, "Ben Hogan intended to start making the finest golf clubs anybody had ever played with—and eventually maybe even the balls to go with them."

That could explain why Hogan openly played a Titleist golf ball at the 1953 Masters, two months before his meeting with Cowen at Mac-Gregor headquarters. It also was Hogan being Hogan. When it came to golf, he did things his way.

The formal split came later that summer despite the company's last-ditch effort to convince its star player to tee up the Tourney ball. It was too late. The Hawk refused to play what he considered to be inferior golf equipment and balls—and he was going to do something about it. He would start the Ben Hogan Golf Company.

      •   •   •

In 1953 there was nothing in Hogan's tournament play to indicate he had the slightest concern about his flap with MacGregor. Not since 1930 when Bobby Jones won his era's four majors—the British Amateur, British Open, U.S. Open, and U.S. Amateur, named the "Grand Slam" by sportswriter O. B. Keeler—had a golfer accomplished so much in a single season. Hogan entered six tournaments and won five, including three of the four majors, the Masters, U.S. Open, and British Open. The fourth major, the PGA

Championship, overlapped the British Open, so Hogan crossed the Atlantic for what would be his first and last Open championship on British soil. Not only did he win all three major championships he entered, he shattered each of their scoring records. The Hawk's three major wins in 1953 became known as the "Hogan Slam," and he was named Associated Press Male Athlete of the Year.

Playing in six tournaments in a season was a limited schedule by anyone else's standards, but not for a man who had narrowly escaped death and whose doctors thought he might never walk again. Before an automobile accident on a foggy Texas highway, Hogan played dozens of events in a season.

A former caddie, nineteen-year-old Ben Hogan joined the PGA Tour in 1931. "I didn't think I was good enough to win anything as a professional," Hogan said, "but I figured if I played enough I might make some money."

He lasted one month before he ran out of money. Two years later Hogan tried and failed again. On his third attempt, in 1937, after marrying Valerie Fox, the stubborn Texas pro stuck. A slew of wins followed his first individual victory in 1940 as he topped the money list for three consecutive years. Hogan was a winner, but he still played in Byron Nelson's shadow and had yet to capture a major.

After serving stateside in the Army Air Corps for two years during World War II, Captain Hogan was discharged in August 1945 and returned to Fort Worth to resume his golf career. Nelson, whose career had continued uninterrupted because of a blood condition that disqualified him from military service, was still on top, called "Mr. Golf" by sportswriters.

Over the next three and a half years, Hogan won thirty-seven tournaments, including thirteen in 1946 and ten in 1948, the first man to collect double-digit wins in two separate seasons. One of those victories was his long-sought first major, the 1946 PGA Championship in Portland, Oregon, a match-play event until 1958. A highly anticipated face-off with rival Nelson, who lost in the quarterfinals, didn't materialize, and "Lord Byron" retired from full-time tour play. As Nelson became a gentleman rancher in rural Texas, Hogan assumed the mantle of America's best golfer, with Sam Snead a close second, the two in a class of their own. Hogan was the new sheriff on tour, and he struck fear in the psyches of his opponents.

"The little man is the only one in golf I've been afraid of," confessed tour standout Lloyd Mangrum, a sentiment shared, if not verbalized, by others.

On his tenth try, Hogan added a U.S. Open to his résumé at Riviera Country Club in Los Angeles in the summer of 1948. His 72-hole total of 276 broke the eleven-year-old record held by Ralph Guldahl by 5 shots. He also won the Los Angeles Open at Riviera in 1947 and 1948, and henceforth the course was known as "Hogan's Alley." Following his Open triumph, the Hawk won five straight tournaments, including the Inverness Four-Ball with partner Jimmy Demaret.

Power Golf, Hogan's first golf instruction book, hit the bookshelves in April of that season. Packed with 120 drawings and detailed instruction on everything from the grip to how to play in bad weather, *Power Golf* was a forerunner of modern golf instruction. The first two sentences of the introduction summed up Hogan's underlying belief.

"Contrary to anything you may have read on the subject, there is no such thing as a born golfer," he wrote. "Some have more natural ability than others, but they've all been made."

The words were autobiographical, for Ben Hogan was the embodiment of a made golfer.

•   •   •

William Ben Hogan was born on August 13, 1912—the same year as Byron Nelson and Sam Snead—in Stephenville, Texas, the youngest of three children. Hogan's brother, Royal, was the oldest, followed by a sister, Princess. On February 13, 1922, Ben's father, a blacksmith named Chester who suffered severe bouts of depression, fatally shot himself in the chest with a .38 revolver in the front parlor of the Hogan home. As Hogan biographer Curt Sampson wrote, "At the age of nine, Bennie Hogan's childhood was shot through the heart." Chester Hogan's suicide would remain a family secret for decades.

The family moved to Fort Worth, and Bennie, as he was known in his youth, discovered golf when a friend told him that carrying a golf bag paid better than selling newspapers. To join the caddie ranks at Glen Garden Country Club, twelve-year-old Bennie had to win a fistfight with a bigger, older boy. The young caddie sometimes slept in a sand trap so he would be at the front of the line when golfers arrived for their weekend rounds. Golf went from occupation to obsession, and three years later Hogan faced the best player in the caddie yard in the club's annual Christmas caddie tournament. Bennie lost in a playoff, beginning his lifelong rivalry with the more talented Byron Nelson.

At seventeen, Bennie became a club pro for Oakhurst, a 9-hole course near downtown Fort Worth. The young pro's game featured a long swing built for distance. To compensate for the strong Texas winds and his small stature—Hogan was 5'7" and had a slight build, later prompting sportswriters to call him "Bantam Ben," a nickname he disliked—Bennie's ball flight was a low hook. It made him an unusually long hitter for his size. It also made him habitually wild.

"I hate a hook," he later said. "It nauseated me. I could vomit when I see one. It's like a rattlesnake in your pocket."

Later, the hook nearly drove Hogan from the tour, but quitting wasn't in his DNA. Practice was.

"Practice was his greatest insight and his biggest advantage," wrote Sampson. "Whether it was due to his world weariness, his dislike of company, or a Calvinist belief in redemption through work, Bennie Hogan could stay on the practice tee like nobody else. His diligence was amazing because he had no model for it and because he got almost no immediate rewards from it."

One enduring story is that Hogan practiced until his hands bled, soaked them in brine, then resumed his relentless practice sessions. How he finally conquered the hook became a part of golf lore, popularly known as "Hogan's secret." It was a weakened left-hand grip. It was a cupped left wrist. It was the right knee. Whatever helped Hogan solve his swing flaws and mold himself into a champion golfer, he discovered it through long hours on the practice tee, or "digging it out of the dirt," the famous Hogan mantra.

There was no disagreement. Golf legend Bobby Jones marveled at Hogan's work ethic in the foreword to *Power Golf.* "I thought I was a hard worker at this game. I thought Hagen and Sarazen were hard workers. But Ben Hogan is the hardest worker I've ever seen, not only in golf, but in any other sport."

Hogan's real secret had always been in plain view. He simply outworked everybody.

The Hawk's ten-win 1948 season that included two majors put any lingering doubts to rest. He was the undisputed king of golf. After more than a decade of scratching and clawing his way to golf's summit, seemingly nothing could have stopped Ben Hogan except a Greyhound bus.

•　　•　　•

On February 2, 1949, Groundhog Day, Hogan swung his Cadillac onto Highway 80 in Van Horn, Texas, en route to Fort Worth five hundred miles to the east. He and Valerie were anxious to return home after the season-opening tour events, two of which Hogan won, the Bing Crosby Pro-Am and the Long Beach Open.

Encountering patches of dense fog and a surface thinly coated with ice, Hogan switched on his headlights and crept along the two-lane highway. At their snail-like pace, it would take hours longer to cover the hundreds of miles to Fort Worth. In minutes, the comforts of home would become even more distant for the Hogans.

Alvin Logan wanted to stay on schedule. The twenty-seven-year-old Greyhound bus driver and thirty-four passengers were traveling westbound, the opposite direction from the Hogans, when Logan decided to pass a six-wheel freight hauler lumbering along the fog-shrouded road. Seeing no vehicles ahead, Logan swung the ten-ton coach into the passing lane and accelerated to fifty miles per hour up a slight incline.

Seconds later, at 8:30 A.M., the bus and Cadillac collided on a small bridge that crossed a culvert. Hogan saw the oncoming headlights in his lane but was trapped on the bridge with no escape route. He let go of the steering wheel and threw himself across the passenger seat to shield his wife from the head-on crash. It saved his life.

The impact drove the steering column into the sedan, catching Hogan's left shoulder and fracturing his collarbone. The Cadillac's five-hundred-pound V-8 engine also slammed into the car's interior. Hogan's face struck the dashboard, and his left leg was crushed. In addition to the fractured collarbone, he sustained a double fracture to his pelvis, a broken left ankle, and a cracked rib. Valerie's injuries were minor.

In the confusion that followed, none of the thirty-eight people left the scene to find a phone and report the accident. A Texas state trooper arrived and radioed for help. Ninety minutes elapsed before the battered golfer received medical attention and was loaded into an ambulance. Hogan was in a state of delirium, fading in and out of consciousness. At one point during the long ambulance ride to El Paso, he gripped an imaginary golf club in his hands and waved back a gallery to the left of a dreamy fairway.

．　　　．　　　．

While eating breakfast that morning in El Paso, a young golf pro overheard a waitress say there was a terrible accident east of Van Horn. A short while later, with lights flashing and sirens screaming, two police motorcycles and an ambulance sped by as the golf pro headed in the opposite direction to San Antonio for the Texas Open. The next morning Jack Fleck read in the newspaper that Ben Hogan was near death in an El Paso hospital.

．　　　．　　　．

Arriving at El Paso's Hotel Dieu Hospital in critical condition, Hogan rallied over the next few days, and his condition progressed from fair to good. Cards, letters, and flowers poured into Hogan's hospital room as news of the accident was splashed across the front pages of the nation's newspapers. A story line emerged that would change how the public regarded the aloof golf champion: Ben Hogan sacrificed himself to save his wife. Hogan was a hero.

Publicly, hospital personnel expressed satisfaction with the patient's progress. Privately, Hogan's doctors doubted whether the golf great would walk again without assistance and all but ruled out tournament golf. Then things took a sudden downturn. A blood clot traveled from Hogan's left leg to his right lung, causing a sharp pain in his chest. More large clots broke free, each one a certain death sentence if it blocked a main artery.

There were few medical options in 1949 and no effective blood-thinning drugs. They decided to operate. Newspapers prepared obituaries.

Dr. Alton S. Ochsner, the country's top vascular surgeon and a Tulane University professor, flew to El Paso to perform the high-risk surgery. It was a complex, highly invasive two-hour procedure to enter Hogan's abdomen and tie off the inferior vena cava, the blood's primary pathway from the lower body to the heart and lungs. Valerie prayed in the hospital chapel.

On April 1, Ben Hogan, weighing 120 pounds, left the hospital on a gurney and boarded a train for Fort Worth, completing the journey he and his wife had begun two months earlier.

• • •

Fourteen months later, in June 1950, the Hawk limped to the 1st tee of the U.S. Open at Merion Country Club in Ardmore, Pennsylvania. Defending champion Cary Middlecoff called him "a walking miracle." Hogan would play in the national championship, but each step would be a painful reminder of the accident that mangled his lower body and the lifesaving operation that permanently hampered his circulation.

Hogan would endure a two-hour ritual for the rest of his playing days. After rising, he would soak for an hour in a tub of hot water and Epsom salts. In the next hour, he would swallow aspirin, apply liniment, and wrap his legs with elastic bandages. It was as if he were preparing to do battle on the football gridiron rather than walk country club fairways.

Hogan's Lazarus-like comeback began the previous September when he was the nonplaying captain of the U.S. Ryder Cup team in matches hosted by England. Weeks later, in early December, Hogan played 18 holes at Colonial Country Club in Fort Worth, his first round since the

February accident. Then he sent in his entry for the 1950 Los Angeles Open.

The sight of Ben Hogan playing tournament golf again sent shock waves through the press, golf fans, and fellow tour pros. The fact that he nearly won, losing in an 18-hole playoff to Snead, was even more shocking. Legendary sportswriter Grantland Rice summed up, "His legs simply were not strong enough to carry his heart around."

Golf fans and the public at large gobbled it up. So it made perfect sense that Hollywood hitched its wagon to America's newest sports icon. Starring Glenn Ford as Ben Hogan with Anne Baxter playing Valerie, *Follow the Sun* debuted in March 1951. It was the first motion picture ever made about a golfer, the story of Hogan's near-fatal accident and miracle comeback. A technical adviser on the film, Hogan "drove everybody nearly mad," according to his golf partner Jimmy Demaret. Much of Hogan's dissatisfaction was justified, especially the ungolferlike movements of Ford. The critics gave the film favorable reviews, although some labeled it "contrived" and "ingratiating." Hogan responded in typical Hogan fashion—with silence. Upon another viewing of *Follow the Sun* in the last years of his life, he wept.

For Hogan, a comeback was the only option. It had little to do with sentimentality or adulation, even though the public outpouring of support did seep through his tough exterior. Golf was his life. Regardless of what doctors or anyone else might say, the Hawk would find a way to play.

At the 1950 U.S. Open at Merion, the "walking miracle" with the bandaged legs and steel will opened with a 72 on the par-70 layout, a good start. In the second round cramps struck like thunderbolts as he trudged to the 12th tee. Playing with intense pain, Hogan fired a 69 and trailed 36-hole leader Dutch Harrison by 2 shots. Could he survive the 36-hole final day, a ten-mile marathon of Open golf?

Hogan arose at 5:30 A.M. to prepare for his 9:30 A.M. tee time. By noon, cramps again viciously attacked his legs. The hobbled champion gamely played on, finishing with a 72 that left him 2 behind leader Mangrum with 18 holes to go. When Mangrum and others fell back on the outward 9, Hogan took the lead. The pain in his legs had become so acute that his caddie took his ball out of the hole and playing partner Middlecoff marked his ball at times. On the 12th tee, Hogan reached out and grabbed an arm to avoid falling after hitting his drive.

"I thought he was going to collapse," Middlecoff said.

By the time he reached the 72nd hole, Hogan had surrendered his 3-shot lead and needed a par on the challenging 448-yard finishing hole to get into a playoff with Mangrum and George Fazio. He hit a solid drive into the fairway but still faced a wood or long-iron shot from a slight downhill lie to the 18th green. The fairway was lined by thousands of spectators as he reached for his 1-iron, a difficult club to strike well under the best of circumstances. The Hawk made perfect contact. Directly behind Hogan, Hy Peskin, who had set his camera on a spectator's shoulder, snapped one of golf's most famous photographs. As the masses craned their necks, Hogan's 1-iron shot rocketed through the air and landed safely on the distant green, stopping 40 feet left of the cup. He limped up the rise to the putting surface and surveyed his long putt. His first effort was too strong, leaving a nervous 4-footer. He took little time and holed his par to tie Mangrum and Fazio.

The next day, against all reasonable odds, Hogan won the 18-hole playoff and was crowned national champion for the second time. Penalized 2 shots on the 16th green, Mangrum carded a 73. Fazio had a disappointing 75. The Hawk shot a 69.

Hogan had completed what some considered to be the greatest comeback in the history of sports. A stone plaque in Merion's 18th fairway marks the spot where he struck the famous 1-iron shot. It was the last shot Hogan hit with the club, which, along with a pair of his shoes, was stolen moments after his playoff victory.

Playing in his first U.S. Open, Iowa pro Jack Fleck missed the cut.

•   •   •

The Hogan Slam began in April 1953 at Augusta National Golf Club. The Hawk toured Bobby Jones's masterpiece in rounds of 70, 69, 66, and 69 for a 14-under-par total of 274, obliterating the Masters tournament record. Golf legend Gene Sarazen called it the greatest four scoring rounds ever.

Nearly impossible to satisfy, Hogan even impressed himself. "That's as good as I can play," he said.

Everyone except defending champion Julius Boros had to play in a 36-hole qualifying tournament to make the field of the 1953 U.S. Open to be played at Oakmont near Pittsburgh. That included Hogan, even though he had a near monopoly on the title with three wins in the previous five Opens. As Sampson noted, "Making Hogan qualify for the U.S. Open was like running a credit check on John D. Rockefeller." The two extra days on the golf course cost Hogan a muscle strain in his back.

Oakmont was a brute—long, thickly treed, and heavily bunkered. It also featured large, lightning-quick putting surfaces, including a few that sloped from front to back. It was the kind of unforgiving championship course Hogan excelled on. Wearing a cardigan sweater to warm his aching back, the Hawk shot an opening 67 and took a 3-shot lead. A 72 in the second round left him 2 ahead of Snead, a marquee matchup for Saturday's final two rounds. Despite being the leaders, Hogan and Snead wouldn't play together. At the time, the USGA didn't pair players based on their scores, nor did the leaders necessarily tee off in the final group.

Whether intentionally or not, the USGA pairings benefited Hogan, who teed off at 9:00 A.M. (Earlier starters generally face better course conditions.) Contender Mangrum followed at 9:30 A.M., and Snead drew a 10:00 A.M. starting time. Hogan's peers accused the USGA of favoritism. Middlecoff was so miffed that he quit during the third round after knocking his approach shot at the 10th onto the Pennsylvania Turnpike. In the meantime, the Hawk posted a 73 for a 1-shot lead over Snead after 54 holes. In the final round on Oakmont's brutal finishing stretch, Hogan carded par, birdie, birdie. His closing 71 was good for a 6-shot victory over a fading Snead, runner-up in the National Open for an agonizing fourth time.

It was a record-tying fourth U.S. Open for Hogan. In his second U.S. Open appearance, finishing 26 strokes behind Hogan, Jack Fleck tied for fifty-second.

•   •   •

Would Ben Hogan enter the British Open? That was the burning question. The answer, finally, was yes. It was one of the best decisions Hogan ever made. He had accomplished everything in American golf. The 1953 British Open, as it turned out, was for immortality.

Hogan arrived in Scotland two and a half weeks early to prepare for the Open Championship at Carnoustie, a municipal links course bordered by the Firth of Tay. Everything was foreign to him—the smaller British ball, Scottish turf, bare fairways, slow greens, varying flagsticks, and unraked bunkers. He didn't like it and made a crack to the greenskeeper, which didn't go over well with his hosts. "I've got a lawn mower back in Texas," he said. "I'll send it over."

In the end, the Scots revered Hogan. They called him the "Wee Ice Mon" for his cool demeanor under pressure. During practice, qualifying, and the four rounds of the championship, thousands chased after the Wee Ice Mon. They were mostly invisible to Hogan, whose singular focus was a two-week crash course in links golf. Just as no one practiced like Hogan, neither did anyone study a golf course like him. Everyone had to qualify, including defending champion Bobby Locke. The Hawk made the field with rounds of 70 at Burnside, a neighboring course, and 75 at Carnoustie.

The first day of the tournament was cold and blustery. Struggling with his pace on the slow greens, Hogan shot a 73 and trailed leader Frank Stranahan, an American amateur, by 3. Two downpours soaked Hogan in the second round. Good ball striking and more lackluster putting resulted in a 71, leaving him just 2 behind coleaders Eric Brown and Dai Rees—but he was getting sick.

On Saturday, in addition to facing a 36-hole final on those legs, Hogan was burning up with a 103-degree fever. He took a shot of penicillin and headed out into the wind and cold for his 10:27 A.M. tee time. A steady 70 in the third round tied him for the 54-hole lead with Argentine Roberto De Vicenzo. After opening with four pars in the final round, the Hawk birdied the 5th and 6th holes to take sole possession of the lead. He charged home with a 34 on the inward 9 and a final-round 68, a competitive course record, to win the famed Claret Jug by 4 shots.

On both sides of the Atlantic, superlatives rained down on Hogan like a Scottish storm. On his first try, he had not only won the world's oldest golf championship, he had captured the hearts of fans in golf's founding country. He would never go back. Upon his triumphant return to America, a smiling Ben Hogan dressed in a gray business suit and riding in an open Chrysler limousine was hailed by 150,000 people in a ticker-tape parade along Broadway in New York City. It was the first time an American golfer had traveled the famous parade route since 1930, when the conquering hero was an amateur named Bobby Jones.

• • •

Ben Hogan and Pollard Simon, a Dallas construction tycoon and investor, met Hogan's friend real estate agent Dan Greenwood at a single-story brick building on West Pafford Street in Fort Worth not long after Hogan's historic victory at Carnoustie. It was a large warehouse with an attractive front side for offices and had never been occupied. The price tag was $50,000. Hogan and Simon decided it would be the home of the new Ben Hogan Golf Company.

Hogan set up his factory on West Pafford Street as if he were preparing for a major championship. He hired an elementary school classmate named Claribel Kelly as his secretary. The two got along like siblings. He supervised the purchase and installation of club-making equipment and personally hired and trained the employees who would make clubs to his fanatical standards. After a union organizer appeared at the plant, Hogan made a blunt speech to workers on the factory floor, telling them he wouldn't pay them one more cent than he could afford until he and his investors made some money. If employees didn't like his terms, they could collect their pay and leave. No one did, and the union talk died.

The first sets of Ben Hogan irons were nearly a year in the making. They came off the production line in May 1954 at the same time their namesake was defending his title at the Colonial Invitational. Hogan shot 69 and 71 and then abruptly withdrew, complaining of a pulled muscle in his left knee. His knee wasn't the only sore point. The initial production run of Hogan irons was seriously flawed. At a glance, they were gorgeous examples of traditional forged blades, but a closer look revealed terribly inconsistent borings (the holes where the shafts were inserted). One club pro who acquired a set wondered if Hogan's workers knew what they were doing. Hogan knew the answer. He shut down production and searched for better assembly workers. Meanwhile, Hogan's sales staff collected orders, and a few dozen sets were shipped to prominent club pros. That wouldn't do.

It was as if Hogan had hit one out-of-bounds and reteed his golf ball. He scrapped the clubs and started over. It wasn't that simple for Simon. Throwing out $100,000 worth of clubs was more than the investor could bear. He crunched the numbers and came up with $150,000 in lost revenue. Simon met with Hogan and agreed to part ways, telling friends it was "one of the saddest days of his life."

Hogan had a factory, a workforce, a rejected production run of irons, and no money. He knew where to get some, though: the Fort Worth National Bank. He borrowed a reported $450,000 to buy out Simon, using his name and personal fortune as a loan guarantee. Shortly thereafter longtime friend Marvin Leonard came to Hogan's rescue. Leonard recruited a group of investors that included singer Bing Crosby, New York Yankees owner Dan Topping, and Wall Street broker Paul Shields. Hogan's name was removed from the note, and the Ben Hogan Golf Company got back to doing what it was in business to do: making the best golf clubs in the world.

4

COLONIAL

At the same time Jack Fleck admired the Hogan clubs in Skip Alexander's pro shop, the Ben Hogan Golf Company—now almost a year removed from the scrapped irons—was still struggling to make clubs that would satisfy Ben Hogan. In fact, the set Hogan used were the only clubs the factory had produced to his lofty standards. One could suppose it worked in favor of the obscure Fleck, whose letter inquiring about Hogan clubs arrived at 2912 West Pafford Street in March 1955. The Iowa pro didn't have to wait long for an answer. He received a letter from general manager Charlie Barnett less than ten days later: Hogan approves. Send us your specs.

Fleck was thrilled. He didn't know it at the time, but he would be the first pro besides Hogan to play the new Precision model irons. A pro's clubs are his tools of the trade, and Fleck was on his way to a set made by the world's greatest player. His club specifications—the lie, shafts, grips, swing weight, and dead (total) weight—were standard. Upon receipt of Fleck's instructions, the Hogan factory would make up a set of irons with standard-sized leather grips, standard length and lies, and medium-flex shafts. He would also acquire a Hogan 3-wood and 4-wood. Two non-Hogan clubs would remain in his bag: a Tommy Armour driver, a persimmon wood with added weight and length (the shaft measured 44¼ inches, perhaps making Fleck's driver the longest on tour), and his Bulls Eye blade putter that was so uncooperative much of the time. Barnett invited Fleck to drop by the Fort Worth factory and check on his new clubs during the Colonial National Invitational Tournament—if Fleck earned an invitation to the May event.

The Colonial was played at Colonial Country Club in Fort Worth, a course opened in 1936 by Marvin Leonard, who thought Texas should have a championship golf course with bentgrass greens. When he failed to convince area clubs to pursue his vision, Leonard bought a patch of scruffy land along the Trinity River and hired renowned golf course architect John Bredemus to transform acres of dirt and brush into a championship layout. In the ensuing decades, Colonial would be judged one of the toughest par-70 golf courses in the world.

The Colonial Country Club hosted the 1941 U.S. Open won by Craig Wood, the first National Open played south of the Mason-Dixon Line. It was a rousing success with players and fans alike, and Colonial officials reasoned an annual tournament would be a popular event and an ongoing source of civic pride. If Leonard built Colonial, then Hogan mastered it. He rallied from six shots back to win the inaugural Colonial Invitational Tournament in 1946. Hogan won again in 1947 and repeated his back-to-back wins in 1952 and 1953, both after trailing by six shots. Like Riviera in Los Angeles, the Colonial Country Club became known as "Hogan's Alley."

Because of the pros' respect for both Hogan and the Colonial Country Club, the Colonial National Invitational Tournament had considerable prestige and a sizable purse by the day's standards. Only the top tour players were invited to enter Hogan's hometown tournament. They didn't include Fleck. His only faint hope of playing in the Colonial would be to receive one of two "Champions' Choice" invitations reserved for up-and-coming players who otherwise wouldn't be eligible to play in the event.

Created in 1953, "it was a tournament policy Ben had a direct hand in shaping," wrote James Dodson, "no doubt recalling his own years of struggle when an invitation to a quality event would have meant the world to his confidence."

Fleck, who had never finished higher than fourth in a tour event, had no reason to expect a Champions' Choice invitation that spring. His thoughts were elsewhere.

After the St. Petersburg Open where he discovered the Hogan irons, Fleck drove south for the Miami Beach Open. He made the cut but finished 3 shots out of the money. Two weeks later he arrived in North Carolina for the Greater Greensboro Open, where another surprise was in store for him.

      ·   ·   ·

If Colonial was Hogan's Alley, then Greensboro was the golf playground of Samuel Jackson Snead. Snead won the inaugural Greater Greensboro Open in 1938, after which play alternated between Starmount Forest Country Club and Sedgefield Country Club. It made no difference to Snead, who won on both courses, capturing Greensboro titles in 1946, 1949, and 1950. The dapper, athletic Snead was a splendid ball striker whose silky smooth swing was especially effective in North Carolina. Someone theorized that he played well at Greensboro because it was his last event before returning home to Hot Springs where he could eat his mama's home cooking.

Home cooking or not, Snead had won all along the pro circuit, near and far from home. Coming into the 1955 season, he had accumulated seventy tour victories, including seven majors. Not bad for a hillbilly kid who grew up fashioning makeshift golf clubs out of sticks.

At Starmount Forest Country Club, Snead played steadily in the last two rounds to win his fifth Greensboro title. He would go on to win three more times for a total of eight victories at one tournament, a PGA Tour record. Fittingly, the address of Starmount Forest Country Club later became 1 Sam Snead Drive. While Snead was adding hardware to his trophy case, Fleck was trying to regain his tournament form. The Iowa pro didn't improve much on his previous performance in Miami, finishing in a tie for twenty-fifth place. His check for $25 wasn't enough to cover his caddie fee.

Meanwhile, in Fort Worth, Colonial tournament officials had made their Champions' choices. One invitation would be extended to Dow Finsterwald, a PGA Tour rookie who had recently completed a hitch in the U.S. Air Force and was part of a new breed of tour pros that had honed their games at colleges instead of rising through the caddie ranks. Other promising newcomers who had played collegiate golf included Gene Littler, Mike Souchak, Ken Venturi, Billy Maxwell, and Arnold Palmer.

Finsterwald was a worthy Colonial selection. A 1952 graduate of Ohio University with a slight build and deft short game, he had recorded a top-five finish on tour while still in the air force. The Athens, Ohio, native became hooked on the game while saving money one summer to go to the World Series. He decided to spend his earnings from sweeping locker rooms and cleaning showers at the Athens Country Club on a set of golf clubs instead of World Series tickets. His investment in golf would pay off for years to come.

While Finsterwald's selection was no surprise, the other Champions' Choice was. At Greensboro, a PGA Tour official found Fleck and delivered the news. "How'd I get in that?" he asked. He knew of the strict criteria for making the Colonial field, including the Champions' Choice invitations.

Although he never found out why he was selected, Fleck believed Hogan had something to do with it.

"Why he chose me, I had no idea," Fleck said a half century later. "I still don't know why."

Was Ben Hogan a do-gooder, someone who would help a struggling young pro?

•   •   •

About to run out of money for a third and perhaps final time on tour, Hogan received assurances from Henry Picard, a twenty-six-time tour winner and head professional at the Hershey Country Club in Hershey, Pennsylvania. Mike Krak, later an assistant to Picard, recalled his former boss's encouragement to a struggling Hogan.

"Picard told me that his exact words to Hogan were 'Don't leave the tour. You have the best swing out here. If you run into a financial problem, let me know. I'll take care of it. I'll back you.'"

Hogan would never forget Picard's help and felt so indebted that he included a dedication to Picard in *Power Golf.* He got by without financial backing from Picard, but "knowing that help was there if I needed it enabled me to forget about my troubles." It wasn't the only time Picard took an interest in the professional development of Ben Hogan. He also recommended Hogan for the head pro job he vacated at Hershey.

A virtually identical scenario played out in 1953. The struggling young pro was Gardner Dickinson; the veteran player offering help was Ben Hogan. After playing with Hogan for the first time at the Pan-American Open in Mexico City and "choking like a dog," Dickinson joined Hogan's gallery the following week in Fort Worth at the Colonial National Invitational Tournament. A small gesture during the first round became a turning point in Dickinson's career.

On the 6th fairway Hogan handed the young pro a tiny piece of paper, which read, as recounted in Dickinson's memoir *Let 'Er Rip*, "Gardner, I don't know what your financial situation is, but if you run out of money, don't quit. This is my unlisted phone number. You call me, and I'll get you some money."

Hogan's offer was a huge boost to Dickinson, who went on to earn tournament checks the rest of that season. He never had to call Hogan for money, but knowing he could made all the difference. Later Hogan hired Dickinson as his assistant pro at Tamarisk Country Club in Rancho Mirage, near Palm Springs. While the Hawk pounded balls all winter long in the warm desert sun, Dickinson gave lessons to Hollywood stars such as Jack Benny and the Marx Brothers.

History repeated itself in another way. Just as Hogan had dedicated his book to Picard after Picard's encouragement and show of support, Dickinson dedicated his book to Hogan as a tribute to his longtime golf mentor. Dickinson did something more: He named his son Ben.

•   •   •

At Greensboro, Fleck had received his second piece of surprising news from Fort Worth in a month's time. Why it happened, how it happened, wasn't clear. The game's greatest player had apparently taken more than a passing interest in the Iowa club pro. As he headed to the Virginia Beach Open, Fleck's excitement for an early May trip to Fort Worth was building. These were thrilling developments for a thirty-three-year-old pro who was desperately trying to establish himself on tour.

Five-time tour winner Chandler Harper began a springtime hot streak with a win at the $15,000 Virginia Beach Open, not far from his home in Portsmouth. Fleck finished in a tie for twenty-second worth $170 in winnings. The tour's next stop was Las Vegas, Nevada, for the Tournament of

Champions, a winners-only field that didn't include Fleck. Facing an open week, his next destination was Fort Worth for the Colonial National Invitational Tournament and a visit to the Ben Hogan Golf Company.

The distance between Virginia Beach and Fort Worth was 1,400 miles, a long and lonely automobile trip on two-lane highways that passed through numerous cities and small towns. (The Interstate Highway System would be authorized by President Dwight Eisenhower the following year and take several years to complete.)

Everybody drove. Well, almost everybody. A pilot who owned his own plane, Johnny Bulla flew. Snead and Hogan were his occasional passengers. Men crisscrossed the country with fellow pros, or their wives and kids, or both. Accompanied by his wife and child, Larry Tomasino pulled a trailer on the winter tour from Detroit to Miami to Los Angeles to Pebble Beach and back to Michigan. Arnold Palmer also towed a trailer in 1955, his rookie season. "My wife said to me, 'I love you and I'll do anything you want, but I'm not going to live in a trailer ever again,'" Palmer later said, chuckling.

Finsterwald said the long car rides spawned close friendships. "We all liked each other, really," Tomasino added.

Some of the legs on the tour, such as Phoenix to San Antonio, were quite long. Players would travel a couple of hundred miles after the tournament ended and drive the rest of the way the next day. They would wash clothes on Tuesday, play a practice round on Wednesday, and tee it up in the tournament on Thursday.

After buying his first car when he got his head pro job—and no longer needing to arrange rides with other pros—Fleck mostly traveled solo. "I was a loner," he said.

It was tough driving. He had to be alert. One time his alertness may have saved his life. Fleck was driving to Greensboro to meet his wife after visiting South Carolina club pro Melvin Hemphill for help with his golf swing. As he was traveling along a two-lane highway at sixty-five miles per hour, a man in a pickup truck pulled out from a side road. Fleck swerved and dove onto the passenger seat while keeping his grip on the steering wheel. He missed the truck but lost control of his car, skidding off the pavement into someone's front yard.

The pickup truck driver came running and apologized profusely. "I never saw you coming!" he exclaimed.

Fleck got out, checked the tires, and headed down the road. "I didn't want to be scared to drive at full speed, so I just got going again," he said.

In late April of 1955, it was full speed ahead for Jack Fleck. Fueled by his recent good fortune, the excited pro rolled across the South toward Fort Worth. He couldn't wait to see those new clubs. He didn't know it at the time, but each mile was bringing him closer to his first face-to-face encounter with his idol, Ben Hogan.

•   •   •

Fleck was waiting at the Ben Hogan Golf Company when the office door swung open at 8:00 A.M. on the Monday before the Colonial National Invitational Tournament. He introduced himself to the secretary, Claribel Kelly, and told Hogan's grammar school classmate he had stopped by to see how his new clubs were progressing. Kelly asked him to wait a minute and stepped into an adjoining office. General manager Charlie Barnett hadn't arrived yet, but the punctual company president had. Moments later Ben Hogan appeared. After years of admiring Hogan from afar, Fleck now stood in the presence of his idol. The club pro and the golf legend shook hands and talked for a few moments. Fleck recalled Hogan's sincere interest in him. Hogan was pleased that Fleck would soon be playing Ben Hogan clubs and refused to accept payment for the set. Then Hogan's secretary ushered Fleck into the plant, where a Texas pro named Ivy Martin was placing leather grips on his new set of Ben Hogan irons.

Fleck looked around and saw large cardboard barrels filled with clubs. Gathered like orphans, they were the production-run rejects that drove off investor Pollard Simon. Martin explained that the flawed clubs would be shipped to driving ranges in Japan. Based on Hogan tales through the years, Japan wasn't the only destination for the rejected irons. One story: Hogan had the clubs buried in an unmarked grave in a field behind his factory. Another: He had the heads melted down and sold for scrap to Cadillac, his automobile company of choice. A few discarded sets supposedly never left the company premises, collecting dust bunnies for decades in a storage bin above the men's restroom.

Fleck's set, however, would see immediate action. Martin said the clubs would be ready the next day. Fleck returned the following morning at 8:00 A.M. and picked up his new irons, except for the not yet completed pitching and sand wedges. It felt like Christmas morning for the Iowa pro. Word traveled at Colonial to top pros such as Lloyd Mangrum, Jimmy Demaret, and Cary Middlecoff that Fleck had set foot in the factory, sparking good-natured jealousy.

"They all said they had never gotten past the front office," Fleck later said. "Why did he like me? I'll never figure it out, unless it was that I had grown up poor and worked hard like he had."

Fleck was anxious to try out his new clubs and spent several hours hitting balls after his Tuesday and Wednesday practice rounds at Colonial. Yet he used his old sticks, a set of Tommy Armour Silver Scots, in the tournament's first round. Old irons or new irons, Colonial was a tough track that would test his game to the fullest.

"If you missed those smaller greens and missed the bunker next to it, it was going a long way on the hard dry ground," he said.

Balls could easily roll out-of-bounds or into water hazards, and the wind blew constantly. This was Texas, after all.

Fleck started well, shooting an even-par 70. It placed him in a tie for second with Johnny Palmer, 1 stroke behind red-hot Chandler Harper, who led with a 69 despite a 2-stroke penalty due to a lost ball. Paired with Harper in the second round, Fleck shot a respectable 72 that landed him in fourth at the tournament's midway point. Playing partner Harper was in another world, racing to a record 7-shot lead after a 65 that included another 2-stroke penalty.

The press took notice of the solid play of the little-known Iowa pro, especially when he announced he would change clubs in the middle of the tournament. New irons? Why switch clubs when you're in contention?

"These are good clubs," Fleck said. "I've been practicing with them for two or three days. They're Hogans."

Nonetheless, the press remained baffled.

Harper went on to win by 8 shots, his second title that spring. Finsterwald finished alone in second, confirming the wisdom of the special invitation. The other Champions' Choice, however, struggled after putting the new Hogan irons in his golf bag. Fleck faded over the final 36 holes to a disappointing twenty-fourth-place finish and received a check for $108.33.

Two weeks later in Kansas City Fleck was approached by two Wilson representatives who wanted to sign him to an equipment contract. One was the Wilson salesman who called on him at his two Davenport golf courses; the other was a vice president from Wilson's home office in Chicago. They offered him $1,500 to play Wilson clubs. It was the customary fee in contracts with the big four golf equipment companies: Wilson, MacGregor, Spalding, and Hillerich & Bradsby. Fleck asked about a percentage of gross sales of Wilson equipment sold at his two pro shops. The vice president said he could sign for a fee or a percentage of sales, but not both. Fleck, who had never been offered an equipment deal, turned Wilson down.

That same week the two Hogan fairway woods arrived. Fleck used them in the $20,000 Kansas City Open and finished in a tie for eighteenth, banking $293. Except for his Tommy Armour driver and a Bulls Eye putter made by John Rueter Jr. in Rueter's garage, Fleck would be a Hogan man throughout his bag.

The U.S. Open at the Olympic Club in San Francisco was one month away. Only two men would play Hogan clubs at the national championship— the legend himself and Fleck, if he could qualify. Hogan would be bidding for a record fifth U.S. Open title. Fleck just wanted to make the field of golf's greatest championship and continue his two-season quest to succeed as a full-time player on the PGA Tour. He had another incentive to get into the U.S. Open field. The Hawk would personally deliver Fleck's two remaining Hogan irons, a pitching wedge and a sand wedge, in San Francisco. There would be no special invitation this time. Jack Fleck would have to play his way into the national championship.

— 5 —

THE QUALIFIER

In 1955, $10 could buy ten pairs of nylon stockings, a baseball glove, or a muffler at Sears, Roebuck and Company. It was also the entry fee for the fifty-fifth Open Championship of the United States Golf Association to be contested June 16, 17, and 18 at the Olympic Club in San Francisco, California. "Entry must reach USGA office by 5:00 P.M. on Friday, May 20," the application stated in two places. "Late or incomplete entry is not acceptable. Do not telegraph or telephone." Jack Fleck completed his application and mailed it to the USGA at 40 East Thirty-eighth Street in New York City. He would attempt to advance through the sectional qualifier at Lincolnshire Country Club in Crete, Illinois, forty miles south of Chicago on the Illinois-Indiana border.

Sectional qualifying rounds of 36 holes would be held the first week of June at twenty-five sites around the country. The Open field, consisting of both professionals and amateurs, would be limited to 162 players through qualifying or exemptions. Nearly everyone had to qualify. There were few exemptions in 1955: only seventeen players, or roughly 10 percent of the field. Exemptions were awarded to the last five U.S. Open winners, the top ten finishers including ties from the previous year's Open, and 1954 champions of the U.S. Amateur, PGA Championship, British Open, and British Amateur. An exemption was also granted to the head professional at the host golf course. Among those select few who would bypass qualifying were defending champion Ed Furgol, Olympic head pro Johnny Battini, and Ben Hogan, winner of three of the previous five U.S. Opens.

In addition to Fleck, 1,511 players would vie for the 145 remaining spots in the Open field, including semiretired Byron Nelson. The 162 men who made it into the Open field would play for a $20,000 purse. The winner would receive $5,000, a gold medal, and custody of the Championship Trophy for a year. The championship was commonly called the "National Open" during the era. There was no bigger golf tournament. The Masters had not reached its current prominence, the British Open was a cross-Atlantic expedition many American players didn't attempt, and the PGA Championship was still a match-play tournament, a major of lesser stature.

"The golfers snarl," later wrote Pulitzer Prize–winning sports columnist Jim Murray. "They don't like the qualifying. They don't like the tricked-up course. They tell you they'd rather win the Used Edsel Open or the Sasparilla Open or the Upper Sandusky Four-Ball or the Tijuana Lower Open, because the money is better. But don't let them kid you. The U.S. Open is the big apple."

Fleck had qualified twice. The first time was in 1950, when Hogan won his second U.S. Open at Merion sixteen months after the car accident. Fleck made it through a sectional qualifier close to home at the Wakonda Country Club in Des Moines but missed the 36-hole cut at Merion. His next Open appearance was at Oakmont in 1953, the site of Hogan's record-tying fourth National Open title. Fleck's rounds of 76, 76, 77, and 80 for a total of 309 were good for fifty-second place. It was slow progress for the Iowan. Another interruption came in 1954. Playing in a 36-hole sectional qualifier at Cincinnati, he 3-putted six greens and missed qualifying by a stroke. He was so agitated that he drove through the night to the next tour stop at Virginia Beach.

The $15,000 Fort Wayne Invitational lay ahead of Fleck prior to his U.S. Open sectional qualifier on June 6. Fort Wayne was where the year before he had stormed off the course after the tour supervisor accused him of cheating. Dow Finsterwald opened with a 65 and never looked back, posting a 19-under total of 269 and a 3-shot victory over Doug Ford. It was a breakthrough for Finsterwald, the first of eleven PGA Tour wins that included the 1958 PGA Championship.

"At that time a tour win entailed an invitation to the Tournament of Champions," Finsterwald said a half century later. "It was a big step in my tournament career."

While Finsterwald was fulfilling his promise, Fleck finished sixteenth at Fort Wayne and won $230, the kind of middling finish that had become his trademark. He had earned just shy of $2,800 in thirteen events.

Fleck drove home to Lynn, Craig, and his two Davenport golf courses for the one-week break before the Open qualifier. The season was half over, and the allotted time to prove himself and cash bigger checks on tour was slipping away. Unlike at Fort Wayne, Colonial, Virginia Beach, and Greensboro, he had to qualify to make the elite Open field. It was a 1-in-10 shot, but Fleck was no stranger to long odds. If he could play well on June 6, he would secure his spot at the Olympic Club in San Francisco—and keep his appointment with Ben Hogan.

•   •   •

Crete, Illinois, was a town of 2,500 people located a short drive south of Chicago. The village was settled in the mid-1800s and served as an important stop along the Underground Railroad. With rail and interurban lines tying it to its large metropolitan neighbor, Crete became a commercial hub and desirable suburb.

In 1925, Chicago interests bought land on Crete's eastern edge to build Lincolnshire Estates, a housing community that included four planned 18-hole golf courses as part of Lincolnshire Country Club. Course No. 3, designed by Scottish architect Tom Bendelow, whose portfolio included famed Medinah and East Lake, was the site of the Chicago-area sectional qualifier for the 1955 U.S. Open. Opened in the late 1920s, it had relatively narrow, tree-lined fairways spread across flat and gently rolling terrain. Water came into play on several holes. The bentgrass greens were small and "very tricky," according to one player in the '55 qualifier.

Fleck crossed the Mississippi River and drove through the farmland of northern Illinois on the three-hour trip from Davenport to Crete. Two pressure-filled 18-hole rounds lay ahead. Only nine men would advance out of the Chicago sectional.

Monday, June 6, dawned cool, wet, and breezy. More than fifty years later, Fleck's memory of the 1955 season was surprisingly sharp, but the features and contours of Lincolnshire Country Club had faded over the decades.

"It was a good course, but I don't remember much," he said on the drive to a Champions Tour event in North Carolina. What he did recall was the conditions that day. "I was an early starter. I played 34 holes in a cool rain."

The sun appeared as he finished with rounds of 73 and 73 for 146. Fleck was convinced he wouldn't qualify. The sun is out now, he told fellow player Errie Ball. The later scores will surely be lower.

Ball was the head pro at Oak Park in Chicago, a Welshman who befriended Bobby Jones at the British Open during Jones's Grand Slam year of 1930. Ball came from a family of golfers. His father was a friend of six-time British Open champion Harry Vardon. At Jones's urging, Ball came to America to take an assistant pro job at East Lake Golf Club in Atlanta and played in the inaugural Masters Tournament in 1934.

"I didn't feel too scared or nervous at all in the first one [Masters] because it was more relaxed," Ball said. "Bob Jones made it that way."

Ball had played Lincolnshire on several occasions. In addition to the dampness, Ball recalled the wind and hills.

"You had to really watch it and use your head. I never really did like the golf course," he admitted. "It was like a trick golf course."

Lincolnshire's small greens—and greens in general—gave Ball fits. "I never had much trouble from tee to green, but I had a lot of trouble with putting and I developed the yips."

Despite his reservations about the course, Ball came in at 145, a shot better than Fleck. As he drove around the circle drive to leave the club, he spotted Fleck on the practice putting green.

"How did you do?" Ball asked.

"I don't think I'm going to qualify," Fleck replied.

"I'll bet you a dollar you qualify."

"There's some players still out. I'm hanging around here putting, just to keep loose."

"I still bet a dollar that you make it."

Then Ball eased his car into gear.

"I'll see you in San Francisco," he said, as Fleck waited anxiously on the putting green. Would he?

That same day the other Colonial Champions' Choice and recent first-time tour winner was still on a roll. Dow Finsterwald was low medalist at sectional qualifying in Cincinnati with a 66-71 for 137. Recent two-time winner Chandler Harper led all 1,512 players in nationwide qualifying with a 67-67 for 134 at Chevy Chase, Maryland.

At the North Carolina sectional qualifier in Fayetteville, Fleck's friend Walker Inman secured one of three available spots. In Cleveland, Mike Krak lost a two-hole playoff but would get into the Open field as an alternate. At Fort Worth, Billy Maxwell, Fred Hawkins, Ernie Vossler, and six others qualified under the intent gaze of an exempt player turned spectator, Ben Hogan.

At Lincolnshire the final players streamed off the course in the late afternoon and tallied their scorecards. Errie Ball's math had been correct. With the qualifying mark set at 147, Ball's 145 and Fleck's 146 were in. They would see each other in San Francisco after all. The course and conditions had proved tough. Ball's 145 was second best to medalist Ed Oliver's 143.

"He still owes me a dollar," Ball said, chuckling, a half century later in reference to the friendly wager, although Fleck said Ball refused payment through the years.

"He said, 'I want you to owe me,'" Fleck recalled.

.   .   .

With the U.S. Open nine days away, Fleck would spend the short break from tournament golf at his Davenport golf courses and prepare for the trip west. Early Tuesday morning, the day after he qualified at Lincolnshire, he was regripping and refinishing his golf clubs when an elderly man named Ralph Riley walked into his pro shop. No one else was around. Riley congratulated Fleck on his tournament play. Thanking Riley, Fleck admitted that he had not come close to winning a tournament.

"Do you pray to win a tournament?" Riley asked.

"No, you don't pray to win a golf tournament," replied Fleck. "Sickness or death or something that's real important, yes."

Riley stepped away and then returned a few minutes later. "OK," he said, "then pray for the power and strength to compete."

Jack Fleck was raised in a Christian home by hardworking, God-fearing parents. Presbyterians, the Flecks bore witness to the Good Book, the Protestant work ethic, and raised their children with a firm but loving hand.

"We had to toe the mark," said Jack's sister Shirley.

It took with Fleck, whose straitlaced ways included an aversion to cigarettes and alcohol, although in later years he would occasionally allow himself a glass of wine with dinner.

"He doesn't drink, smoke, or even drink coffee," Lynn once said, laughing. "Why, he thinks cigarettes cause everything from dandruff to athlete's foot."

Despite his Christian roots and squeaky-clean lifestyle, the chance encounter with Riley challenged Fleck's view of prayer. Dare he bring golf into his petitions to God? Was it OK to ask for the power and strength to compete?

"That made sense to me," he decided, "not asking for a specific thing . . . only for the Lord to help me."

．　　　．　　　．

On Wednesday night Fleck packed for San Francisco. As an itinerant golf pro, he knew the drill and routinely gathered his items for the trip, chief among them clean clothes and his prized Hogan clubs. Two items, however, were not the usual stock-in-trade of a tour pro. For Fleck, bringing along his Motorola record player and Mario Lanza records was as important as packing enough socks. The record player with accordion-style speakers had been a Father's Day gift from Lynn. He had once shot a low score at the Phoenix Open the morning after listening to classical music in a friend's home.

While other tour pros smoked, drank, played cards, and went out to dinner and the movies, Fleck mostly kept to himself, leading a monklike existence. He rarely hung out with the other players, whether in the locker room or elsewhere. He was not one of the guys.

"Jack wasn't a rabble-rouser," Inman said. "He didn't carouse like a lot of the guys did, didn't gamble, didn't drink, was a straight shooter. I was the same way."

Hawkins, who associated with fun-loving types on tour such as Jimmy Demaret and Cary Middlecoff, acknowledged that Fleck didn't fit the mold. "Jack Fleck has always been a different kind of person," Hawkins, who partnered with Fleck at the Legends of Golf, later said. "He's just different—I wouldn't say anything really against him—but he's different. He doesn't have any great buddies out there."

Hawkins's repeated use of the word "different" made it seem like Fleck was from another planet, which, as far as the pro golf circuit was concerned, he was. Among Fleck's differences was a penchant for healthy eating long before it was a fad. Like others, he preferred dining in cafeterias because they were economical, but he also favored them because he could go through the line and carefully select the foods he wanted to eat. His diet consisted largely of vegetables and fruits. He ate chicken but avoided red meat. He shunned processed baked goods such as white bread and rolls, calling them "poison."

Fleck also was a devotee of Hatha yoga, an exercise regimen he picked up from a book given to him by a Michigan man. "Hatha" means health, and Fleck was an enthusiastic proponent of the yoga technique, buying and selling yoga books in his golf shops and on tour.

"He was a conscientious guy who wanted to be a good player," In-man said, "and that showed in his lifestyle and the way he practiced and the way he played and the way he took care of himself."

Another difference that didn't endear Fleck to some of his golf peers was his avoidance of money games, which was how many pros supplemented their incomes on the tournament trail. There were limited opportunities to earn money in golf. Club jobs, equipment contracts, and tournaments were the primary ways, although none of them were lucrative for most pros. Some players made as much or more money gambling and hustling. It was how they survived and got from town to town.

Fleck discovered that playing for money on off days wasn't for him. He learned an expensive lesson in Texas when he lost a few hundred dollars in a practice round with Doug Ford and Ted Kroll. It was money he couldn't afford to lose, so he vowed to not play in big money games from that point on. Sometimes other players chided him, saying the money games would toughen him up for tournament competition. Nevertheless, Fleck went his own way, instead working on his shotmaking and learning the golf courses, paying little attention to the number on the scorecard until the tournament began. It was just one more way he didn't fit in.

During his hours away from the golf course, Fleck could be found exercising and meditating in his motel room. Nearby the Motorola record player played the calming classical sounds of tenor Mario Lanza. Born in Philadelphia, Lanza was a prodigy who began singing in local operas and went on to worldwide fame through the stage, radio, concerts, and movies during the late 1940s and early 1950s. In 1954, Lanza's recording of "I'll Walk with God" from the sound track of the movie *The Student Prince* became a major hit. With music by Nicholas Brodzky and lyrics by Paul Francis Webster, the song ended, "And I'll never walk alone while I walk with God," words that were particularly meaningful to Lanza fan Jack Fleck.

"Nothing was more soothing to me than hearing him sing 'I'll Walk with God,'" Fleck later said. "His singing put me in a wonderful frame of mind."

With his Hogan clubs, phonograph, and Mario Lanza records safely stowed, Fleck climbed into his Buick early Thursday morning for the solo two-thousand-mile trip across the Great Plains, Rockies, desert, and Sierra Nevadas to California's Bay Area. Forty-nine hours later on Saturday morning he rolled into Daly City and registered at the El Camino Motel on Mission Street. The motor court was just a short hop from the Olympic Club. There was a good cafeteria nearby.

Eight miles away in downtown San Francisco, his lean tour days far behind him, Ben Hogan was staying at the upscale St. Francis Hotel on Union Square, one of the city's most elegant accommodations. Among his possessions was an extra set of new Ben Hogan Precision wedges.

PART
II

—6—

THE RECORD

Ben Hogan was two months shy of his forty-third birthday when he arrived in San Francisco two weeks prior to the start of the 1955 U.S. Open Championship. The luxurious confines of the St. Francis on Union Square—a hotel erected in 1904 by the wealthy Crocker family as part of their attempt to make San Francisco the "Paris of the West"—could not mask the persistent complaints of Hogan's battered body. The grueling physical demands of tournament golf since the terrible accident had become almost too much for the hardscrabble Texan who lived to dig golf balls out of the dirt.

He wondered aloud if his time in tournament golf was drawing to a close. "If I'm lucky enough to win here, I doubt if I will ever play in an important tournament again. It's just too hard."

Hogan never played more than seven tournaments in a year after the near-fatal bus collision in February 1949. He focused on the major championships, and the U.S. Open was the one he coveted most. It suited his splendid long game, obsessive preparation, course management, and mental toughness.

Author Robert Sommers wrote that Hogan "was perhaps the best striker of the ball who ever lived, at least as fierce a competitor as Bob Jones, and no one ever prepared for a tournament with more intelligence or insight. He had one other knack that transcended the others; he could hit the ball to where he wanted it to go."

Ben Hogan and the U.S. Open were made for each other.

There was another compelling reason for the Hawk to enter the '55 National Open, even on bad legs: It offered him an appointment with history. Hogan's four U.S. Open titles at Riviera in '48, Merion in '50, Oakland Hills in '51, and Oakmont in '53 tied him with two men in the golf record books.

The first man to win four U.S. Opens was a Scot named Willie Anderson who immigrated to the United States in 1896. Anderson's first title came in 1901 at Myopia Hunt Club in Massachusetts. During the day of hickory-shafted golf clubs and out-of-round golf balls, Anderson tied Alex Smith at 331 (neither man broke 80 in any round) and then won in an 18-hole playoff. The Scot took home the trophy and $200. Then, beginning in 1903, Anderson did what no man since has accomplished: He won three consecutive U.S. Open titles. The streak included a record round of 72 in 1904, a phenomenal competitive score at the beginning of the new century. Anderson died at the age of thirty-one just five years after his final victory in 1905. The official cause was epilepsy, although at least one writer suggested the Scot drank himself to death.

Bobby Jones, the other man to win four U.S. Opens, was the dominant golfer of his era and considered by many in the mid-twentieth century to be the greatest golf champion of all time. When Jones, a lifelong amateur, retired from tournament golf at the age of twenty-eight, he had amassed thirteen major titles, including a quartet of National Opens won in a seven-year stretch from 1923 to 1930, the year he won what became known as the Grand Slam, an elusive standard of golf excellence for decades to come. Upon his triumphant return to American soil after winning the 1930 British Open at the Royal Liverpool Golf Club, Jones was honored with a ticker-tape parade down Broadway in New York City.

With a win at Olympic and record fifth U.S. Open title, Hogan would pass Anderson and Jones, setting a new mark that would surely stand for a very long time. However, Hogan and some of his most ardent supporters would claim in the ensuing years that he already owned five Open titles when he arrived in San Francisco.

Hogan won the 1942 Hale America National Open, a wartime tournament staged by the USGA, the PGA of America, and the Chicago District Golf Association after the USGA decided to cancel the U.S. Open. The U.S. Open did not resume until 1946, the year after World War II ended. Similar to the U.S. Open, the Hale America tournament featured national qualifying, a strong field, and USGA medals for the winner, runner-up, and low amateur. Propelled by a second-round 62, Hogan took home the winner's gold medal, which was nearly identical to the medal awarded to U.S. Open champions. For the purposes of the record book, however, the Hale America National Open would be regarded as a cosponsored tournament played to support war efforts rather than a USGA-sanctioned national championship.

.   .   .

A third-round 76 thwarted Hogan's assault on the record books at the '54 Open at Baltusrol Golf Club in suburban New Jersey, where Ed Furgol prevailed with a 4-over-par total of 284. Hogan finished in a five-way tie for sixth place, another top ten for a man who had not finished lower than sixth in the U.S. Open since 1939. Excluding the war years during which the National Open was canceled, the Hawk had posted a stunning series of finishes in ten appearances: four wins, two thirds, a fourth, a fifth, and two sixths. Besides the war years, the only interruption to Hogan's streak of high Open finishes was in 1949 when he was recovering from the accident.

An astonishing fact: Hogan had played his best tournament golf since the death-defying accident, winning six majors in five seasons, including the Hogan Slam trio in 1953. Coming into the 1955 U.S. Open, he had captured four of the previous seven national championships, a dominating run by golf's dominant player.

"In years to come, I am sure, the sports public, looking back at his record, will be struck by awe and disbelief that any one man could have played so well so regularly," wrote Herbert Warren Wind in the *Sports Illustrated* U.S. Open preview article titled "The Age of Hogan."

In June of 1955, was Hogan an aching and aged golfer? Most definitely. Was he washed up on the eve of another U.S. Open? Most would have not dared to think it.

Errie Ball later described Hogan, whom everyone looked up to, as the Tiger Woods of his day. Late in his life, Tommy Bolt insisted that Hogan was the greatest player he had ever played with, even greater than Jack Nicklaus. Arnold Palmer said all the players respected Hogan's game.

The Hawk's reputation as a hard worker stood out in players' minds. Dow Finsterwald noted the many golf balls Hogan constantly hit, and the singular concentration that kept his mind on his work.

Bolt agreed. "As a golfer, he could outconcentrate anyone else. He just overpowered them with concentration. He kept his mind on what he was doing. That's how he beat everybody. His mind never left his business."

Hogan was the only player Bolt ever saw get a standing ovation on the practice tee.

He was like a machine, recalled Shelley Mayfield, a tour and club pro who played a regular game with Hogan in later years. "I have never seen anybody better than Ben Hogan from tee to green."

Despite fawning respect and a sterling U.S. Open record, Hogan was battling Father Time. He dragged himself around championship golf courses hampered by a set of worsening wheels. As the U.S. Open approached, some even reported they detected clues of Hogan's decline.

Wind, for one, offered evidence: occasional missed fairways, popped-up approach shots falling short of their mark, and missed putts in the nerve-jangling 5-foot range. Normal occurrences for most competitive golfers, these were considered to be telltale signs that the machinelike Hogan had lost some of his precision.

There was something else. The Hawk's swing looked different. It was shorter and on a flatter plane. The swing change was intentional, Hogan's plan of attack for Olympic's tilting fairways, although it escaped the scribes.

It would have come as no surprise to Fred Hawkins, a frequent Hogan practice partner who would drive from his home in El Paso to Hogan's Fort Worth turf for some friendly competition prior to tournaments. A head taller than Hogan, Hawkins was a good iron player and even better with the putter.

"The top players are making continuous adjustments," Hawkins later said. "... Hogan was always trying out something different. I mean, it sounds stupid to say that for a guy of his caliber, but that's just the nature of the game. Everybody is making adjustments all the time."

New York Herald Tribune sportswriter Al Laney later said, "In our ignorance, we thought Ben had adjusted his game to his own physical limitations and that he was at last playing with impaired weapons. We ought to have known better, to understand that he was adjusting to the new conditions just as he had at Carnoustie."

If Hogan knew of such talk, it would have only served as further motivation. Doubters were nothing new. They had been around since the beginning when the young Texan fought a wicked hook and aborted his first two attempts to make it on the tour. If anything, the doubters just made the world's most obsessed golfer work harder.

On the eve of the National Open, Hogan cataloged a handful of slights in a rare interview granted to *Sports Illustrated*'s Joan Flynn Dreyspool. They had been saying he was through for a decade. When he started out, they said he was too small. A well-known golfer said he would never make it. They criticized his swing. They said his first win would be his last. It was just luck.

"It seems to me that every time somebody said I couldn't do something," Hogan told Dreyspool, "I just got more determined."

The Hawk had a chip on his shoulder long before he had a limp. It drove him.

As Hogan assessed the difficult task that lay ahead of him in San Francisco, there was one foe that commanded his full attention. Although irritating, it wasn't the press. Nor was it the field of 161 other golfers, even though it was one of the strongest U.S. Open fields ever. Hogan's chief concern was the 18 holes at Olympic's Lake Course. Each hole would be a battle in miniature to be planned and executed across three days and four rounds of pressure-filled championship golf.

This was as much a part of Hogan's greatness as his uncanny ability to consistently strike pure golf shots. No one prepared as thoroughly as Ben Hogan for a major championship. As he was soon to find out, Olympic would live up to its namesake, Mount Olympus, a tall, rugged peak that, according to Greek mythology, was the seat of the gods. If Hogan was going to rewrite the record books, he would have to find a way to scale one last mountain.

— 7 —

THE COURSE DOCTOR

Although it was the national championship in name, the U.S. Open was primarily an East Coast and Midwest tournament in location. Of the fifty-four previous U.S. Opens, only four had been played west of the Mississippi River, and until the Olympic Club was awarded the fifty-fifth edition, only one U.S. Open had been contested on the West Coast. The first West Coast Open also happened to be the first of Hogan's four Open wins—the 1948 championship contested at Riviera Country Club in Los Angeles.

If Ben Hogan found Olympic to be a severe test, then perhaps he had himself to blame. At Riviera, as Hollywood stars such as Humphrey Bogart and Gregory Peck looked on, Hogan obliterated Ralph Guldahl's U.S. Open scoring record of 281 by 5 shots. Jimmy Demaret, Hogan's playing partner in team events, came home with a 69 in the final round to break Guldahl's Open mark by 3 strokes. Sunny Jim held the record for fifty-six minutes. Hogan's 276 would stand until Jack Nicklaus bettered it by a shot at Baltusrol nineteen years later.

It seemed to be no coincidence that U.S. Open golf courses got tougher following Hogan's record-breaking parade at Riviera. The USGA prided itself on conducting the most rigorous championship in golf. Par became sacred for American golf's governing body. All but one of the next six Open winners leading up to the 1955 contest finished over par. Courses such as Oakland Hills in Michigan, site of the 1951 championship, became the stern defenders of golf's scoring standard. Oakland Hills measured nearly 7,000 yards, a long course in the day of small-headed, wooden clubs, with thick rough and cavernous bunkers. Hogan called it ridiculous. He won nonetheless, posting a 7-over-par total of 287, 11 shots more than his 1948 record-setting performance.

"I'm glad that I brought this course, this monster, to its knees," he famously said.

In June 1955, another treacherous U.S. Open course lay ahead of the Hawk and his fellow pros, this one on the edge of the Pacific.

.   .   .

In the summer of 1918 after a five-year search for a suitable property, the Olympic Club, a prestigious athletic club with champions in multiple sports, stumbled upon an ideal site to fulfill its golf aspirations. The economic consequences of World War I had helped decide the issue. The Lakeside Golf Club, which opened in 1917, was in financial trouble. Lakeside and the Spring Valley Water Company, owner of the acreage on which the 18-hole golf course sat, made a proposal to Olympic's membership: take over the lease with options to buy the land from the water company and four acres owned by the golf club. The deal was too good to pass up. The membership unanimously approved.

The Olympic Club exercised the purchase options by 1922 and acquired adjoining parcels until the club had amassed 371 acres that stretched from the Pacific Ocean to near Lake Merced. Ten miles southwest of down-town San Francisco, the property was distinguished by bluffs and rolling sand dunes. Only one dirt trail—about the width of a motorcar—snaked its way onto the acreage.

Designed by Wilfrid Reid, an English professional who accompanied British greats Harry Vardon and Ted Ray to play in the 1913 U.S. Open won by American amateur Francis Ouimet, the original Lakeside course would soon vanish. The Olympic Club had acquired enough land to design and build two 18-hole golf courses and construct a massive Spanish-style clubhouse.

Two 18-hole layouts were carved out of the dunes and bluffs: the Lake and Ocean courses, both designed by William "Willie" Watson and con-structed by Sam Whiting, the club's golf pro and superintendent. Watson and Whiting later teamed to build Harding Park, a municipal course on the east side of Lake Merced, and Watson had a hand in several other American courses, including Interlachen, a future U.S. Open site in Min-nesota.

With Watson and Whiting's work complete, the Lake and Ocean courses opened in May 1924. The impressive new clubhouse, a California motif of yellow stucco with a Mediterranean red tile roof, followed a year later. Soon after, winter storms rendered the Ocean Course unplayable, prompting the redesign and reconstruction of both courses by Whiting. The new Lake and Ocean courses opened in 1927, the year that marked the official start of Ryder Cup matches between the United States and Great Britain.

The Lake Course was the more demanding of the two layouts, gain-ing a reputation throughout America for its beauty and difficulty. Char-acterized by rolling terrain that sloped toward Lake Merced to the east, the course matured into a thick parklike forest, with thirty thousand Marietta pine, gnarled California cypress, cedar, eucalyptus, and other native trees lining its 18 holes. The fairways, many of which doglegged, were narrow. The greens were small, sloped, and well bunkered. There were no water hazards and few fairway bunkers at the Lake Course. This woodland masquerading as a golf course didn't need them.

Although the trees were not full grown in the 1920s, the Lake Course was a difficult layout from the outset and earned high praise from the world's greatest amateur, Bobby Jones, who called it "the best in the west" after shooting a 75. Early-day pros such as Walter Hagen, "Lighthorse" Harry Cooper, Leo Diegel, Tommy Armour, Olin Dutra, and Macdonald Smith (who became the Olympic Club's first pro) also found the Lake Course to be tough sledding.

Although it wasn't a regular stop on the pro golf trail, the next generation of great players—including Byron Nelson, Ben Hogan, and Sam Snead—had occasion to test their skills on the Lake Course. None of the game's best subdued the forested terrain along Lake Merced. It made the Olympic Club a good match for the United States Golf Association, an organization that existed, in large part, to conduct the world's most demanding golf championships.

Nonetheless, with U.S. Open courses getting longer and tougher, the Lake Course's 1920s design, length of 6,432 yards, and par of 71 made it vulnerable to the best field in golf. The situation called for action. After visiting Baltusrol, site of the 1954 Open, Olympic Club tournament committee members made plans to modify the Lake Course to make it a worthy test for the likes of Hogan, Snead, and others who would grace their fairways.

They had the right man for the job. It was the same man who had turned Oakland Hills into the monster that frightened, angered, and humiliated the world's best golfers. His name was Robert Trent Jones.

Jones, who would turn forty-nine one day after the 1955 U.S. Open, was a Cornell University graduate who studied to become a golf course architect. After completing his coursework in landscape architecture, agronomy, horticulture, surveying, hydraulics, economics, and public speaking, Jones partnered with a Canadian golf course architect named Stanley Thompson for a decade. The pair's projects stretched from British Columbia to Argentina.

Jones then launched his own practice and built an impressive client list that included the states of New York and New Jersey and companies and organizations such as International Business Machines, General Electric, and the United States Military Academy. He designed golf courses and recreational developments, but his fame would come in golf. Throughout a seven-decade career, Jones would design or redesign more than five hundred golf courses, spawning a golf course architecture dynasty that continues today with his sons, Robert Trent Jones Jr. and Rees Jones.

By 1955, Jones was known in golf circles as the U.S. Open course doctor who made house calls, having performed major surgery on Oakland Hills and tuning up Baltusrol Golf Club prior to the '54 Open.

"Jones was an amplifier," wrote Curt Sampson. "He put tail fins on Oakland Hills. Bigger, longer, tougher, more: the new Oakland Hills fit perfectly with other examples of fifties excess such as poodle skirts, hula hoops, and Elvis."

After criticism of his redesign of the par-3 4th hole at Baltusrol's Lower Course, Jones, playing with Baltusrol pro Johnny Farrell, teed a ball and struck it with his 4-iron. The ball cleared the pond, landed on the green, and rolled into the cup, an ace. Jones turned and said in his high-pitched voice, "Gentlemen, the hole is fair. Eminently fair."

A small man with a round face and broad smile, Jones appeared harmless, even jovial. In contrast, his handiwork—enormous bunkers, ponds and creeks, tight fairways, heavy rough, and undulating greens—was downright sinister. Many of golf's best were not fond of his work. Some openly loathed it. Criticism did not deter Jones, for he held to a simple, uncompromising philosophy.

"The shattering of par without a proper challenge is a fraud," he said. "I make them play par."

Jones set out to make the Lake Course a worthy battleground for the world's best golfers and their modern weapons. With higher-quality steel shafts, forged irons, persimmon woods, and more consistent golf balls, equipment was on the advance. Jones would attempt to counter whatever edge players had gained.

Compared to recent Open courses, the Lake Course presented a different set of challenges for the designer to overcome. Jones would turn the Lake Course's apparent weaknesses into strengths. He stretched the course—the shortest to host the U.S. Open since Merion in 1950—adding nearly 300 yards. Already tight, especially with overhanging trees that stood up to 100 feet high, the fairways were narrowed to a width of 25 to 40 yards. Bunkers were expanded and reshaped to guard openings to the tiny greens and crowd pin placements. In the absence of water, heavy bunkering, and sheer length, the course doctor pulled one more thing from his bag of tricks: rough.

The Lake Course rough was an Italian rye grass sown in the early 1920s. It was strong, clumpy, and thick, with single stalks measuring three-eighths of an inch wide. The stout grass was unlike anything the players had seen—and they'd seen nearly everything. The rough alongside Olympic's narrow fairways would be graduated, ranging from a height of 2 to 5 inches if a player strayed more than 5 yards off the fairway. The grabby rough also would hug the putting surfaces, a severe penalty for inaccurate approach shots.

As Jones laid his plans, it was apparent that he would need to do something about the Lake Course's easiest birdie opportunities. For starters, he changed the par on the 461-yard 17th hole from 5 to 4. Jones himself called it "controversial" and said "even the best pros will find reaching it in two extremely nerve-racking." The 7th, a straightaway 266-yard par 4, was the weakest hole on the course. The green was wide open and begged to be driven. So Jones wrapped a new horseshoe-shaped bunker around the front of the green and turned the fairway into rough. He devised a small landing area called the Dewdrop, putting a premium on accuracy from the tee box. Lastly, he placed a crown contour on the center of the green. There would be no easy birdies at the 7th.

A par-4 dogleg to the left, the 14th hole underwent the greatest change. Jones tightened the broad fairway to favor tee shots down the left-hand side, but not without significant risk. Trees and a steep slope hugged the dogleg. A pulled or hooked tee shot could disappear into the trees or, worse, roll down the hill into a nasty barranca, a graveyard for misdirected Titleists and Spalding Dots. Jones also modified the greenside bunkers to narrow the opening to the putting surface.

There would be no carefree strolls to Olympic's large stucco clubhouse—at least not by way of the course's three finishing holes. The 16th hole, a 603-yard par 5, required three robust shots to reach its small green in regulation. The long, uphill par-4 17th, the converted par 5, would be unreachable in 2 for most of the 162 players in the field.

The 18th hole was a straightaway par 4 that measured only 337 yards. Jones noted that it "may prove to be the glamour hole of the course." Bordered by a slope on the left and trees on the right, the 18th funneled downhill to a narrow landing area and rose up a steep slope to a small, tilted green set in a natural amphitheater. Cleared of trees and vegetation for the Open, the hillside surrounding the 18th green would accommodate thousands of spectators eager to see the world's best players strike their final shots of the championship.

On the scorecard, Olympic would play 6,700 yards and to a par of 70,

35 on both the outward and inward 9s—but the scorecard was deceiving. The Lake Course would play longer and harder than anyone expected. Jones's modifications bore responsibility, but so did San Francisco's cool, damp weather. The city was a fog- and mist-shrouded landscape, the ground perpetually blanketed with heavy dew. Golf balls flew shorter distances in the thick, chilly air, and roll was minimal on Olympic's lush, wet fairways. The rough would grow to unprecedented heights, strangling the hopes of the 162-man field.

Hogan would call Olympic the longest short course in the world. When asked more than three decades later to name the toughest championship course he ever played, Hogan said, "The Lake Course at Olympic in the 1955 Open stands out in my mind."

After assessing his work, the course doctor pronounced that Olympic was fit for competition "and should prove a thorough examination in golf." Little did he know how many would receive failing grades.

— 8 —

"A TERROR, START TO FINISH"

At the *San Francisco Chronicle,* one of the city's top dailies, a team of veteran sports scribes was gearing up for the first staging of a major professional golf championship in the Bay Area. As the golf and sports world began to focus its attention on Olympic in early June, the copy cranked up in the offices of the *Chronicle Sporting Green,* the paper's sports section. Sports editor Bill Leiser would oversee the coverage; sportswriters Bob Goethals and Art Rosenbaum would report all the action. The typewriter of Rosenbaum, a Bay Area golf authority, would be among the busiest in the local and visiting press throng.

It was typing, not writing, that landed Rosenbaum his job at the *Chronicle* in the late 1920s. He never left, spending seven decades at "the Voice of the West," as the paper proudly called itself in the mid-1950s. Rosenbaum perfected his dexterity for the newfangled machine after his sister brought home a typewriter keyboard chart from secretarial school. He later got an audition from sports editor Harry B. Smith at the *Chronicle*'s Fifth Street offices.

"I was using ten fingers, bang, bang, bang, and most of them were just one- or two-finger guys," Rosenbaum said. "He said, 'You're hired.'"

One of six children, Rosenbaum was a genial man and respected sports-writer who sometimes befriended the stars he covered, among them New York Yankees great Joe DiMaggio and, later, the San Francisco Giants' Willie Mays. This was not unusual during an era when the press and pro athletes were on chummy terms and coverage rarely strayed from the field, court, or course.

On Tuesday, June 7, the lead item in Rosenbaum's "Overheard" column was the upcoming visit of the American president. "Even a Democrat will agree that it's only a coincidence that President Eisenhower plans to be in San Francisco about the same time as the U.S. Open golf championship is being competed," Rosenbaum wrote.

Eisenhower, popularly known as "Ike," would attend a meeting to cel-ebrate the tenth anniversary of the United Nations. Connecting the presi-dential visit with the National Open was good copy. The president's golf obsession was a national punch line.

"If he slices the budget like he slices a ball, the nation has nothing to worry about," once joked comedian Bob Hope.

Ike was an unabashed golf enthusiast who took the ribbing good-naturedly. He installed a practice green on the White House lawn in 1954 and visited Augusta National so often—twenty-nine times in all—that the club built and named a cabin for him. The thirty-fourth president would play nearly nine hundred rounds during his time in office, second only to Woodrow Wilson.

Because of security concerns, Rosenbaum suggested Eisenhower's only exposure to the Open would be through the screen of his hotel suite televi-sion set. Millions of other TV viewers would tune in along with the president. Television was becoming mainstream, and *I Love Lucy,* a screwball comedy starring Lucille Ball and her husband, Desi Arnaz, was America's hit show. A 1953 episode anticipating the birth of Lucy's son attracted 15 million more viewers than Ike's inauguration the following day. The show was among a handful of popular situation comedies—*The Adventures of Ozzie and Harriet, Father Knows Best,* and later *Leave It to Beaver*—that portrayed family life in the 1950s as a wholesome existence with happy endings. In increasing numbers, American families were spending their evenings gathered around the television instead of the radio.

The 1955 U.S. Open would be the third national golf telecast. Lindsey Nelson would anchor the one-hour final-day coverage for NBC-TV, with Gene Sarazen providing commentary. For the first time at a National Open, Sarazen would grip a microphone instead of a golf club. Sarazen, nicknamed "the Squire," was a seven-time major winner who had played in every U.S. Open since 1920, winning the championship twice, in 1922 and 1932. The Squire was also the inventor of the modern sand wedge, a heavy short iron with ample loft and a wide sole designed to dig golf balls out of bunkers. As players at Olympic were soon to find out, the sand wedge would also be a weapon of choice to extract golf balls from the thick rough surrounding the Lake Course's tiny greens.

.   .   .

On Wednesday, eight days before the start of the tournament, Rosenbaum trailed America's top golfing tandem as they sped around the Olympic layout in a brisk two-and-a-half-hour practice round. Hogan and Snead didn't keep score, and when their golf balls landed in the rough, they kicked them back into the fairway. The pair hit multiple approach shots to gauge distances and judge the effect of the course's sloping terrain. At the finishing hole, while several Olympic members watched from the clubhouse on the hill behind the green, Hogan and Snead struck two tee shots apiece before launching their final approaches toward the putting surface. The two golf stars gave a unanimous two-word assessment of the Lake Course: "very tough."

Snead elaborated. "Man, if some of the eastern boys knew how tough this course was, they wouldn't even bother to come out."

On Thursday, with gloomy skies overhead, Hogan and Snead were joined for a practice round by Byron Nelson and Cary "Doc" Middlecoff, the reigning Masters champion. Middlecoff had just stepped off an airplane, and it showed. His golf ball made frequent visits to the rough, and the former dentist struggled to a 77. Middlecoff gave up his dental practice in 1947 to pursue a pro golf career. With a swing envied by Bobby Jones, he won the 1949 U.S. Open, although he later said, "Nobody wins the Open. It wins you."

After narrowly qualifying to get into the field, genteel part-timer Nelson was giddy about his practice round alongside Hogan and company. Byron needed just 24 putts and carded an even-par 70, tying Hogan for low round in the group.

Snead moaned about the weather after shooting a 74. "All my aches and pains come out again on a day like this. My hand hurts and my back hurts. I won't play well if it stays like this."

Hogan was tight-lipped about his own physical complaints, but his limp was easy to spot as he clutched his right leg several times during the round. He occasionally fell off the pace of his playing partners, lagging 30 yards behind. Hogan's drives also trailed those of the other players by 20 to 30 yards. It appeared the Hawk was struggling to keep up.

Whatever Hogan was doing to prepare for the championship—and whatever his perceived limitations—he appeared to be unconcerned, even relaxed. He hummed and whistled the popular *Davy Crockett* theme song as he toured the Lake Course, amusing the gallery of four hundred people.

.　　.　　.

For others, practice rounds at Olympic were more likely to produce whining and cursing rather than humming and whistling. The course doctor had gone too far. Ed Oliver had his first look at Olympic on Sunday, four days before the start of the tournament. Nicknamed "Porky" because he carried 240 pounds on a 5'9" frame, he returned to the locker room after losing twelve balls in six holes.

"The way that course is playing I'm going to need all the balls I can get," he said.

Oliver wasn't the only one hunting golf balls as if on safari. Some later said that more golf balls were lost at Olympic than the previous ten national championships combined. Nor were golf balls the only thing that went missing. One caddie who ventured into the deep rough to search for a ball could not find the golf bag he had set down in the tall grass.

The Lake Course was getting into players' heads. Players warned each other not to practice too much on the rough-infested layout. Some pleaded with their golfing brethren to avoid hitting recovery shots from the maniacal rough. "It was like striking a shot out of a deep bed of day-old linguini," later wrote Bill Fields.

The greens were no bargain either. First, they were too small to be receptive to long approach shots, complained many players. Second, the greens were filled with *Poa annua*, a weedy grass that made the putting surfaces tricky to decipher and bumpy to putt. "The greens were hard to read," remembered Detroit club pro Larry Tomasino.

On Sunday, the *Chronicle Sporting Green* published an aerial photograph of the Lake Course with a headline that read, AND HERE'S THE COURSE—A TERROR, START TO FINISH. The pairings for the first two rounds appeared halfway down the page. One might have wondered if all of the

135 pros and 27 amateurs would bother to show up on Thursday for the start of the tournament.

Despite the terror that lurked alongside Lake Merced, the par defenders at the USGA would pick up where the course doctor left off. Tournament officials would select a set of pin positions for each green, balancing difficulty with fairness, although it was a subjective exercise and a source of consternation for the players who had to maneuver their golf balls to the challenging hole positions. The front aprons of the greens would be soaked with water to discourage run-up shots, but there would be no liberal watering of the putting surfaces, which would play harder and faster as the championship progressed.

An occasional ray of hope broke through the increasing gloom at Olympic. On the same day that Oliver aborted his practice round and ordered more golf balls, Dick Mayer threatened the competitive course record of 65. Mayer, a promising young player, had almost won the U.S. Open the year before at Baltusrol. A par at the 72nd hole would have given him the victory. Instead, he carded a tragic triple bogey to finish third, 2 shots higher than Furgol's winning score.

Mayer showed good form that spring. A month earlier he had won the Kansas City Open, the same event where Jack Fleck had received his Hogan woods. Alongside Hogan and Claude Harmon in a Sunday practice round, the blond thirty-year-old pro chipped in for an eagle and recorded three birdies en route to a 66.

"I was playing so good and dropping so many putts that even Ben Hogan smiled along about the 17th hole," Mayer said.

Being noticed by Hogan was no given. The Hawk was famous for blocking out all on-course distractions, including his playing partners. Once while playing in the 1947 Masters with Harmon, Hogan was so pleased with a rare birdie at the par-3 12th hole that he mentioned it to

Harmon as they walked to the 13th tee. It didn't occur to Hogan to congratulate Harmon on his hole in one. He hadn't noticed it.

Alas, Mayer's 66 during the practice session would be his best round on the Lake Course and a score no one would match in the tournament. When the shots counted from Thursday through Saturday, only five players would break Olympic's par of 70 and there would be just six rounds in the 60s. Labeling the Lake Course a "terror" was no exaggeration.

—9—

THE YOUNG GUARD

News arrived that veteran Lloyd Mangrum had dropped out of the tournament. Pegged as one of "the Old Guard" favorites in *Sports Illustrated*'s U.S. Open preview, the forty-year-old Mangrum was recovering from a rib separation injury suffered in late April at the Tournament of Champions in Las Vegas. The 1946 U.S. Open champion and a winner of more than thirty PGA Tour events, Mangrum was a contender every time he teed it up. The Texan, along with George Fazio, was part of the 18-hole playoff at Merion in 1950, Hogan's miraculous comeback victory and second U.S. Open title. Mangrum's withdrawal meant one less battle-tested adversary for Hogan. For Mangrum, it meant not hacking through the Lake Course's rough with a tender rib cage.

Whether Hogan gave it a passing thought or not, the withdrawal of a player of Mangrum's caliber was significant. Besides Hogan, there would be 161 golfers in the field, but only a small percentage of them were given any realistic chance of winning. The prestige of the national championship and the difficulty of the course made it improbable that a middle-of-the-pack player, club pro, or amateur could hold his game together for four tournament rounds and win golf's most coveted prize. It rarely happened.

Defending champion Ed Furgol was an exception, although he had won twice on tour before edging Gene Littler and Dick Mayer at Baltusrol. In addition to Furgol, the names on the U.S. Open trophy in the postwar era were Mangrum, Worsham, Hogan, Middlecoff, and Boros. Four of the six were future Hall of Famers. The best players triumph at the U.S. Open. That was the conventional thinking. Moreover, it was the blueprint of the USGA.

Sports Illustrated published a lineup of fifteen serious contenders for the U.S. Open title, a full-color photo spread broken into three parts based on age and experience: the Old Guard, the Middle Guard, and the Young Guard. Each player appeared in a separate photograph striking a casual pose beside his golf clubs contained in a leather-trimmed canvas carry bag, unlike the enormous logo-adorned bags of later years. Most smiled or wore a sly grin, as if they had just made a birdie. The entire group was on display to demonstrate the sport's fashion-forward consciousness. In both appearance and golfing prowess, they were an impressive lineup. No one would have been surprised if the U.S. Open winner came from this group.

The Old Guard consisted of Hogan, Snead, and the absent Mangrum. Hogan, forty-two, wore his familiar white linen flat cap and a navy blue knit shirt. Snead, listed as forty-one, was actually forty-three, born in May the same year as Hogan. The Slammer was outfitted in his trademark coconut straw hat and a V-neck sweater. Sporting a pencil-thin mustache, forty-year-old Mangrum was noteworthy on two counts: his cardigan sweater and baseball-style cap, both new fashion trends on the fairways. The baseball-style golf cap with its stiff crown and long bill was introduced by Palm Springs pro Eddie Susella. Six of the fifteen players in the spread covered their domes with the sport's newest headgear. The alpaca cardigan worn by Mangrum came in fifty colors and was considered to be serious competition for cashmere. Hogan's fellow Texan was also singled out for his mink "club mittens," otherwise known as headcovers.

Four men comprised the Middle Guard: Middlecoff, thirty-four; Boros, thirty-five; Tommy Bolt, listed as thirty-six but actually thirty-nine; and Chick Harbert, forty. Along with Middlecoff, Boros was a U.S. Open champion, the 1952 winner at Northwood Club in Dallas. A Connecticut native and former accountant, Boros had an easy, relaxed manner on the golf course. There were no wasted movements by the silky smooth Boros; he never took a practice swing and never dallied over any shot.

Nicknamed "Thunder Bolt" and "Terrible Tommy" for his famous temper, Bolt was already a two-time winner in 1955, a player of enormous talent according to his peers. "Tommy Bolt was the best ball striker I ever saw," Hall of Famer Billy Casper would say.

Harbert was the reigning PGA champion and a seven-time winner on the PGA Tour who would go on to be a playing captain on the 1955 U.S. Ryder Cup team. The week before the U.S. Open, Harbert teamed with Furgol in Washington, D.C., to win the Canada Cup (now the World Cup).

Despite the many accomplishments of the veteran players, the most intriguing group was the Young Guard. They were the future of the game, loaded with talent and full of aspirations. One of them, Arnold Palmer of Latrobe, Pennsylvania, would become one of the game's all-time greats. However, Palmer's reign as golf's king would not begin for a few years, at which time he would capture his first of four Masters in a six-year span. By April of 1964, the handsome and charismatic Palmer would have a vast following—"Arnie's Army"—single-handedly launching tournament golf in the television age. That June, Palmer was a tour rookie and winner of the 1954 U.S. Amateur. His first tour victory would come in August at the Canadian Open. Shown wearing an off-white V-neck sweater with a light blue golf cap in his hand and his head slightly cocked to one side, golf's future monarch was no more touted than the others who graced the magazine spread. The twenty-five-year-old Palmer was just one of an eight-player cast of promising young players that included Shelley Mayfield, thirty-one; Mike Souchak, twenty-eight; Peter Thomson, twenty-five; Bob Rosburg, twenty-eight; Billy Maxwell, twenty-five; Bud Holscher, twenty-four; and Gene Littler, twenty-four.

The reigning British Open champion—his first of three consecutive Claret Jugs—Aussie Peter Thomson would not play at Olympic. The other seven players were on the scene, and despite their youthful vigor and nerves, they were discovering that the short, wet Lake Course was an intimidating foe.

Mayfield, hatless and fair-haired, had enjoyed recent success on the West Coast. The Long Island–based pro had won in Palm Springs in January at the Thunderbird Invitational. More than fifty years later, he recalled many aspects of the Lake Course, especially the rough. "It was the highest rough I think I ever saw," Mayfield said. "In places, it was knee high and maybe a little more."

During practice and tournament rounds, tournament officials mobilized a small army of forecaddies to spot players' golf balls. They were positioned in landing areas along the fairways and also stationed by the greens, where golf balls are usually easy to locate. Yet Olympic was far from the usual case. Mayfield recalled a practice round during which he struck a shot that landed left of the 17th green, a few feet from where one of the young spotters was standing.

"The forecaddie had to duck to keep the ball from hitting him, and we have still not found that ball," he later said.

Holscher, a Southern California native and former member of the Santa Monica Junior College golf team, had reason to expect to play well in San Francisco. He was a California State Junior College champion and had one tour win, the 1954 Labatt Open. On June 3, in a field of 157 players, he tied for low medalist with Ralph Evans in the Southern California section of U.S. Open qualifying at L.A.'s Bel-Air Country Club.

Maxwell, the 1951 U.S. Amateur champion, had broken through for his first PGA Tour win in late March at the Azalea Open in Wilmington, North Carolina. Maxwell's opposite in terms of size, the burly Souchak, a former member of Duke University's football and golf teams, won back-to-back events in Texas in February and was the tour's leading money winner coming into the U.S. Open with more than $15,000 in winnings. Souchak set a 72-hole scoring record of 257 (27 under par) at the Texas Open that included a first-round 60, an 18-hole scoring mark that would stand for more than two decades until a tall, rail-thin pro named Al Geiberger shot 59 in Memphis. The long-hitting Souchak, shown wearing a stylish powder blue alpaca sweater and matching cap, was capable of overpowering golf courses, although Olympic's Lake Course bore no resemblance to San Antonio's Brackenridge Park.

Yet among the constellation of young players, it was another Californian who was garnering a large share of pretournament attention. The loudest thing about Gene Littler may have been the red sweater he was wearing in his Young Guard photograph, but the golf game of the unassuming, boyish-looking Littler was making plenty of noise. The 1953 U.S. Amateur champion had nearly won the National Open at Baltusrol, finishing a shot behind Furgol. A native San Diegan who played collegiate golf at San Diego State, Littler had the rare distinction of winning a PGA Tour event as an amateur, the 1954 San Diego Open. Now a pro, he had collected early-season wins in Los Angeles, Phoenix, and Las Vegas. Upon his arrival in the Bay Area, Littler was considered to be a worthy opponent for Hogan and the man to beat according to some of the sport's veteran onlookers. For the duration of the championship, he would be staying at the Palo Alto home of another face of the Young Guard, his good friend Bob Rosburg.

•   •   •

Robert Reginald Rosburg took up golf at the age of three. He was a graduate of Stanford University, where he had been a standout in two sports—baseball and golf—and nearly chose the diamond instead of the course as his field of work. "Rossie," as he would become known, turned pro in 1953 and won the Miami Open the following year. The Stanford grad had something else going for him coming into the national championship. He had been a member of the Olympic Club during his youth.

"I played there a lot," Rosburg later said. "My dad joined when I was about ten or eleven years old, and I had played it that whole time. It was a great golf course. The juniors got treated pretty well."

One member who didn't have fond memories of the young Rosburg was baseball Hall of Famer Ty Cobb, one of the sport's greatest batsmen and a terror on the base paths who retired to the West Coast and wielded a different kind of stick on Olympic's verdant fairways. The fearsome "Georgia Peach" was humiliated by the twelve-year-old Rosburg in the first flight of Olympic's club championship. The match ended on the 12th hole, with boy beating man 7 and 6.

"I remember him getting mad at himself for not playing better," Rosburg said, "but he was nice to me. He shook my hand."

Two weeks before the start of the U.S. Open, Rossie may have felt worse than Cobb did after their club championship match. The Bay Area pro was so ill with the flu that he dropped out of the final round of the Palm Beach Round Robin tournament in Long Island, New York. While Rosburg lay in bed, Snead collected his second win of the season and a check for $3,000. The following day Rossie arose from his sickbed for a 36-hole U.S. Open qualifying tournament in the New York section. Competing for twenty-three spots in the best qualifying field in the country because most of the tour pros were entered there after playing on Long Island, Rosburg beat them all with a score of 138, including a sparkling 66 on the final 18.

Accompanied by Littler, Rosburg returned home to a measles-infested household. His youngest child, Debbie, was recovering, and his two sons were expected to break out with the tiny red bumps at any moment. Littler had the measles as a kid, so he didn't have to worry about being infected by the Rosburg clan. The National Open gave him plenty to think about.

The day after he qualified, Rosburg was identified by the *Chronicle* as one of the Open favorites because of his intimate knowledge of the Lake Course. It made sense. He had logged many rounds on its tree-lined fairways and small greens. However, even for Rossie, Olympic was different, a much more menacing course that June.

"Being a member," he said, "I didn't think it would play quite so hard as it did. It was unbelievable how tough the golf course was."

Another thing stood out, a common refrain from the players.

"It was the toughest rough I've ever seen there," Rosburg said. "You hit it in the rough and you didn't have much chance. At the end, they couldn't even move it out of the rough some of the times."

While Rosburg wondered who stole the Lake Course and replaced it with a hairy beast of a championship layout, a handful of local writers focused their attention on his houseguest. *San Francisco Examiner* sports editor Harry M. Hayward unveiled the consensus pick of Rosenbaum, himself, and two others.

"We got together," Hayward wrote. "Dug up the dope. Came up with the answers: They won't bust par of 280 for 72 holes. And if you gotta pick one man, you gotta pick Gene Littler."

They made a good case. After winning the season-opening Los Angeles Open, Littler was dubbed "the hottest thing in golf . . . the greatest prospect to come along in many years." Even the great Bobby Jones was enraptured, calling the San Diegan's swing "perfect." Jones, Sarazen, and others had identified their successor to Hogan and Snead. It was Gene Alec Littler.

At Olympic, though, the heir apparent to Hogan was having the same problem as others: The golf course was getting the best of him. Three days before the start of the tournament, Littler counted 84 strokes at Olympic. Snead's aches and pains might have subsided after a 68. Other practice round scores trickled in: Jerry Barber and Doug Ford, 74; Arnold Palmer, 75; Bud Holscher, 76; Dow Finsterwald and Al Zimmerman, 77.

Littler's 84 did not faze Sarazen, who opined from his suite at the Fairmont Hotel. He called the Open field the best in twenty years. While he thought Hogan and Snead were still great shotmakers, he didn't expect either man to win in San Francisco. The Squire was in love with the youth, whom he called clean-cut, bigger, taller, and better trained. The game had changed before his eyes, and Sarazen stuck by the young man who had already won three times that season.

"Littler is still my pick," he said.

However, Littler's good friend and weeklong host detected something overlooked by others.

"He couldn't handle the rough," Rosburg said a half century later. "I played a practice round with him and he might have shot 85. He was shanking it out of the rough. I think he kind of lost his confidence."

—10—

186 HOLES

The host city of the U.S. Open was a dazzling smorgasbord for the senses. During their hours away from the pressure-filled tournament, the golfers could take in San Francisco's many sights and exciting nightlife. Steaks and drinks awaited them at Trader Vic's. Singer Peggy Lee was performing at the Fairmont. The cinema featured *The Seven Year Itch*, the latest Hollywood blockbuster starring Marilyn Monroe and Tom Ewell. Theaters and newspapers showcased Monroe in scandalous promotional posters and advertisements on which her billowy white dress blows up around her waist to reveal her well-proportioned gams.

San Francisco's charms, however, would have no effect on at least one golfer, a midwesterner whose idea of nightlife was listening to classical music and turning in early. While Hogan lodged at San Francisco's largest hotel in the heart of the city, Jack Fleck checked into his modest room at the El Camino Motel in Daly City, a short drive south of San Francisco.

Built around 1950, the El Camino was U-shaped and contained a few dozen rooms, all with doors to the outside facing the parking lot, a car-friendly, one-level configuration that was spreading throughout America as the hospitality industry sought to accommodate the growing number of budget-conscious overnight travelers.

Fleck unpacked the Buick for the weeklong stay. His Hogan clubs and record player set aside and his clothes put away, he assessed the layout of the room and decided to rearrange the furniture. More than a half century later, the motel owner's grandson said Fleck turned around the bed. It puzzled him, an odd footnote to Fleck's long-ago visit that had passed from his grandfather to father to him. Maybe it had something to do with Fleck's yoga, he guessed. No, Fleck turned the bed so his head would face north, considered a benefit by those who believed in the positive magnetic energy of the North Pole. Whether or not the direction mattered, the repositioned bed was good to Fleck. He would sleep long and soundly for the duration of the championship.

After settling into his motel room on Saturday morning, Fleck made the fifteen-minute drive to the Olympic Club to get in a practice session. He had four and a half days to prepare for the championship. The entry from Davenport was determined to make the most of it.

The first order of business was to hire a caddie. It would be a local man. Caddies, as a group, were not the professional bagmen they are today. They didn't travel with players. They were locals who worked at the golf courses where the pros played, hiring on for the week. They made little money. They typically only gave advice when asked, and it was usually minimal. It often wasn't helpful.

"Sometimes the caddie was pretty good," Shelley Mayfield later said, "and sometimes he didn't know anything."

It was rare for Mayfield to seek advice. "I don't ever recall one time in my life asking a caddie, 'How does this putt break?' Never. Ask them about a club? 'I don't know. It must be some kind of an iron. I don't think it's a wood.' Or, 'It's a long way.' You got no help there at all."

The caddies' credo of "show up, keep up, shut up" that became a popular mantra in later years was the perfect job description for the 1950s bag toter.

After arriving at the course, Fleck drew a number, the method used to assign caddies. He got Emil Schroder, an older-looking man. Actually, Schroder was not that old—forty-three—but there was something about the caddie's appearance and demeanor that concerned the pro. Could Schroder keep up?

After completing his first trip around the Lake Course, Fleck had his answer and was ready to make a caddie change. "I thought he would never make all the rounds of practice I planned to play," he said. "I paid him for the Saturday afternoon round and said he should get another bag."

There was another thing: Fleck believed Schroder was a drinker. The caddie pleaded for his job. Fleck relented, but not without a warning. If Schroder was late or smelled of drink, he was through. The trial round over and the terms settled, the two men went to work. Schroder was true to his word and remained sober for the duration of the tournament.

That Saturday Fleck bumped into a player whose locker was only a short distance from his—Ben Hogan. The Hawk delivered the Ben Hogan Precision wedges that completed Fleck's new set. "He was just very nice," Fleck remembered of their brief encounter. Hogan wished him the best of luck with the new clubs, and Fleck took the shiny new wedges and genuine encouragement from his idol straight to the golf course.

"I just started practicing and playing with them," he said.

Whether in later years when player equipment changes became a well-choreographed undertaking or in the 1950s when some players spent days or weeks fussing with new clubs, putting brand-new wedges into the bag on the eve of an important championship could be regarded as either a bold or foolish move. With the U.S. Open rough and heavily bunkered greens, wedge play would be critical to every player's fortunes at Olympic.

"You might think, 'Gee, that's strange,'" Fleck later said of putting new wedges into play just days before the National Open. Strange or not, he had felt a kinship with the Hogan-model irons from the time he first saw them three months earlier in St. Petersburg. Now the set was complete, and he couldn't wait to break the wedges in on the Lake Course's damp turf.

Fleck imitated Hogan in at least one important way: "He practiced very hard," Larry Tomasino said.

Fleck's practice philosophy was built on playing as much golf as possible. His health regimen of eating right, doing yoga, meditating, and getting eight hours of sleep fueled his grueling practice schedule. He felt he had no other choice if he wanted to succeed on tour. Fleck later pointed out that Littler, although nine years younger, had many more years of competitive experience. He figured it would take thousands of rounds to catch up with Littler and other pros. At Olympic, he cut into the large deficit. It's hard to imagine that anyone played more practice holes—Fleck recorded 186 in four days—leading up to the start of the tournament.

The par-3 8th hole was a short distance from the clubhouse, which enabled Fleck's three consecutive 44-hole practice days beginning on Sunday. Each day he made two entire loops of the layout, and then played the first 8 holes a third time, after which he made the short walk to the locker room. He cut back on Wednesday, the day before the tournament started, playing *only* 36 holes. One might wonder if Schroder had second thoughts about his practice-obsessed employer.

Fleck also hit dozens of balls on the practice tee. His three swing keys were rhythm, timing, and balance. The Iowan's swing with his Tommy Armour driver was long and loose. A later series of swing-sequence photos demonstrated the source of his wiry power. Standing tall at address, his long arms forming a V, Fleck made a big and wide shoulder turn. The club traveled well past horizontal as he coiled, his left knee kicking in to the right and the left heel well off the ground. Then he was all arms and legs as he pulled the extralong persimmon driver down and through, both feet replanted on the ground just before impact.

"He did not have a real beautiful swing like a Walker Inman or Jay Hebert . . . ," said Mike Krak. "Jack had a decent swing but he worked real hard at it. If you were picking people for a golf team and you had your choice of guys—not know[ing] what their heart is—you would have never picked Jack for his golf swing."

Although pounding balls on the driving range helped hone his golf swing, spending time on the golf course was the core of Fleck's tournament preparation. He wanted to learn everything he could about the Lake Course before the shots counted. Fleck paced off yardages, a method he had been using since 1947 after watching Hogan practice on the winter tour. He recorded the locations of trees, bunkers, and other landmarks and objects on the course scorecard. He paced off distances to the first third and second third of each green, which allowed him to compute accurate yardages for his approach shots to various pin positions. It was, in effect, a forerunner of the modern yardage book. As odd as it may seem today, an era when tour pros and amateurs alike have exact or near-exact yardages, the technique was still uncommon as the '55 U.S. Open approached. In addition to having a more accurate knowledge of distances—there were few yardage markers on public or private golf courses at the time—Fleck also focused on how far he could hit each club. The game had been played mostly by sight, feel, and intuition. Although all three were critically important in golf, Fleck had added another element to the mix, the use of actual distance data. It was an innovation that was helping him a great deal.

Fleck reached many of the same conclusions about Olympic as did other players. The 6,700-yard course played deceptively long. The misty, cool June weather made the Lake Course a permanent moisture pad. He took note of the jungle that bordered the edges of fairways and greens. Instead of shying away from the cabbage, he dropped balls into its depths and practiced shot after shot around the edges of the putting surfaces and bunkers.

Other players issued a friendly warning to Fleck. Do not play too many practice rounds, they said. Stay away from that rough. For the Iowa club pro, however, the long hours of practice had an entirely different effect. They built his confidence. He knew it would take pinpoint tee shots and iron play to navigate Olympic's narrow layout. It played to his strengths, a dependable game from tee to green. Fleck hit a straight ball and was sneaky long off the tee. Sometimes his drives would move slightly to the right, a slider, as he called it. He thought Olympic was a fair course and knew the key to U.S. Open success: Hit it straight and stay out of the trees.

Indeed, hitting the ball straight would keep a player away from trouble and allow him to find the thimble-sized greens. Although players were hitting the golf ball farther than ever, precision mattered most on championship layouts such as the Lake Course. Keeping the ball in play was a common strategy that was exceedingly difficult to execute under National Open pressure.

Yet Fleck's greatest concern revolved around his uneasy marriage with the shortest club in his bag. What kind of week would he have on the Lake Course's greens? He lacked confidence and never expected to hole a lot of putts. His habit of opening his Bulls Eye blade and stroking sidespinning putts didn't help matters. He was like other players who were mediocre or weak putters: good on the fairways, not so good on the greens.

"It always haunted me," Fleck later said about his putting. "The other part of the game seemed easy to me."

Fellow pro Johnny Bulla later said Jack Fleck "could really drive it and iron it." What Bulla couldn't understand was how Fleck missed so many little putts.

While the press chased Hogan, Snead, and Littler, Fleck and his caddie walked Olympic's fairways in obscurity. They were not entirely alone, however. During his Monday and Tuesday practice rounds, a man named George Tompkins trailed Fleck as he rounded the course. Tompkins was an Olympic Club member and president of Overseas National Airways, a charter airline that transported passengers and freight. He would be a roving marshal during the tournament, stationed between the 10th and 13th holes. The friendly and outgoing Tompkins introduced himself to Fleck. The Iowan now had a tiny U.S. Open fan base. He would spot Tompkins each day of the tournament near the 10th green, where the two men would exchange greetings and small talk. Their budding friendship would be more important than Fleck could know early in the tournament week.

· · ·

Although Fleck often practiced alone, he was also joined for pretournament rounds by Walker Inman and Mike Krak, his practice partners and occasional companions on the circuit. Tour rookies Inman and Krak were as invisible as Fleck.

Inman saw Fleck from the vantage point of someone who was eight years younger with far less tournament experience. "He hadn't won a lot of tournaments," Inman later said, "but he was a successful tournament player and knew how to play and compete."

In fact, Fleck hadn't won a single golf tournament, except for a possible local or regional event in his native Midwest. As Tommy Bolt would later say, "Nobody knew who he was—he had never won a caddies tournament." Still, to Inman, Fleck was an older and more seasoned competitor, a tournament player he looked up to.

Actually, Inman and Krak were just happy to be in the 162-man field. For most players, it was a major accomplishment to tee it up in the U.S. Open. They were the cream of golf, among the one in ten who survived nationwide qualifying. Each player had one National Open on his résumé: Inman played as an amateur in the 1952 championship in Dallas won by Julius Boros; Krak's lone Open was the year before at Baltusrol, where he missed the cut.

Inman's one Open could not have prepared him for Olympic. He had never seen rough like the thick Italian rye at the Lake Course. Not in Dallas, where the grasses were a different variety and considerably drier. Not anywhere. Although he would play in at least half a dozen more U.S. Opens, it would be his first and last experience with rough so long and treacherous. "If you hit a ball out in the rough, it was gone," he said. "You couldn't find it."

The Georgia native remembered a practice round during which he, Fleck, and two other players lost nine balls between them. He also recalled the 14th hole, where a patch of rough beyond the primary cut stood taller than the golfer. To document the absurdity, a lady snapped a photograph of the slim 5'11" Inman standing beside the high grass.

It's hard to overemphasize what a shock the course was to players' senses. Inman heard players talk of practice-round scores in the mid- and high 80s, and an occasional round in the low 90s. It was a major embarrassment for men whose livelihoods depended on their peerless skill on the fairways. One player confided to him, "Man, I hate for people back in Fort Worth to see these scores I'm shooting. They'll think I'm out here just fooling around and they're sponsoring me. I wish they could see the golf course, because they couldn't break 150."

—— NEIL SAGEBIEL ——

The thick canopy of pine, cypress, cedar, and eucalyptus trees that lined the fairways also made an indelible impression on the rookie. "It was dark under those trees, even in the middle of the day. I never will forget that."

As he reflected on the '55 Open more than a half century later, the setup of the Lake Course dominated his memories, a lush and beautiful layout with a sinister dark side—severe rough, tight fairways, an untamable golf course.

Inman and his buddies certainly couldn't tame it. During his four practice rounds played with Fleck and others, he didn't remember anyone breaking 80.

On Wednesday, Al Mengert, an assistant on Claude Harmon's staff at Winged Foot, joined Fleck, Inman, and Krak for a practice round. Teams were drawn and a small wager was made.

"The day before the Open," Krak said, "he [Fleck] and Al Mengert played Walker and I, and we just absolutely killed them. We beat them six or seven different ways for a two-dollar Nassau." (A Nassau is a popular type of golf bet that includes a separate wager on the front 9, the back 9, and the full-18 scores.)

Like others, Krak marveled at the course preparations, in particular the narrow opening into each green and the heavy grass that rimmed the putting surfaces. He reasoned all the chipping and putting practice in the world wouldn't improve his chances in the 8- and 10-inch grass that swallowed golf balls 5 feet from the green. Greenside shots were gouges with wedges rather than chips with an 8-iron or 7-iron. Even with the most lofted clubs in the bag, golf balls flew out of the thick rough with overspin, scurrying across the putting surface and sometimes off the other side. There would be no easy up-and-ins on the Lake Course.

For Krak, winning a practice-round bet was not the confidence booster

110

it might normally be. The challenge for Krak and the rest of the field was the Lake Course, and the examination, as course doctor Jones called it, was about to begin.

"There was only one way to play Olympic," summed up Robert Sommers. "Hit the fairways and hit the greens." It happened to be the hallmark of the man who hand-delivered Fleck's new wedges, for as Sommers noted, "No one did this better than Hogan."

Many of the players agreed.

"Everybody said Hogan's going to win," Inman said. "They set this up where he'll win for sure because nobody can put the ball in play as good as he can."

At the end of his long practice sessions, Fleck returned to the El Camino and ate his meals at the cafeteria a few blocks away. Except for the soothing vocals of Mario Lanza, the evenings passed quietly in his motel room. The par-70 layout was to his liking.

"I could drive the ball and I loved the golf course," he said.

At least one person concurred.

"It was a perfect golf course for him because you had to hit it straight," Krak said, "and he could hit it straight."

—11—

FINAL PREPARATIONS

The news appeared in the *Chronicle Sporting Green* on Tuesday, two days before the start of the tournament. O.C. [OLYMPIC CLUB] IS ORDERED TO TRIM ROUGH read the headline. It was not a pleasing development for Lake Course superintendent Elmer Border. Border felt he had religiously followed the meticulous instructions of the USGA in preparing the course for the national championship, a process that had begun months in advance of the tournament. He had been on the job less than a year, and all agreed the course was in immaculate condition. From December to April, the superintendent spread forty-three tons of fertilizer across the Lake Course, the first such feeding in a quarter century. The ravenous fairways and outlying areas grew and thickened prodigiously. As the USGA later reported, "The condition of the fairways and the greens was excellent. It was almost impossible to get a bad fairway lie."

However, the rough had gotten out of hand—"It was a grass that just grew like crazy," Walker Inman said—and the loud complaining had reached the ears of USGA executive director Joe Dey. Complaints about the toughness of a National Open golf course were not new to Dey, whose skin may have been as thick as Olympic's rough when it came to such criticisms. The debate raged every June when the game's best pros and amateurs faced what they considered to be a tricked-up par defender such as Oakland Hills, Oakmont, or Baltusrol. It was before the days of USGA on-site monitoring leading up to an Open championship, a practice that began the following year. This time Dey conceded the crazy-growing rough needed an extensive trim after he arrived in San Francisco.

Dey would later say it was a misunderstanding. A year earlier amid concerns the rough at the Lake Course might not grow to U.S. Open standards, club officials, led by tournament chairman Robert Roos Jr., began to let the edges of the course thicken. In the month preceding Dey's arrival, the rough was not cut at all, making it extra thick and juicy from the perpetual coastal dampness.

It looked like a long-postponed haircut. With new last-minute instructions from Dey, Border and his crew took a lot off the sides. The first cut of rough, which formed a 6-foot-wide collar alongside the fairways and had grown to 5 inches, was cut to 2 inches. The next cut of rough, exceeding a foot in some areas, was trimmed to 4½ inches. Sections of rough about 7 yards and farther from the fairway went untouched, reaching a foot high.

Dey also ordered two other changes. The small Dewdrop landing area on the short par-4 7th hole was extended by 5 feet on all sides after pros insisted they couldn't find the sliver of fairway with their tee shots. In addition, the fairway of the narrow par-4 5th hole was widened by 12 feet.

The eleventh-hour changes to the golf course stressed Border and his large crew, but they responded in soldierlike fashion. The haircut completed, the Lake Course looked stunning. If the freshly groomed course now appeared easier to play, it was a cruel deception.

With the stage set for the start of the championship, the discussion about what score it would take to win at Olympic intensified. Before the rough-cutting announcement, there was a near-unanimous view among the early-arriving professionals that a score of 4 to 8 over par would claim the trophy. However, many players changed their minds as they gazed upon a manicured Lake Course with shorter rough.

Defending champion Ed Furgol led the chorus of those who predicted a score of par or lower would win on the lakeside layout. The thirty-eight-year-old veteran arrived in San Francisco on Monday fresh off a double victory in international matches for the Canada Cup, where he captured the individual title as well as the team competition with Chick Harbert. Playing well coming into the National Open boosted the confidence of the reigning champion, and his comments were tinged with a past winner's certainty about what it would take come Thursday.

Furgol told the press that Olympic was 20 percent easier than Baltusrol and par golf would be needed to win. Nonetheless, the Lake Course still commanded his respect. Two weeks earlier he noted it was the tightest Open course he had played in his eleven appearances. "It takes a .22 rifle for accuracy and a .30-30 for carry," he said. "There is a big premium on the second shot."

·   ·   ·

A tall, lanky New York native who resided in St. Louis, Furgol served as recent proof that the national championship could produce a surprise winner. Furgol was an established tour player—he had won the Crosby and the Phoenix Open—but he was no Hogan, Snead, or Mangrum. Nor was he a Middlecoff, Boros, or Bolt. He called himself a "nobody in golf" before he whipped the field at Baltusrol.

It was a reminder of how tournament golf—and the U.S. Open in particular—was among the most democratic of sporting events. At its essence, there was nothing subjective about the game. A player was not subject to the whims of coaches or judges or other outside influences. Sure, a ruling might affect an outcome, but it was a rare occurrence. The number on the scorecard was all that counted. Whether an amateur or professional, a star or an unknown, if a player scored well enough among the hundreds of qualifiers, he gained entry to the elite U.S. Open field. If he posted the lowest score during the championship, he took home the trophy. There were no judges, no style points, no consolation prizes. Nothing could be fairer. Success or failure rested almost entirely with the individual.

It was a game, qualifying system, and championship that gave players such as Furgol a chance to compete against the sport's best—and he claimed the nation's most coveted golf prize with only one good arm.

Furgol fell from playground equipment and shattered his left elbow at the age of twelve. Withered and crooked at the elbow, his arm was never the same. Despite the deformed left arm, so integral to the swing of a right-handed golfer, he pursued golf and became a champion. Like others, he put in long hours at the driving range and on the golf course. Unlike others, he focused on fitness long before golfers did much more than walk the course. From the age of eighteen to twenty-five, he ran every day to build his stamina and skipped rope to improve coordination in his hands, arms, and legs.

Furgol was a story of courage and perseverance in overcoming a physical obstacle. After his win at Baltusrol, thousands of letters from people with physical disabilities jammed his mailbox, including correspondence from teens and military personnel who had taken up the game despite injured limbs. They congratulated the heroic golfer and sought his advice. Furgol, with the help of his wife, Helen, answered each letter. He was a grateful man living a dream from which he didn't want to wake up.

Two weeks before defending his title, he said, "For a man with a shriveled arm, I've done well. I'm satisfied."

. . .

Sam Snead wasn't. There was no satisfaction in second place, and in a long illustrious career that had produced seventy-two wins, including seven major titles, Snead had been the bridesmaid in the National Open on a record four occasions: 1937, 1947, 1949, and 1953.

"A guy's got to finish first or nothing," he said on Monday in the locker room. "Nobody cares about second place. It doesn't pay off."

Snead would know, having been jilted at America's altar of golf far too often. In 1939 at Philadelphia he needed a bogey on the par-5 finishing hole to win, although he didn't know it at the time. Playing ahead of other contenders, Snead thought he'd better go for birdie and made a triple bogey to finish in fifth place. Byron Nelson won his only Open that day.

The biggest bruise to Snead's ego may have come at the 1947 National Open in St. Louis when he lost to Lew Worsham. Snead birdied the 72nd hole to force an 18-hole playoff. The next day, holding a 2-shot lead with 3 holes to go, he was poised for victory. Yet Worsham drew even as they came to the final hole, where both players faced short par putts. Snead went first. Just as he was ready to draw back his putter, Worsham stepped in and asked for a measurement to verify which player was farther from the hole and determine order of play. It was Snead by an inch. After the unnerving wait, he again settled over his ball and missed the 30½-inch putt. Worsham tapped in to win by a stroke. Some considered it to be the ultimate display of gamesmanship. Responding to the criticism, Worsham later said, "All I can say is I have many fond memories of St. Louis in 1947."

Snead disagreed with Furgol's assessment of the Lake Course. "I still feel a man can be over par for the four rounds and win this thing," he said. Someone nearby said Snead was the man to beat, but, talking with reporters, Sam didn't hear the comment.

.　　.　　.

The Bay Area pinned its hopes on three local golfers in the U.S. Open field. In addition to Bob Rosburg, they were Bud Ward, a pro at San Mateo's Peninsula Country Club and low man in San Francisco section qualifying, and Harvie Ward (no relation to Bud), an amateur star who sold cars at a Van Ness Avenue automobile dealership owned by Eddie Lowery.

A member of the USGA Executive Committee, Lowery was a mover and shaker in amateur golf. He also happened to be the former caddie of Francis Ouimet, the boyish amateur who beat British professionals Harry Vardon and Ted Ray in an 18-hole playoff to win the 1913 U.S. Open. Lowery was known for taking promising amateur golfers under his wing. Harvie Ward was one of Lowery's golden boys. Ken Venturi, who would make his U.S. Open debut the following year, was another.

While Rosburg was a "practice-round flop" on Tuesday, Harvie was touring the Lake Course in style. Ward, a member of the nearby San Francisco Golf Club, was a strong contender for the U.S. Open title. It was nearing the end of an era when the best amateur golfers could match shots with the top professionals. That June, Ward was considered to be one of the best golfers in the world.

.　　.　　.

Edward Harvie Ward Jr. first roamed a golf course in bare feet as a boy growing up in a small town in eastern North Carolina. Much of the time he felt grains of sand between his toes as he honed his putting stroke on sand greens. Good-looking and loaded with Tobacco Road charm, Ward would tread America's lush golf pastures with abundant talent and sheer joy for years to come. He attended the University of North Carolina, where, in addition to taking a degree in economics, he became the Tar Heels' first All-American golfer. His first noteworthy victory came in 1948 in the prestigious North and South Amateur at nearby Pinehurst. The following year the talented Tar Heel was crowned NCAA champion. Life and golf came easily to the convivial North Carolinian, a frat boy and heartthrob with a canvas golf bag slung on one arm and a gorgeous coed hanging on the other.

Ward's promising amateur career took off at the beginning of the new decade. In 1952, he won his first of back-to-back Dogwood Invitationals, one of the nation's top amateur events. That same year he crossed the Atlantic and won his first major championship, the British Amateur, one of the two most prestigious amateur tournaments in the world, the other being the U.S. Amateur. Only nine Americans had won the British Amateur. Ward did it on his first try despite a diet still influenced by postwar rations.

"Hell, I ate enough Dover sole to swim back to the United States," he later said.

The following summer in Massachusetts Ward played in his first Walker Cup, an amateur team competition between America and Britain. Ward won both his 1953 matches and would go on to post a perfect 6–0 record in three Walker Cup appearances. In 1954, he added the Canadian Amateur to his impressive golf résumé. The only major title that eluded Ward, the king of amateur golf, was the U.S. Amateur.

It was during his victorious 1952 trip to Scotland that Ward met Lowery, who was attending the British Amateur along with other USGA officials. Lowery urged the North Carolinian to move to San Francisco. The climate was agreeable for year-round golf, and Ward could hire on to Lowery's sales staff at Van Etta Motors. The following year Ward and his wife, Suzanne, packed up and moved to the Bay Area. Cars and golf were his trades, but selling automobiles never kept him from the fairways. It was honorable to compete as an amateur, and Ward—not lacking anything with a cushy sales job and a membership at the San Francisco Golf Club—was an amateur through and through.

As "Doc" Middlecoff donned the Green Jacket at the Masters in April, Ward finished in a tie for eighth. Harvie had proven he could play with the big boys. With a win at the Lake Course, he would be the first amateur to hold the U.S. Open title since Johnny Goodman won at Pebble Beach in 1933. It would be no surprise. He was that good.

Arnold Palmer, who competed against the Tar Heel in college, called Ward a "great player." Ken Venturi went further in his praise. "Take Nicklaus at his best and Ward at his best. I'll take Ward."

. . .

On Tuesday, while others tiptoed around Olympic as if it were an outdoor cathedral of horrors, both Wards stockpiled pretournament confidence by hitting bold shots on the course's toughest holes. Harvie carded a 1-over 71 that included six birdies. Bud fired an even-par 70, but Harvie, with a gallery of three thousand in tow, was the preferred Ward among the fans. His group's popularity was no doubt aided by the inclusion of Littler, Nelson, and Rosburg.

Snead and Hogan were also spied on the premises. Snead's practice session going poorly, he picked up after a few holes. Hogan camped out on the driving range, striping practice shots into a stiff breeze. He avoided the Lake Course the final two days before the start of the championship, instead slipping off with Claude Harmon to the nearby Ocean Course to simulate the wind conditions and shots he would need once the tournament started. The Hawk surely had a score in his mind. All that was left to do was make sure he had all the shots in his bag.

Shelley Mayfield later marveled at Hogan's ability to pick winning scores. "Believe me, it wasn't over one or two shots away. I don't know how he could predict it like that, but he could."

Even TV commentator Gene Sarazen unpacked his clubs for an 18-hole round to see for himself what all the hollering was about. The Squire fashioned a respectable 77 and pronounced that the Lake Course would be the best test of golf in twenty-five years. Porky Oliver, however, was nowhere near Olympic. He was in downtown San Francisco having a shaft repaired after getting his club tangled in that wet, thick jungle the USGA called rough.

The rough still gave the players the willies. The most frightening realization was that the eleventh-hour trim mattered not. Players determined they would lose fewer balls. Otherwise the mow job made little difference. If anything, Rosburg thought the shorter 2-inch rough that bordered the fairways was more difficult to play from than the longer rough. He noted that the golf ball had a tendency to sit up in the 4- and 5-inch rough, but the ball sank to the ground in the shorter cut, making excavation and control problematic.

Inman agreed. "It was very difficult even to hit out of the first cut. It wasn't sitting up to where you could get it to the green."

Herbert Warren Wind observed that hitting more than a 6-iron from the rough was "quite impossible." Nelson and Inman said a trip to the rough would cost a player a stroke. It was what the par defenders at the USGA intended.

The course, as if to prove it was not totally ridiculous, surrendered two holes in one on consecutive practice days. Ohio amateur Ed Meister aced the 187-yard par-3 13th. The following day a forty-six-year-old Atlanta pro and Eastern Airlines pilot named Elmer Reed sent a 2-iron shot into the cup on the 220-yard par-3 3rd hole. One might have imagined the course doctor nodding his head and saying, "Eminently fair."

·   ·   ·

The tension was high on Wednesday as the field made its final preparations for the championship. Tommy Bolt, however, was grinning from ear to ear. Bolt's concluding practice session had produced a sensational 66, tying him with Mayer for low round during drills. Bolt, who had a reputation as a strong player on tough courses, was in top form as the clock ticked closer to his 8:48 A.M. Thursday starting time. He liked his chances so much that he picked himself to win.

The *Chronicle*, which handicapped the players as if they were thoroughbreds, did not regard Mr. 66 as highly. The newspaper's favorite, at odds of 3–1, was the man of U.S. Open sorrows, Sam Snead, who was playing well coming into the championship. There was also a prevailing belief that time was running out for the forty-three-year-old. Perhaps Olympic offered his last best chance to break the U.S. Open jinx. Next was Masters champion Middlecoff at 4–1, followed by 6–1 favorites Mayer and Harvie Ward. The fifth name on the list was Hogan, a 7–1 pick along with Furgol and Chandler Harper. Housemates Rosburg and Littler were listed at 8–1. Farther down were Bolt at 15–1 and Arnold Palmer at 20–1.

In his final pretournament report, Rosenbaum wondered about Hogan's fitness and endurance. Hogan was anticipating another operation stemming from the accident. "I don't know if I can go 72 holes," he said.

Along with the large silver trophy and winner's check of $5,000, the U.S. Open champion could expect $60,000 from endorsements, exhibitions, and personal appearances. Hogan didn't care about any of that. His name was already on the trophy four times, and he had all the money he needed to lead a comfortable life in the Fort Worth suburbs. Hogan would attempt one more 72-hole journey in the hopes that he could limp past Bobby Jones and Willie Anderson and into the record books as the first five-time winner of the national championship.

After assessing the favorites, Rosenbaum threw in a final thought, as if he needed to allow for every conceivable outcome.

"By Saturday night, the new Open champ could very well be a suddenly well-known unknown."

The sports scribe was an accidental prophet—except he would be off by one day.

—12—

THURSDAY: ROUND 1

Addressed to Robert A. Roos Jr., general chairman of the USGA Open Championship, the Western Union telegram from the White House read:

ON THE OCCASION OF THE 1955 NATIONAL OPEN GOLF TOURNAMENT MY GREETINGS GO TO ALL PARTICIPANTS AND SPECTATORS. I KNOW THIS TOURNAMENT WILL ONCE AGAIN AFFORD A DISPLAY OF GREAT GOLF, AND I WISH I COULD BE THERE TO SEE IT.
DWIGHT D EISENHOWER

The president's greeting appeared in the championship's official program, 262 pages of tournament information that sold for a dollar. Pictured beside the reproduced telegram, Ike is shown taking his stance with putter in hand and decked out in golf attire that includes a pair of oxford-style shoes and a brimmed hat like Sam Snead's. President Eisenhower would arrive in San Francisco late that weekend for the United Nations' tenth-anniversary commemorative session. On Thursday morning, when the first group was set to tee off in the fifty-fifth National Open, the First Golfer was 2,800 miles away in Washington, his putting green nearby on the White House lawn if he needed a golf fix.

A few minutes before their 8:00 A.M. starting time, Ted Gwin, Ralph Arnold, and Bob Moore arrived on Olympic's 1st tee. As was the case for each of the day's fifty-four groupings, the three men would play together during their Thursday and Friday rounds, after which the field would be cut to the lowest fifty scorers and ties. Those with morning tee times on Thursday would begin their Friday rounds in the late morning or afternoon, a method to facilitate, as much as possible, equal playing conditions for all the competitors. On Saturday, the 72-hole championship would conclude with the third and fourth rounds, a total of 36 holes, which was customary until 1965, the year following winner Ken Venturi's near collapse in stifling heat at Congressional in Washington, D.C.

The sky was uncharacteristically bright for a June morning, and the warmth of the early sun chased away the cool fog and mist that habitually settled over the Lake Course. A hint of a breeze stirred the eucalyptus trees and Marietta pines as Gwin, Arnold, and Moore looked out on the 530-yard 1st hole, one of only two par 5s on the par-70 course, a dogleg to the right that could be reached in 2 by long hitters. The first decision for the three players was how much of the dogleg to cut with their tee shots, if any. Trees hugged the right side, and anything wide of the fairway was trouble. Beyond the 1st green were 6,170 more yards through 17 narrow corridors lined by tall trees and thick rough. All terminated at small closely mown greens with holes that were four and a quarter inches in diameter, each freshly cut early that morning in spots designated by the USGA. The 18 hole positions would move each day of the championship.

Practice and the collective angst of the field were recent history. Now every stroke counted. One by one, the three players were announced, teed their golf balls, and struck their opening shots. The championship was under way.

. . .

Even though he wouldn't tee off until 10:00 A.M., Ben Hogan had already been up for hours when Gwin, Arnold, and Moore sheathed their wooden clubs and stepped onto the 1st fairway. Rising early in his room at the elegant St. Francis Hotel, Hogan began the two-hour ritual to prepare his ailing lower limbs for 18 holes of tournament golf. He drew a hot bath and lowered his body into the tub to soak in Epsom salts. Afterward, he gulped down aspirin and rubbed liniment on his legs. Lastly, he wrapped his legs in elastic bandages and wriggled into his pleated trousers. Three days and 72 holes of championship golf lay ahead. If things went his way, Hogan would return to Fort Worth as a five-time U.S. Open winner and retired golf champion. If his aching legs could carry him to one more major victory, there would be nothing left to achieve.

In Daly City, Jack Fleck, also an early riser, had stretched, showered, shaved, and prayed when he departed his room at the El Camino Motel to eat breakfast. With a 10:40 A.M. starting time, there was no need to hurry to the golf course. Logging more than nine full practice rounds in five days, he had crammed hard for the U.S. Open examination. The Iowa club pro, whose best Open finish was a tie for fifty-second, had an ambitious goal: a top ten finish that would exempt him from qualifying for the 1956 U.S. Open. Upon his arrival in Daly City the previous Saturday, Fleck had penned a letter to John O'Donnell, the sports editor of his hometown *Davenport Democrat*. He suggested that O'Donnell ask the newspaper's publisher for permission to travel to San Francisco to attend the championship. In his note to the editor, he also made his predictions, including his desire

125

to crack the top ten, although it would later be reported that Fleck had picked himself as a dark horse to win the U.S. Open.

In Davenport, Lynn Fleck was already at work in the Credit Island golf shop to serve the steady stream of early-morning golfers. She would listen to the radio in the background for news about the national championship in San Francisco. Busy and efficient, Lynn wondered in idle moments how her husband would do in his third U.S. Open. All tournaments were important, but this was the most important of them all, another chance to prove he could compete with golf's best and earn his way on the PGA circuit. Halfway through the '55 season, Fleck would improve and record higher finishes or he would be off the tour in eighteen months. San Francisco was one more stop in a string of diminishing opportunities for the Iowan.

•   •   •

In groups of three, the 135 pros and 27 amateurs teed off every eight minutes until the day's final group struck their first shots at 3:04 P.M. Less than a week before the summer solstice, there would be ample daylight for tournament golfers accustomed to playing 18 holes in under four hours. A round that exceeded four hours was considered to be snail-like play.

Despite the chamber-of-commerce weather, the golf course bared its teeth from the outset of the championship. In addition, the players felt the added pressure of the U.S. Open as they fanned out on the Lake Course. There was no use pretending this was Baton Rouge, Virginia Beach, or Fort Wayne. Not even the great Hogan was immune to the National Open pressure cooker. He simply had the sturdiest game and mental makeup to deal with the nerve-wracking competition, although his putter was known to let him down at crucial moments in recent championships.

The day's program awaited spectators as they streamed onto the grounds. It featured a players listing, complete with Thursday and Friday groupings and starting times, and cost twenty-five cents. The spectator instructions were not unlike those issued today. "This is the players' competition—treat them as you would like to be treated if you were playing. Be silent and motionless when a player takes his stance and throughout his stroke." Spectators were advised to walk and never run. Cameras, except those belonging to the official press corps, were "prohibited completely on course." Marshals were stationed throughout the course to "help you enjoy the Tournament. Please cooperate with them at all times." There was one other important spectator instruction—an innovation in conducting golf championships—printed in capital letters: "STAY BEHIND THE GALLERY ROPES." It was only the second U.S. Open at which gallery ropes had been strewn alongside fairways and around greens. The USGA erected 2,250 metal stakes and strung twelve miles of rope at Olympic, just as it had the year before at Baltusrol. The governing body of U.S. golf gave several reasons for the added effort of roping the entire golf course. For one, it helped to preserve the playability of the course for the competitors. When allowed to roam freely, spectators left fairway-marring footprints and trampled the rough along the fairways' edges, lessening the difficulty of recovery shots. Gallery ropes also provided players a wide-open course and mostly spectator-free paths as they made their 18-hole loop. Players no longer had to fight their way through large galleries milling about the golf course.

Fred Hawkins later recalled how the days before gallery ropes benefitted the game's stars. "Before the ropes came up, they used to pack around the greens—the good players had a gallery—and they fired into the greens and seldom went over because it hit somebody and stayed right on the edges."

The gallery ropes were still a novelty at a golf tournament. The U.S. Open would be a zoolike experience, with spectators standing at a distance behind the roped barrier and observing the rare species of championship golfer in his native habitat. Tournament officials wouldn't rely solely on the printed spectator instructions. Supervised by gallery chairman Stanton Haight, an army of volunteers was mobilized to ensure proper gallery decorum. Some wore helmets, which, as the *Olympian* reported, "gave them an imposing look and also were a fine safeguard from a hooked or slice liner that might have caused a fractured skull or a concussion of the brain should a misdirected ball carom off the bare dome."

•   •   •

Tommy Bolt was impossible to miss as he arrived on the 1st tee for his 8:48 A.M. starting time. He wore a pale blue long-sleeve sweater over a black shirt, pastel green slacks, and a pink baseball-style cap. A 66 fresh in his memory banks, Bolt had proven to himself that he could handle the brutal U.S. Open layout. Thunder Bolt just needed to keep a lid on his famous temper and play his enviable game, a game superior from tee to green to nearly everyone's except Hogan's and Snead's. Off he went with Robert Sweeney and Bo Wininger.

At 9:04 A.M., Chandler Harper, the low qualifier among the more than 1,500 U.S. Open entrants, teed off in a group that included 1940 U.S. Open champion Lawson Little. Two groups later, Bud Holscher, one of the Young Guard, struck his opening shot of the championship. At 9:44 A.M., the tournament's youngest player left the first tee, a seventeen-year-old amateur from Bethesda, Maryland, named Deane Beman. Beman would go on to an impressive amateur career before turning professional and later serving for two decades as the PGA Tour's second commissioner. Meanwhile, Hogan was on the grounds warming up for his fifteenth U.S. Open, the same number of appearances as his rival Sam Snead. His possible appointment with history would begin at 10:00 A.M.

The Olympic Club buzzed with activity as midmorning approached. Players, members of the press corps, and spectators flowed onto the property by way of Skyline Boulevard, a coastal highway situated a short distance to the west of the golf course. Still others entered admission gates along John Muir Drive, which bordered Lake Merced to the east of the Lake Course. No advance planning or details were overlooked. Parking, logistics, and course access were sufficiently organized to enable 9,300 spectators to attend the opening round on Thursday. Those numbers would swell on Friday and Saturday, resulting in galleries the USGA termed "unusually large." The Burns Detective Agency manned the six entrance gates, monitoring credentials, ensuring proper access to various areas, and safeguarding the thousands of dollars of gate and concessions receipts.

There were several hospitality and merchandise areas. Spectators could avail themselves of more than a dozen food tents, where 125 servers sold hot dogs for thirty-five cents and hawked hamburgers and beer for half a dollar apiece. A two-foot-long cardboard periscope with reflecting mirror, a viewing device designed for spectators wedged in large galleries, was available for a buck. More than four thousand of the odd contraptions would be sold during the championship. Some spectators stacked one periscope on another to gain an additional viewing advantage. The course contained nine sets of bleachers—six of them on the final 9 holes—making it a more spectator-friendly venue. Many of these features of a major tournament venue would be amplified in the years to come.

Tournament courtesy cars and sponsorship by a major automobile company, destined to become a growing monetary influence on the game and a perk for tour pros, were also in evidence at Olympic. The Dodge Motor Car division of the Chrysler Corporation donated ten new automobiles to ferry players and members of the press between their downtown hotels and the Olympic Club, although many used their own vehicles.

Player facilities at Olympic represented another area of expansion and improvement for the golfers, as noted by Byron Nelson in a bylined article that appeared in the official program. "The facilities of a club that hosts a tournament such as the USGA Open mean to me almost as much as the preparation of the golf course," Nelson wrote. The pro recalled tournaments where he shared lockers in cramped quarters, waited his turn to shower, and stood in line at a food shack to grab a sandwich between rounds. Olympic, Byron wrote, "has wonderful clubhouse facilities." The food was more than adequate, and the private locker and shower facilities gave the players "almost as much lift . . . as hitting par on the toughest hole."

There would be few hiccups during the tournament. The USGA and other officials later paid high compliments to the Olympic Club and its members, although there was at least one silly mishap. In an attempt to avoid cars along the 4th fairway of the Ocean Course, which was being used for parking, member Tony Glesener lost control of his automobile and skidded into a sand trap. Glesener, whose golf balls had visited the bunker on several occasions, confessed it was the first time he had driven his vehicle into the trap. Instead of a sand wedge, Glesener required a tow car to escape the bunker.

•   •   •

If Hogan failed in his attempt to win a record fifth U.S. Open, it would not be due to lack of preparation. "No man," reported England's *Golf Monthly*, "not even Henry Cotton at the peak of his enthusiasm, has ever put so much into the preliminary preparations for a golf title."

"He went all out for that type of tournament, the Open," Dow Finsterwald said. "Whereas a lot of guys would just come in and play two, maybe three, practice rounds, he'd go in a week ahead of time and do a lot of things in preparation."

It actually began several months earlier at Seminole Golf Club in Florida, a winter ritual for Hogan during which he honed his game alongside Claude Harmon. The Hawk's knee ached when the weather turned cool, so he headed to Florida. "He spent a lot of winters there at Seminole," Shelley Mayfield said.

In preparation for the U.S. Open, Hogan began a four-month practice regimen in February at Seminole, a course he later called "the best schooling ground." He practiced hard, losing fifteen pounds in a few days. It began each day at 10:00 A.M. with two hours of chipping and putting, playing every stroke as if it were a shot in a tournament. He took a break at noon for a light lunch and then set up shop on the practice range, starting with the short clubs and working his way through the bag until finishing with the woods, a practice phase that lasted four hours. Hogan always had a specific target in mind on every shot. He imagined water hazards, trees, foliage, and bunkers as he struck balls to various spots in the practice area, bending shots and controlling their height to match the situation he had conjured in his mind. Afterward he often headed to the course to play 9 holes.

When Hogan arrived at Seminole, he hadn't played a round of golf in four months. When he left, the sharpness had returned. Still, he needed some tournament competition, so he played in the Seminole Pro-Amateur, Masters, Colonial Invitational, and Greenbrier Open.

With two weeks of practice at Olympic complete, course-management plans laid, and a winning score hidden somewhere in his mind, all that remained before his tee time was a warm-up on the driving range and brief work on his troublesome putting stroke on the practice green. Hogan would not attempt to force anything on Thursday.

"The morning of a tournament I sort of weigh my capabilities at the time," he explained in *Sports Illustrated*. "I don't try to extend myself and do something I know I can't do."

Hogan's caddie was Tony Zitelli, an Olympic Club regular. Even a player of Hogan's stature utilized local caddies. The caddies wore numbers so spectators could identify the caddies' players. Zitelli was number 48. In Hogan's case, it was unnecessary. He was the game's most recognizable player. A man of few words, Hogan would not chitchat with Zitelli. He was all business, and his caddie was expected to match his serious demeanor. Zitelli surely didn't mind. For a caddie, there could be no higher honor than toting the bag of golf's greatest champion.

With Zitelli by his side, the Hawk arrived at the 1st tee a few minutes before 10:00 A.M. and exchanged greetings with his playing partners, Jack Burke Jr., an ex-marine and fellow Texan with ten tour wins, and Dick Mayer, who had shot the surprising 66 alongside Hogan during practice. Burke had the honors and walloped his drive on the par 5. Mayer was next, and then all eyes were trained on the man introduced as a four-time Open champion. Hogan cut an unmistakable figure. He wore light-colored pleated trousers, a dark long-sleeve V-neck sweater, and English-made leather golf shoes, each with an extra spike. A white linen flat cap covered his thinning hair. After teeing his golf ball, the Hawk wasted no time. He set his feet, waggled the long wooden club, and unleashed his first drive into the morning air. He handed the club to Zitelli and strode from the tee. The first of four 18-hole battles was joined. Hogan hoped he could go the distance.

•   •   •

Johnny Battini was the head professional of the Olympic Club, a post he had held for fourteen years. With a large membership, two 18-hole courses, and weather that allowed year-round play, it was a big job. Battini had help—a teaching pro, a shop assistant, a caddie master, and his wife, Betty. She had worked alongside her husband since 1941 when Battini had no one to serve as a starter or supervise caddies. A temporary arrangement became permanent, and Betty, popular among members, was the indispensable other half of one of golf's few husband-wife teams. A photograph in the official program showed the pair smiling at each other. Betty wore cat's-eye glasses, lipstick, and a button-down sweater, her hand resting on her hip. Johnny attired himself in a tie, sweater, casual jacket, and brimmed hat, his right hand holding a lofted iron.

Dating back to 1917, Battini had deep roots at Olympic. Macdonald Smith, the club's first head pro, hired Battini as an assistant and taught him everything he knew. Battini followed his mentor east to the Lakeville Golf Club on Long Island in 1925 and qualified for the 1926 and 1927 U.S. Opens. "There's the future Open champion of the world if he wants to play for it," Smith once said. Battini preferred the rhythms of club pro life, though, and never seriously pursued a competitive career. After a stint as an assistant at the San Francisco Golf Club and a decade at the nearby Millbrae Country Club, Battini returned to the Olympic Club as head pro, a job that was his for as long as he wanted to stay.

Whether called a "single-unit electric car" or "electric caddie cart," early models of powered golf carts were appearing at Battini's club. No one saw any harm in the novel machines. They allowed physically infirm golfers and old-timers to ride instead of walk on the Lake and Ocean courses. However, one local reporter lamented the potential threat to caddies who might lose their jobs. "Golf just wouldn't be golf to millions if such would happen," he wrote, unaware that club caddies would decades later be nearly extinct as a result of powered golf carts.

Battini had many other things on his mind on Thursday. Namely, how would he play? The USGA granted the head pro of the host club an exemption to play in the U.S. Open. Battini would set aside his duties and reach for his clubs for his 1:28 P.M. starting time. The round would be memorable for the affable home pro.

• • •

The 10:32 A.M. threesome was a glamour grouping if there ever was one. All three players—Cary Middlecoff, Mike Souchak, and Harvie Ward— were serious contenders for the title. Middlecoff was anxious to get started. Ward had played like he owned the joint during practice rounds while his professional counterparts couldn't crack 80.

"I might use a million one of those three days," Ward said, "but I'm not afraid of the place." It had been twenty-two years since Johnny Good- man was victorious in a Chicago heat wave, the last amateur to claim the national title. Could Harvie? There were many believers as he departed with Middlecoff and Souchak.

Among those who didn't chase after Ward and company, some may have reached for their pairings sheet to identify the golfers who followed in the 10:40 grouping. Many, if not all, of the spectators would not have recognized the men by sight—Larry Tomasino, Walker Inman Jr., and Jack Fleck, a trio of no-namers, part of the invisible supporting cast of pro- fessional golf. Tomasino was a club pro from Detroit, a long hitter who nearly won the 1953 Michigan Open. Tour rookie Inman had been in the money just three times in his career, earning $276. The fact that Fleck was the most successful tournament player of the three would have mat- tered to no one that morning. As Bill Rach later wrote, the Iowa pro was "attracting less attention than a hot-dog vendor." There were, however, an older couple who stood near the 1st tee and fixed their gaze upon Fleck: Dr. Barton, Fleck's father in golf, and his wife. Along with a friend, they would follow Fleck every round of the championship.

It was the type of grouping expected from the USGA. In large part, names played with names and no-names played with no-names. For In- man and Fleck, being grouped together was the first break of the cham- pionship. Playing alongside a friend during the intense pressure of a U.S.

134

Open on a brutal golf course was a morale booster in an otherwise lonely, soul-searching expedition. The tour comrades would face the first 36 holes together. Maybe one or both would make the cut.

After being introduced, each to a smattering of polite applause, the three men teed off: Fleck first, Tomasino next, and Inman last. Then they disappeared down the 1st fairway, their anonymity still intact.

. . .

None of the early-morning groupings made a dent in par on the opening 9. Reed, the airline pilot, posted an even-par 35. Few would better or match his number on a so-called perfect scoring day. Yet one who did was playing a few groups behind Reed. It was Bolt. After starting with three pars and a birdie, Bolt drove into the rough at the long par-4 5th hole. He recovered with a 1-putt bogey, one of four 1-putt holes on the front side that included a 9-footer for par at the 420-yard 9th hole. Bolt was out in 35. A warm putter was heating up.

Two groups behind, Harper recorded 40 strokes on his first 9 holes, as did Holscher and Mayer. Beman carded a 41. It was apparent early on that players were counting more strokes than normal. It wasn't an anomaly. It was more like an epidemic. The bright June skies were exposing what would become the highest first-round scoring in recent U.S. Open history.

Forget birdies. Par was the coveted score at Olympic. Every time a player could mark a par on his scorecard was a cause for celebration. At the U.S. Open, bogeys and those dreaded "others," a double bogey or more, popped up like dandelions in the springtime. No one understood the sanctity of par better than the Hawk, who picked off seven pars on the opening 9. His two bogeys came at the par-4 2nd and 9th holes. He was out in 37, not great by Hogan standards but manageable.

While Mayer was struggling, Hogan's other playing partner had gotten off to a superb start. Burke was out in 34 strokes, 1 under par. After a 3-putt bogey at the par-5 1st, Burke carded consecutive birdies at the 2nd and 3rd holes, rolling in a 40-foot putt at the latter. He parred the next six holes to take the early lead in the championship. Burke was another in a growing line of Texans who could play well when it counted most. The 1952 season was a Texas-sized year for Burke: He won five tournaments and the Vardon Trophy for lowest scoring average on tour. After claiming another title in 1953, the Fort Worth native was winless in 1954. In search of another victory and his first major, maybe Burke was peaking at the perfect time.

Only two players could match Burke's 34 on the front 9: a California pro named Freddie Haas and an unknown from Augusta, Georgia, Walker Inman Jr. Like Burke, Inman picked up two birdies against a lone bogey on the outward 9. The young pro who had failed to record a decent score in practice had charged out of the gate. If Inman could keep it going, the press would be scrambling to stitch together his biography by day's end.

Meanwhile, Fleck started the championship with a bogey at the opening hole. After steadying himself with three consecutive pars, he bogeyed the 457-yard par-4 5th hole. Two bogeys after 5 holes was not great. Nor was it a disaster. He bounced back with a birdie at the par-4 6th hole and finished with two pars and a bogey for a 37, the same score as the other man in the field playing Hogan clubs.

•　　•　　•

By early afternoon, 18-hole scores began trickling in. The best anyone had managed on a sunny, mild, near-windless day at the Lake Course was a 4-over 74. Other early scores ranged from poor to abysmal: a handful of 77s, a pair of 79s, and four scores of 80 or more, including two 84s. Florida pro Bill Meyers shot a horrendous 48 on the first 9 and withdrew from the tournament. Olympic was a thug. It was beating up the field in what was sizing up as an unfair fight. The first scores were like early election returns that predict the outcome. More results from the rest of the field would only confirm the obvious: The Lake Course was winning in a landslide.

Bolt was an exception, a cagey golfer who ducked Olympic's haymaker and landed a few blows of his own. He was erratic with his driver. He later told the press he started slicing his tee shots while practicing with Hogan in Texas. His wedges and flat stick, though, were extremely reliable. Legs nearly straight, shoulders and head hunched over the ball, Bolt swung his blade putter with amazing feel on the small, sloping greens. While playing partners Wininger and Sweeney were shooting 75 and 80, respectively, Bolt waltzed through the back 9 with a magic wand that produced seven 1-putt greens.

It began with a birdie from 16 feet at the 417-yard par-4 10th. Bunkered at the par-4 11th hole, Bolt blasted out and holed a 10-footer to save his par. He sank another par-saving putt of 10 feet at the 12th. At the 187-yard par-3 13th, he landed his tee shot 12 feet from the cup and dropped it for a deuce. While others muttered to themselves, Bolt walked on air. His only stumble came at 14, the lone bogey on his card for the inward 9. He recovered masterfully with birdies on the next two holes, dropping a 7-footer at the short par-3 15th and snaking in a 25-footer on the monster par-5 16th hole. His final 1-putt came on the most difficult hole on the course, the 461-yard par-4 17th. After landing his second shot in a greenside bunker, Bolt's third shot left him 12 feet from the cup. If the USGA had allowed such things in stroke-play championships, Wininger and Sweeney might have conceded the putt to the blazing Bolt, who sank it. A par at the last completed one of the lowest opening-round scores in U.S. Open history. After going out in 35, Thunder Bolt came home with a 32 for a 3-under 67. It was a near-perfect encore to his 66 in practice. The early leader was buoyant. Hogan had twice opened with 67 and gone on to win the National Open. Why not Bolt?

Still, Bolt paid tribute to the Hawk, telling reporters, "Ben Hogan is still out there. I pick him to win the tournament."

Tommy Bolt held the four-time U.S. Open champion in the highest esteem. "He was the greatest player I played with," Bolt said a few months before his death. "I thought Nicklaus was a great player, but Hogan was just a little bit better than him."

No one knew it at the time, but two things had occurred by lunchtime on Thursday. Tommy Bolt would be the only player to break the Lake Course's par of 70 in the opening round. The other: The lowest 18-hole score of the entire championship was already on the board. No one would go lower than 67, and only two would match it. Neither would be named Hogan or Snead.

•   •   •

Behind Bolt lay wrecked hopes and shell-shocked golfers. The threesome that followed Bolt posted scores of 78, 86, and 91. In the next group, Harper and Little shot 81, as did young Beman. Holscher managed a 77. Oddly, a score in the mid-70s was looking pretty good.

While Mayer was struggling to break 80, playing partners Hogan and Burke were playing steady golf. Burke carded a double bogey on the 10th but settled down to play par golf the rest of the way for a 1-over 71, a fine opening round considering the carnage around him. After a birdie, a bogey, and the rest pars on the incoming 9, Hogan tersely suggested his 72 was "par" golf for the championship layout, even though the scorecard disagreed. The remark was a window into Hogan's thinking about the Olympic setup and hinted at what the four-time champion had set as a target score. "His putts hung on the lip everywhere," reported Rosenbaum. Hogan's lone birdie came at the par-4 12th, where he struck a 7-iron to within 18 inches of the hole.

Following a half hour behind, Souchak (73), Middlecoff (76), and Harvie Ward (74) putted out on the 18th green. Their rounds could have been better, but at least none of them had shot themselves out of the tournament. As it has been said, no one has won a major championship on Thursday. However, many players have lost one. A poor start rarely leads to victory in golf's biggest tournaments.

Players with afternoon tee times had begun their rounds, including a 12:40 grouping of former Open champions: Julius Boros, Lew Worsham, and Byron Nelson. Playing in front of them was another anonymous pro, Mike Krak. Over the next two and a half hours, the rest of the fifty-four groupings went off the 1st tee, players such as Dow Finsterwald, Porky Oliver, Shelley Mayfield, Errie Ball, Arnold Palmer, Fred Hawkins, and Johnny Battini.

Had these players seen the scores from the morning rounds? One common approach was to ignore what other players were doing, especially in early rounds. Still, a portion of the field must have checked the early scores if for no other reason than to gauge how the course was playing on a picture-perfect San Francisco day. They learned from the morning scores that the Lake Course was as terrifying under a bright, sunny sky as in fog, drizzle, and mist. The value of this type of sobering information was debatable. How would it affect already fragile psyches?

By midafternoon, the three players in the twenty-first grouping had signed their scorecards. The long-hitting Tomasino—a driving-contest winner against Chick Harbert in '53 and later at the 1956 Pensacola Open, where he won $100 and considered himself a rich man—carded a disappointing 84 after too many drives visited the rough and trees. Although his ball striking was solid—he only missed one fairway—Fleck's balky putting continued on the second 9. Five pars and four bogeys added up to 39 for a total of 76. Meanwhile, Inman came home with all pars except on the long 17th, where few players were reaching the par 4 in the regulation two shots. "Boy, it played long," Tomasino later said, a telling comment from a big hitter. Inman's 70 matched Olympic's par and landed him in second place. He missed just three fairways. Four of the five times he was bunkered he got the ball up and in to save par. If Bolt had accomplished the unfathomable with his 67, Inman had surprised onlookers by bettering the marks of established players like Burke, Hogan, and Souchak. There was another thing about the only man in the field who would match par on Thursday: No one knew who he was.

•   •   •

Another marquee afternoon threesome was the 1:36 P.M. grouping of Ed Furgol, Gene Littler, and Claude Harmon. By day's end, Furgol and Littler, each carding 76, would be lodged in a nineteen-way tie for twenty-second. Harmon finished among the alarming number of players on the wrong side of 80. Littler bogeyed 16, 17, and 18, while Furgol struggled to overcome a poor start. Ed's defense began with a bogey, the product of a hooked second shot into the trees that led to an unplayable lie. At the 2nd, he shanked a bunker shot and hung on for dear life the rest of the way. (The shank, a shot struck too close to the club's hosel, causing the ball to squirt wide of the target at a 45-degree angle, is so dreaded that many players will not utter the word.) "It shook me," Furgol said, "and the rest of the round was played on nerves as I tried to get off the defensive."

The last of the day's star-studded threesomes was the 2:08 P.M. grouping of Doug Ford, Bob Rosburg, and Sam Snead. The first hint of trouble for Snead came at the par-4 4th hole. After three routine pars, Snead eased up on a 5-iron and landed his ball 35 feet from the hole. He cozied his first putt to within 30 inches of the cup and then missed—bogey. He was still in the rough after his second shot on the 5th hole, and the gallery and photographers crowded in to get a look at his predicament.

"You've had those cameras on me every shot I've hit," Snead said. "Ease up, will you?"

He swatted an 8-iron to within 5 feet of the hole. Again he missed the putt and took another bogey. More trouble at the 6th led to a bogey. A par at the short 7th hole stopped the skid, and then came a fourth bogey at the par-3 8th hole when he hit tree branches as hundreds of spectators watched from the slope behind the green. A par at the 9th gave Snead a 39. It was not the start he wanted. It was the start of so many before him.

Olympic's inward 9 was no kinder to the seven-time major winner. Two more bogeys put Snead 6 over after 11 holes. He regained control with three straight pars. On the 15th tee, a fifteen-year-old girl from Chicago named Mary Loretta Dillon, the daughter of a friend, handed him a hamburger. Tossing away half the bun, he ate the burger and then swallowed another bogey. At the 17th, a par 4 the *Chronicle's* Goethals called "murder," Snead hooked his drive into the rough, beginning a series of misadventures that ended with a double-bogey 6 on his scorecard. *Nine over.* Another hook at 18 put him in the tall rough on the left-hand hillside. "I'm not going to break 80," he said, forcing a smile. He viciously slashed the ball out of the hay with a 6-iron, and the ball landed in a bunker 15 yards short of the home green. Snead's sand shot nearly trickled into another bunker across the green, leaving him a 12-foot putt for 79. The man at the nearby main scoreboard picked up his piece of chalk to render the scoring verdict as Snead hunched over the golf ball and gave it a gentle rap. The putt rolled slowly toward the cup, taking the break as it began to lose speed. Snead and the mammoth gallery around the green and on the hillside waited for what seemed like a long time. The ball teetered into the hole. Applause. Cheers. Most of all, relief. He retrieved his ball and chucked it into the sky as if he had won the U.S. Open. A chagrined Snead later walked to his automobile without removing his golf spikes. It appeared that another opportunity to win the U.S. Open had been lost in the Lake Course rough.

Playing partner Rosburg was only 1 stroke better than Snead, shooting a 78 with an ugly 41 on the final 9. Ford, a six-time tour winner, got off to the worst start of the group. He 4-putted the par-5 1st hole for a double bogey. "These greens have me scared to death," he admitted as he approached the 6th green. Ford settled down and finished as one of four golfers on the board with a 74.

It was the same disturbing story as, three by three, players drifted off the Lake Course on Thursday afternoon: Mayfield, 75; Boros and Bud Ward, 76; Nelson, Worsham, Harbert, and Palmer, 77; and Oliver, along with Snead, 79. A few players managed scores that put them among the leaders. Hawkins and a New Jersey pro named Babe Lichardus posted 73s to join Souchak in a tie for fifth. Philippine Open champion Celestino Tugot carded a 74.

Eighty-two in the field of 162 shot 80 or higher. It was ghastly, embarrassing, humiliating. "The crying room at Olympic," reported *Golf World*, "was filled with wailing and gnashing of teeth" as the black scoreboard in the small press room registered unsightly 7s and 8s. Pointing to the first-round scores, *Newsweek* later called the U.S. Open setup "open-air murder." One of the consequences was slow play by that era's standards. The first round, on average, took four hours and twenty-seven minutes.

Those with scores of 80 or higher included Jerry Barber (80), Frank Stranahan (80), Harmon (81), Little (81), Finsterwald (84), and sixty-year-old Bobby Cruickshank (84). Ball, Fleck's qualifying pal, shot an 81. Practice partner Krak had an 82. What had started out well ended badly. "I was even par going to No. 11," Krak later said, "and drove it into the right-hand rough and could not get back to the fairway with a sand iron. I was lucky to find the ball."

Sidelined Open champion Lloyd Mangrum was in the gallery on Thursday and planned to stick around until the championship's conclusion on Saturday. "I'm overgolfed," he joked. "I've walked six or seven holes."

Also among the large throng of spectators was Cameron Dunn, the grandson of Willie Dunn, the runner-up in the inaugural U.S. Open in 1895.

As if to punctuate the field's stratospheric scoring, Olympic head pro Battini came in with 9s of 46 and 50 for a 96. One of five rounds in the 90s, it was Thursday's highest score. Unlike the three players who withdrew after front-9 scores in the mid-40s, at least Johnny had bravely finished his round. Battini knew the Lake Course was going to be a brawler, saying two weeks earlier, "I just wish I didn't have to play it myself." Johnny didn't get his wish, but Open host pros after him would avoid his fate. As it turned out, 1955 would be the last year the home pro was automatically entered in the championship.

18-HOLE LEADERS

Bolt	67
Inman	70
Burke	71
Hogan	72
Souchak	73
Hawkins	73
Lichardus	73
H. Ward	74
Ford	74
Reed	74
Bell	74
Tugot	74

After his 76, Fleck was part of the nineteen-man logjam in a tie for twenty-second. With such high scoring, if he could shoot the same or a better score on Friday, he was likely to make the 36-hole cut.

The first-day crowd of 9,300 was well behaved, producing gate receipts totaling $20,100, which equaled the first day at Baltusrol the year before. There was also thought to be a considerable number of badgeless fans who entered the tournament from their homes along the Lake Course's fairways. Because of the strong gate totals, the USGA increased the purse by 20 percent to $24,000 and the winner's share to $6,000.

It had been a good opening day at Olympic. Unlike the frustrated and embarrassed players, the USGA wasn't particularly troubled by the high scores. The world's longest short course was defending par with the best of them. Somewhere the course doctor might have cracked a grin.

—13—

FRIDAY: ROUND 2

The small pressroom at the Olympic Club was a model of efficiency. It accommodated a hundred-plus representatives of newspapers, wire services, magazines, radio, and TV who had traveled from all parts of the country and beyond to cover the U.S. Open. The media contingent included the local newspapermen: Art Rosenbaum, Bob Goethals, columnist Will Connolly, and photographer Duke Downey of the *Chronicle Sporting Green*; and the team from the *San Francisco Examiner*, which included sports editor Harry Hayward, who served as the head media representative in the pressroom. Prominent Gotham sportswriters Lincoln Werden of the *New York Times* and Al Laney of the *New York Herald Tribune* were on the scene, as were Charlie Bartlett of the *Chicago Tribune* and staffers of golf magazines such as Herb Graffis of *Golf World*, Bill Rach of *Professional Golfer*, and D. Scott Chisholm of the *Golfer*. Herbert Warren Wind, who had begun his career at the *New Yorker*, was covering the action for *Sports Illustrated*, a weekly sports magazine that had published its first issue the previous summer. Also present were reporters from small-town newspapers who were made to feel as important as their big-city colleagues thanks to Dick Smith, a local businessman and Olympic Club member who served as the event's publicity chairman. The industrious Smith was helpful and genial, treating the media with more courtesy than they were accustomed to.

In addition to the standard tables, chairs, and large black scoreboard, the press quarters featured modern equipment that made the scribes sit up and take notice. F. G. Fink, the regional manager of the Underwood Corporation, had donated sixty new Underwood typewriters for use during the national championship. They were a dead solid hit. "The thumpers of the keys appreciated the use of these brand-new, speedy typewriters, enabling them to chronicle the rapidly occurring events with almost lightning speed," the *Olympian* reported. Founded in 1895, Underwood manufactured the first commercially successful typewriter, selling millions of the machines by the end of the 1930s. The typewriter was the 1950s equivalent of the laptop, an indispensable tool of production for the era's reporters.

The press and fans were also treated to a shot-by-shot service provided by the Motorola company. A walkie-talkie system was installed and operated throughout the Lake Course to relay scores and shot information as the action unfolded. Bob Cardinal of the California Golf Club received the transmissions in the pressroom, which included near-instantaneous shot descriptions and hole-by-hole results for groupings of interest. The innovative Motorola service was a forerunner of the high-tech scoring systems and leaderboards of the late twentieth and early twenty-first centuries.

As Friday dawned and people sat down with their coffee and morning newspaper, two story lines highlighted the coverage of the first round of the U.S. Open on the sports pages of America's newspapers. The first was Tommy Bolt's sensational 67, the only subpar round among the 162 players. The other, which underscored Bolt's achievement, was the dismal scoring on the Lake Course.

This was Olympic, so, influenced by the setting and its mythological connotations, Rosenbaum reached for the Greek god Zeus for a comparison for thunderous Tommy Bolt, "known to hurl his jagged shafts to earth"—a reference to Bolt's spreading fame for throwing his golf clubs in fury. "But Zeus was also the god of destiny who controlled mere men," Rosenbaum continued in a story that trumpeted Bolt's first-round performance.

* * *

An Oklahoma native, Bolt, thirty-nine, was a former caddie and construction worker who became the best amateur golfer in Shreveport, Louisiana, a talent that subsidized his blue-collar lifestyle. He was so good and so cocky that he would sell the top merchandise prize before the local amateur tournaments began.

"I'd already have the cash spent before I teed off," he later explained, "which meant I'd have to win to avoid getting in big trouble with the guy who'd bought the prize. That was pressure, boy."

Taking a club job in Shreveport, Bolt turned professional in 1946 but didn't get traction on the PGA Tour until the early 1950s. His first victory came at the 1951 North and South Open. Several more wins followed, including the '55 season titles at San Diego and Tucson leading up to the U.S. Open. In Thursday's aftermath, Thunder Bolt spent as much time talking about his temper as he did explaining how he was the only player to break par at Olympic.

It was an irresistible angle for reporters because Bolt was good copy. He emphasized to the assemblage that his well-publicized temper tantrums had been overblown by the press. "There isn't a man here who hasn't broken a club in exasperation at one time or another," he told reporters.

Bolt's wife, Shirley, came to her husband's defense, saying she could name half a dozen other pros who lost their temper. Yet not all were as skilled at throwing clubs as Shirley's husband. One story that circulated during the week concerned Bobby Cruickshank, who once became infuriated after 3-putting a sand green at Pinehurst. In his attempt to helicopter the guilty putter, Cruickshank landed a blow to his own jaw. He later admitted that it was his best shot of the day. It knocked him out cold.

One thing was certain: Bolt's opening 67 on a tough U.S. Open course was not a fluke.

"Bolt had a chance whenever he played," Rosburg later said. "Tom was a great player when the course got real hard."

He was rested, too. Before arriving in San Francisco, the Bolts had vacationed in Hot Springs, Arkansas, where Bolt picked up a rod and reel and whiled away the days fishing and gigging frogs. It did wonders for his golf game. The 66 in practice followed by a 67 to lead the tournament constituted a hot streak on such a difficult layout. His game had run hot before. Bolt's best competitive round was a 60 at the Insurance City Open, one of three wins in 1954. Of course, this wasn't Greater Hartford, where insurance and birdies were plentiful.

"I'm glad to have that as a platform under me," Bolt said about his opening score. "You won't see many subpar rounds."

The questions that hung in the air: Could Thunder Bolt keep it going? If he didn't, would his lid blow and his clubs fly?

.   .   .

Details were sketchy on the young man in second place after a first round of even-par 70. The *Times*'s Werden referred to Walker Inman as a twenty-five-year-old "unknown freelance pro" from Augusta, Georgia, who had been a professional for five years, even though Inman had spent a chunk of that time serving stateside in the U.S. Air Force during the Korean War. (Inman had been an assistant club pro for some time, but 1955 was his first full season on the PGA Tour. He later called it his rookie season.) Rosenbaum referred to the Georgia native by his full given name, Walker Patterson Inman Jr., adding that Inman "was nobody's choice to be among the leaders." First-round wonders were not unusual at the National Open. More times than not, they disappeared as quickly as they appeared.

Inman, it seemed, was destined to be a golfer. His father once carried a 3 handicap. There was another thing about Walker's daddy: he had been fraternity brothers with golf legend Bobby Jones at Georgia Tech. The two became lifelong friends. Later in life Inman came into possession of movies of his father and Jones playing golf at Augusta Country Club before famed Augusta National Golf Club was carved out of a nursery. Some of his most indelible childhood memories were of the Masters Tournament that Jones started after he retired from golf in 1930. The Masters, which began in 1934, was the only time Jones played in public after retirement. Inman's father wanted his nine-year-old son to see the legend in action. Nearly seventy years later, Inman said he could remember his first encounter with the great Bobby Jones like it happened that very day. Jones stood on the 8th hole when Inman and his father approached the golf great. Say hello to Mr. Jones, his father said. Then Jones addressed the wide-eyed boy.

"He put his hand on my head and he said, 'Walker, are you going to be a golfer like your daddy?' I said, 'No sir, Mr. Jones. I want to be a golfer like you.'"

Young Walker watched intently as Jones made his famous swing with a fairway wood, striking one pinecone after another, whoosh, whoosh, whoosh. If only I could hit the golf ball as well as I hit these pinecones, Jones told Inman's father, I could still win.

Later Inman would watch Hogan, Snead, and golf's other stars when they made their annual trek to his hometown to play in the Masters. He traced their steps on the famed layout and was mesmerized at the sight of Hogan and Snead pounding balls in the practice area. He aspired to play, dress, and carry himself like the men he idolized. "That was my goal, to be one of those guys."

Inman went on to play golf at the Citadel in Charleston, South Carolina, where he competed against a new crop of future golf stars advancing through college golf programs rather than the traditional caddie ranks. Among them were Dow Finsterwald, Gene Littler, Arnold Palmer, and Harvie Ward. Upon graduation, Inman was hired by Henry Picard to be an assistant pro at Canterbury Golf Club in Cleveland, Ohio. He was the same Picard Hogan paid tribute to in *Power Golf* and who hired Mike Krak. Like Jack Fleck, Inman was now giving the PGA Tour a try, testing himself against the game's best.

On Friday morning Inman wasn't thinking about winning the U.S. Open. It would be foolish to entertain that type of thought so early in the championship, even though the young pro was hitting the golf ball on a string. The key to scoring at Olympic was keeping the ball on the fairways, and he was driving the ball with uncanny accuracy through the Lake Course's tight corridors.

"I could drive it good in those days," he later said. "It didn't matter how narrow it was, I'd just take the driver and—bang—hit it right down the middle of the fairway."

Inman did have a goal in mind, the long-held dream of a young boy who grew up in Augusta. More than anything else, he wanted to play in the prestigious Masters. If Inman were to accomplish his goal, he would be the first hometown player to appear in Bobby Jones's invitational. It required a sixteenth-place or higher finish in the National Open.

Teenager Jack Fleck shows off his golf swing.

Courtesy of Jack Fleck

Assistant pro Fleck at Des Moines Golf and Country Club.

Courtesy of Jack Fleck

Fleck (bottom center) and crewmates aboard U.S. Navy rocket ship.

Courtesy of Jack Fleck

Fleck tees off at the Phoenix Open.

Courtesy of Jack Fleck

Fleck's golf swing,
circa 1955.

Courtesy of Jack Fleck

Fleck's near hole in
one in the second
round of the 1955 U.S.
Open.

Courtesy of Jack Fleck

Jack Fleck's climactic 7-foot putt to tie Ben Hogan on the final hole of the 1955 U.S. Open.

Courtesy of Jack Fleck

The prophetic cartoon presented to Jack Fleck the night before the 1955 U.S. Open playoff.

Courtesy of Jack Fleck

Hogan congratulates Fleck after Fleck wins the playoff, 69 to 72.

Courtesy of Jack Fleck

The Hogan woods and irons that beat Ben Hogan.

Courtesy of Jack Fleck

Davenport, Iowa, airport celebration after Jack Fleck's U.S. Open play-off victory.

Courtesy of Jack Fleck

Jack Fleck and wife, Lynn, ride high during welcome-home parade.

Courtesy of Jack Fleck

Fleck's game was on an upswing in 1959.

Courtesy of Jack Fleck

In another playoff, Fleck won the 1979 Senior PGA Championship.

Courtesy of Jack Fleck

Jack Fleck's home club in Fort Smith, Arkansas, in 2010.

Courtesy of Neil Sagebiel

Jack Fleck, eighty-eight, at Hardscrabble Country Club in Fort Smith.

Courtesy of Neil Sagebiel

Fleck with the Ben Hogan 3 wood
in his Fort Smith townhome.

Courtesy of Neil Sagebiel

* * *

After carding a 76 and with his dreamlike win at Baltusrol becoming a distant memory, Ed Furgol changed his mind about the difficulty of the Lake Course. "These greens are as tough as any I've ever played in any Open tournament," he said.

Despite his admission, and with first-round scores averaging within an eyelash of 80, Furgol was in the hunt and knew it. "I don't feel I'm out of contention," the defending champ commented. "I think Bolt could hit a 75 or 76 before this tournament is over."

On Friday, Furgol would again play with Gene Littler and Claude Harmon. All fifty-four groupings would remain intact until the completion of the second round. Only the tee times would change. Off at 10:00 A.M., Furgol's tee time flip-flopped with Hogan's grouping. Hogan, Burke, and Mayer would head out at 1:36 P.M, Furgol's Thursday starting time. The weather was a repeat of Thursday—sunny, warm, and dry by San Francisco standards, a high of 70 degrees. Most of the field hoped their scores wouldn't also be a repeat of Thursday. Another round in the high 70s or dreaded 80s would be hard to explain to people back home, especially under blue skies.

Fleck, who hoped to improve upon his first-round 76, had time to kill. His Friday round with Inman and Tomasino would not begin until 2:16 P.M. It had no effect on his morning routine. He awoke, showered, and shaved in the first light of another gorgeous June day. It gave the Iowa pro the entire morning to reflect on his first trip around the Lake Course and prepare himself for round two. He felt let down. He had recorded a mediocre score despite hitting the ball well.

Like his friend Walker Inman, Fleck was consistently putting the ball in the fairway, occasionally teeing off with his "spoon," a common term for

151

a 3-wood during the era. Rhythm, timing, and balance were his swing keys during his Friday warm-up as the clock ticked toward 2:00 P.M. If only he could putt better on those greens.

As Fleck, Inman, and Tomasino began their second loop on the Lake Course, Sam Snead had risen from the dead. Snead was on the home holes finishing out a 69, a 10-shot improvement that would lift him from also-ran to contender. The round included a sparkling 33 on the inward 9. The powerful Snead was back in sync with his long game, only missing three fairways. The score could have been much better had he not missed a half-dozen putts within seven feet of the hole. Like his chief rival, Hogan, Snead had an ongoing dispute with the putter. His velvet swing didn't translate to the flat stick, nor did forty-three-year-old nerves help his cause on the greens. Despite the turnaround, Snead griped to the press afterward about the rough. "I'm not happy with it," he said, adding that fans didn't like to see the game's stars shoot scores in the 80s.

Playing alongside Snead, Bob Rosburg improved to a 74 and Doug Ford slipped to a 77. At 151 and 152, Ford and Rosburg could expect to survive the 36-hole cut, although they would have to watch the scoreboard over the next several hours to confirm their spots for the final two rounds on Saturday.

Dow Finsterwald, an hour ahead of Snead, made an even more dramatic turnaround. After a Hyde-like 84, Finsterwald posted a Jekyll-like 71, a 13-shot improvement on the fiendish layout. He was still in grave danger of missing the cut, but at least he had shored up his pride with his tidy 1-over effort. Frank Stranahan matched his playing partner's 71 after opening with an 80. Two groups ahead of Finsterwald and Stranahan, an Open champion also rallied. Like Snead after him, Julius Boros, driving the ball beautifully, put a 69 on the large black chalkboard. Boros's playing companion Byron Nelson shot a respectable 74, a 3-shot improvement for the gentleman rancher who rarely played tournament golf.

Would the Lake Course yield lower scores on Friday? Despite early flashes by Boros, Snead, Finsterwald, and Stranahan, the second round wasn't shaping up that way. Group by group, chalk dust flying, the main scoreboard filled up with scores in the high 70s and 80s as it had the day before. Former major champions Claude Harmon and Lew Worsham would find themselves on the wrong side of the cut after rounds of 78 and 79. That afternoon Lawson Little would struggle to an 80 for a two-round total of 161 and announce his retirement from the national championship. Johnny Battini, trimming 11 strokes from his first-round score, would resume his head pro duties after carding an 85.

Johnny Bulla had a different kind of scoring problem. Bulla, playing with Shelley Mayfield and Billy Maxwell, was disqualified when he turned in an incorrect score. The USGA's Dick Butler suspected that Bulla didn't closely review his scorecard before signing for what should have been a 76. The grouping's official scorekeeper gave Bulla a 5 instead of the correct score of 6 at the 6th hole and a 3 instead of the correct score of 4 at the 18th hole. After an opening 82, Johnny was doomed to miss the cut even had he not been disqualified. He put away his sticks and joined the gallery to watch the rest of the championship. Maxwell and Mayfield would be around for the weekend after posting 74 and 76, respectively.

·   ·   ·

With Tomasino still spraying his long drives into the rough and cypress trees, Fleck and Inman got off to a solid start with four consecutive pars. At 457 yards, the 5th hole was the longest par 4 on the outward 9. The hole required an accurate tee shot to cut the tree-lined corner of the right-hand dogleg and set up a favorable approach shot to a green flanked by bunkers. Fleck's drive put him in good position. His long-iron shot to the green was even better, leaving him 22 feet from the hole. It was the kind of putt he couldn't buy on Thursday. Nothing outside of a few feet had gone in. Fleck looked over the birdie putt—he never took long—and settled into his stance. That's when he first noticed it.

"I had some kind of wonderful feeling in my hands over the ball," he said. "I didn't change my grip or stance. It was just a feeling in my hands."

Fleck took back his Bulls Eye putter, stroked the putt, and watched the ball disappear into the cup for a birdie. He handed the putter to Emil Schroder and walked to the 6th tee, 1-under for his round. What had just happened on the 5th green? He felt a new and oddly comfortable sensation in his hands. He didn't know why, but it was nice to see a putt go in the hole for a change.

Fleck teed his ball on the 437-yard par 4 and ripped a solid drive down the left-hand side of the fairway. When he and his caddie arrived at the spot where the ball should have been, it wasn't there. Perplexed, they kept looking. No golf ball. Fleck became uneasy. According to the Rules of Golf, if they couldn't locate his ball within five minutes, it would be declared lost and he would have to return to the tee and play another ball, incurring a stroke and distance penalty. He would likely make a double bogey, or worse, nullifying his rare birdie at the 5th. A well-struck drive tracing the left side of the fairway simply does not vanish. Wait! There it was! The Lake Course had one driveable fairway bunker, a large trap 240 yards from the 6th tee that extended nearly half the distance across the fairway. The ball had rolled into a hole on the lip of the bunker. Fleck was fortunate to locate his ball and avoid a penalty, but he also had caught a bad break. He studied the hole that contained his ball. Was it a gopher hole from which he could take relief, a free drop? No, he finally decided. Another golfer must have visited the bunker and walloped a recovery shot that left a deep gash. His ball had come to rest in the exact spot where sod had been carved out of the bank of the bunker and now shielded the top of his ball. It was an impossible lie. There was no hope of reaching the green—or even advancing the ball 100 yards.

Fleck took his pitching wedge and swung with all his might, tearing into the sod. Amid the flying dirt, the ball popped out and traveled 6 feet onto the fairway. It was a remarkable shot under the circumstances. He was back in play but still had a long third shot to a slightly elevated green guarded by a pair of sand traps. He retrieved his 4-iron from Schroder, settled over the ball, and launched a crisp iron shot into the afternoon sky. The ball touched down on the green and stopped 12 inches from the hole. Fleck tapped in for his par.

(Inexplicably, a bogey was recorded as his official score, a small mystery that surprised Fleck decades later. He had no explanation. According to the Rules of Golf, a player is disqualified for turning in a score lower than actually taken. Conversely—and as in Fleck's case—if a player turns in a score higher than actually taken, the score stands.)

Fleck made a routine par at the short par-4 7th hole. Next was the par-3 8th, the hole where so many of his practice sessions ended because of its close proximity to the clubhouse. The hole measured 139 yards and had a well-bunkered green that sat 20 feet higher than the tee. Fleck's 7-iron flew straight for the pin.

"It hit the flag," Tomasino later said, "and he thought it was off the green."

When the threesome arrived at the green, Fleck's ball was resting less than a foot from the hole. A photograph showed Fleck crouching beside the ball, flat cap in hand. In the background wearing number 61 was Schroder. Up by the 8th green, eyewitness Doug Ford later said Fleck's tee shot ducked into the hole and spun out, a near hole in one. Fleck nudged in his deuce, a second birdie on the outward 9. Things were going his way, and his confidence was growing.

*   *   *

By midafternoon the large galleries had spread across the golf course to take in the action. The spectator count for Friday increased to ten thousand, an enthusiastic end-of-workweek crowd that consumed large quantities of hamburgers, hot dogs, and cold drinks.

A two-page spread in the official program highlighted six of the best spots on the Lake Course to watch the championship. Two prime viewing areas were where Fleck had produced his most exciting moments on Friday's first 9. The area behind the 5th green held several advantages for spectators. In addition to watching players putt out on the 5th, the gallery could watch approach shots to the 5th and 11th greens and tee shots at the nearby 12th hole. There was also an auxiliary scoreboard that listed scores of leading players. Another key vantage point on the opening 9 was near the 7th green. Spectators could watch players hit their approach shots from the Dewdrop landing area and putt on one of the course's trickiest greens; they could also catch much of the action on the 8th hole, where Fleck's 7-iron shot had rattled the flagstick. The 9th tee, where players headed away from the clubhouse area to begin their final 10 holes, was also nearby.

Olympic Club member Lyle Eaton was familiar with these and other highlighted spectator locations, even if he had never seen the Lake Course mapped and diagrammed in such an extensive manner. It was a great source of pride to have the U.S. Open played on your home course, and, despite a long illness, Eaton was not about to miss the championship. He was tickled to be among the large throngs that encircled Olympic's tee boxes and greens and was mesmerized by the long drives of Snead and the game's other bombers.

Besides the one near the 5th green, there were two other auxiliary scoreboards on the golf course, an innovation appreciated by players, tournament officials, and fans. They would be of even greater importance on Saturday during the final 36 holes of the championship. One scoreboard was positioned behind the 14th green. Another was near the 9th green, one of the best spots on the Lake Course to watch play on several holes.

Had Eaton or other Olympic members been at the 9th green on Friday around 4:00 P.M., they would have seen the grouping ahead of Fleck and Inman play their second shots on the straightaway par 4. After his opening 73, Mike Souchak was fading, on his way to a lackluster 79. The ex–Duke football player was in the rough on four of the first five holes. Cary Middlecoff wasn't doing much better and would sign for a 78. However, Harvie Ward putted out on the 9th green for an even-par 35. Birdies at 1 and 5—a wedge to 2½ feet and a 4-iron to 6 feet—were offset by bogeys at the 7th and the 9th. His struggles at the 9th ended with a heroic bogey. Harvie put himself in the knee-deep rough off the tee. A swing with his 4-iron only moved the ball a few feet deeper into the weeds. Watching behind the gallery ropes, Ward's mother cringed. Even Edie Middlecoff, wife of the Masters champion, winced. One disastrous hole could undo a good round and unhinge a golfer. Harvie hacked out of the jungle, hit to the green's fringe, and sank a 35-footer to salvage a bogey, a small miracle. Despite giving back 2 shots in 3 holes, even par was a good score, and the freewheeling Ward was on his way up the leaderboard.

The car salesman the hometown newspaper called the best amateur golfer in the world was completely in character the night before. Unfazed by a 74 that put him in an eighth-place tie 7 shots off Bolt's lead, Harvie did what any contending amateur would do on the eve of the second round of the National Open. Actually, he didn't. He did what Harvie Ward would do—go out on the town. The U.S. Open would not impede his social life. His first stop on Thursday night was a dinner party where he feasted on fried chicken with mashed potatoes and gravy. Calories left no mark on Ward's 149-pound frame. Harvie wielded the knife and fork as sure-handedly as he did his wedges. Not ready to call it an evening, the golfer headed over to the Fairmont to take in the show of singer Peggy Lee. He was home and in bed by 11:00 P.M., a reasonable hour considering a 2:08 P.M. Friday tee time.

Ward arose at 9:00 A.M. and ate a hearty breakfast of eggs, bacon, toast, and coffee. He then headed to the San Francisco Golf Club to practice for the rest of the morning. Harvie arrived at the Olympic Club at 1:15 P.M. and left the 1st tee fifty-three minutes later with Souchak and Middlecoff. As usual, he was loose—or at least appeared to be. Ward was known to chat up his playing partners and joke with the gallery. At the end of 9 holes, happy-go-lucky Harvie was 4 over for the championship and right in the thick of things.

•   •   •

Up ahead, Hogan and Burke were into their second 9 after going out in 37. Mayer, the other player in the group, was working on an 80, destined to miss the cut. On the three-hole finishing gauntlet, first-round leader Bolt was nearing the clubhouse. The hot streak was over. Now the only thing running hot was his famous temper. After a shaky 39 on the outward 9, Bolt ran off four pars and then popped his cork at the par-4 14th. He found the rough, and his 5-iron shot fell 20 yards short of the green. He tomahawked his club six inches into the turf, only the shaft and grip visible sticking out of the ground, like the grave marker of a tee shot that died in the thick rough. He chipped onto the green and sank his putt for a par. Perhaps he looked at the auxiliary scoreboard on his way to the 15th tee. He was still in the lead, but the margin was slimmer, and trouble lay ahead. After a bogey and two pars, Bolt hooked his tee shot on the 18th hole. The ball struck a female spectator and bounced under a large bush. "Pick it up," Bolt said to his caddie as he turned to make the long walk back to the tee. He finished with a double-bogey 6, another scar on a scorecard that totaled 77, or 10 strokes higher than Thursday. Thunder Bolt stomped into the clubhouse and initially refused to discuss his round with a group of reporters that gathered at his locker. Midway through the championship, Bolt stood at 144, 4 over par.

In the group ahead of Bolt, twenty-six-year-old Bob Harris, a former star at nearby San Jose State University and pro at Chicago's Edgewater Golf Club, had caught fire on the front 9, collecting four birdies and five pars for a blistering 31. It was one shot off the U.S. Open 9-hole record of 30 set by Jimmy McHale in 1947. No one among the leaders would touch Harris's 9-hole score, which seemed otherworldly given the severity of the conditions. The Chicago pro returned to earth on the second 9, stumbling home in 40 strokes. Still, a 71 was a fine score no matter how one tallied it up. Harris was in the clubhouse at 148 and within striking distance of the lead. After a 77, a 1-over-par round had shot him up the leaderboard, another testimony to the extreme difficulty of the Lake Course.

•　　•　　•

At the 12th hole, the news had reached Ward that Bolt had skied to a 77 and was in the clubhouse at 144. The messenger was Eddie Lowery, Ward's boss at Van Etta Motors and USGA bigwig. The hometown amateur star could take the lead. Harvie recorded four straight pars to stay even with Bolt and then faltered at the par-4 14th, pushing his second shot to the right of the green and failing to get up and in for a par. He nearly birdied the par-3 15th to regain a share of the lead when his boldly struck 15-foot putt ducked into the hole and spun out. After recording a par on the par-5 16th, Ward arrived on the toughest hole on the course, the long par-4 17th that many players failed to reach in 2 shots. Harvie lashed a drive followed by a 3-wood that touched down on the left portion of the elevated green. The ball bounced right and headed toward the hole as the excited amateur hurried up the fairway to see where it came to rest. No wonder the gallery had burst into cheers. The ball was 3 feet from the cup. Harvie took a bow and did a little jig before sinking the short putt for the rarest of birdies. The hometown favorite held a share of the lead.

Short, narrow, and severe in slope, the 18th was an exquisite finishing hole. While birdies were possible, bogeys were far more probable than one would expect on a 337-yard par 4. With a thick grassy slope to the left and tall trees to the right, the 18th funneled down a slope from an elevated tee. The assignment was to put the ball somewhere in the fairway for a short-iron approach shot to a narrow, tilted green guarded by two fronting and two flanking bunkers. The green and surrounding area formed a bowl, a natural amphitheater for thousands of golf fans. High above, the bunting-draped clubhouse overlooked the scene. Members peered down on the action, sipping cold beverages and cocktails in the comfort of the dining room. From down in the valley of the 18th fairway, players could see the flag but not easily discern the putting surface. Accuracy—especially distance control—was paramount on the approach shot. So was staying short of the hole on the sloped green. Downhill putts on the Lake Course's greens caused heart-quickening moments.

Harvie misjudged his approach, flying the ball over the 18th green into the tall grass. From a gnarly lie, he nearly holed his third stroke for an astonishing birdie. The gallery roared its approval as he sank his par putt for an even-par round of 70 and 36-hole total of 144. Harvie Ward, pride of the Bay Area and amateur among professionals, was tied for the lead at the halfway point of the fifty-fifth U.S. Open.

•   •   •

The spectator guide in the official program designated the 18th-green area as one of the six highlighted spots to watch the championship. Actually, it was the supreme spot, the place to be when marquee players such as Snead, Bolt, Ward, and Hogan walked uphill to the final green and acknowledged the gallery's applause. Come Saturday afternoon, it would be where the final, and perhaps deciding, shots of the championship were struck. The steep slope to the left of and behind the green accommodated thousands of spectators. The gallery also assembled along a small ridge and lined both sides of the fairway in the vicinity of where players struck their second shots. The 18th was an intimate golf stage, and the loud roars that arose from there—as when Ward nearly holed his chip—echoed off the slopes and flowed through the pines.

For one thirteen-year-old boy who sat for hours on the hill behind the 18th green, the setting felt magical. Bill Callan was a junior member at the Olympic Club, which allowed him to attend the U.S. Open along with his father and older brother. In addition to being one of the many keen observers of the tournament action, the junior member served as a scorecard runner. It was his "job" to watch the groupings walk up the final slope to the 18th green and complete their rounds. Callan rubbed shoulders with the players as they came off the final green and signed their scorecards at a small table on a platform with a sign that read RETURN SCORES HERE. Callan then ran the scorecards up the slope to the official scoring room inside the large clubhouse. The boy's participation in the Open championship and his brushes with golf greats stoked a passion for the game and his club that three decades later culminated in his role as Olympic Club historian. On Friday afternoon, he felt the surge of electricity through the large crowd as Ward turned in a scorecard that tied him with Bolt for the halfway lead. Stationed at the 18th green, the scorecard runner would continue to witness the most exciting moments of the championship.

*   *   *

When the cheers rang out on 18 for local hero Ward, Hogan was already finished and looking forward to rest for his weary legs and aching left knee. The sloping terrain of the Lake Course exacted a heavy toll from the forty-two-year-old golfer, but with 36 holes completed, he was halfway home. With one birdie, two bogeys, and the rest pars, he shot 36 on the inward 9 for a 73 and, at 145, stood just 1 stroke off the lead shared by Bolt and Ward. The lone birdie came at the par-5 16th when he drained a 25-footer, doffing his white cap to the appreciative gallery. The 603-yard hole had begun badly. His drive struck a tree branch and bounced into the fairway 175 yards from the tee. He drilled a fairway wood and 2-iron to reach the putting surface and walked off with a gallery-pleasing 4. "Par is 72 for me on this course," he offered after his round. By playing consistently boring golf, Hogan was in his usual spot near the top of the leaderboard.

The most arduous day, Saturday's 36 holes, lay ahead. The Hawk would take it one shot and one aching step at a time. It was a game plan that had worked four times since 1948. If it worked once more on Saturday, Hogan would retire from tournament golf and settle behind his desk in Fort Worth to run his golf equipment company.

*   *   *

Playing nearly two hours behind Bolt, Inman made the turn in even-par 35. Whether or not the twenty-five-year-old Augusta native knew it, he led the U.S. Open. Inman bogeyed 10 and 12 and then reeled off three straight pars. He was 2 over par for the championship and still in the lead when he arrived at the 16th tee. If he could successfully negotiate the difficult finishing holes, he would hold the outright lead at the midpoint of the championship, heady stuff for the rookie who had only cashed three checks on tour. Instead, he rode the bogey train to the clubhouse. Inman's back 9 of 40 gave him a 75 for a 36-hole total of 145. He was tied with Hogan, 1 shot off the lead. An invitation to the Masters was within his grasp if he continued his steady play in the last two rounds. Winning the U.S. Open was not a welcome thought. There was a long way to go, and the young pro would not be well served by allowing his mind to stray into such fanciful places.

Playing alongside his friend, Fleck was also moving up the leaderboard. Beginning with the 22-footer at the 5th, his putter had come alive. There was the near ace at the 8th hole that led to a tap-in birdie and a par at the 9th that completed a front 9 of 34. First Inman, now Fleck.

While nearly everyone was shooting over par and falling away— there were only four rounds of par or better on Friday—Fleck was holding his ground at 5 over for the championship and 1 under for his round. The good feeling in his hands was still there, and his putts rolled true on the deceptive little greens and tumbled into the cup. Good putters such as Ward, Rosburg, Ford, and Finsterwald expected to see putts drop into the hole. For Fleck, the instant transformation was a surprising development. On a brutally difficult Open course, the game was suddenly easier because his putter was more reliable, a friend, not a foe.

After beginning the incoming 9 with a par and a bogey, Fleck 1-putted six of the last seven holes. On the small, banked 12th green, he rolled in a 20-footer for a birdie. He carded pars on the next four holes and then made bogey at the long 17th, hanging a 13-foot par putt on the lip, a rare 3-putt green during his 1-putt binge from the 12th to the clubhouse. He got the stroke back at the last, ironing his approach shot to within 10 feet of the pin and stroking home the birdie for a 1-under 69 that tied him for low round of the day with Snead and Boros. He had caught his friend, making up 3 strokes on the final 3 holes to join Inman at 145. The two unknowns were tied with Boros and Hogan, 1 shot off the lead. Fleck and Inman shook hands on the 18th green. Not only had they both made the cut with ease, they were in contention for the national championship. It was remarkable golf and presence of mind from two players whose combined experience included three U.S. Opens.

A victim of poor driving on the inward 9, Hogan's playing partner Burke fell back with a 77. At 148, Burke found himself tied with Snead and Harris, still within striking distance heading into the final day. In a round during which he only missed three fairways, Gene Littler also crept up the leaderboard with a 73 and was alone at 149.

The club name fit. The course had been an Olympian struggle. Only 10 players in the 162-man field had cracked 150, an alarming 10 over par. Hogan's par of 72, which would total 288 for four rounds, was looking more like a winning score, especially with the 36-hole lead set at 144. He always seemed to know what it would take at the National Open. The only question was whether his sticks and legs would allow him to post the number he imagined in his sage golf mind.

36-HOLE LEADERS

Bolt	67-77—144
H. Ward	74-70—144
Hogan	72-73—145
Boros	76-69—145
Inman	70-75—145

Fleck	76-69—145
Snead	79-69—148
Harris	77-71—148
Burke	71-77—148
Littler	76-73—149

The 36-hole cut was set at 155, eliminating 102 players. Fifty-eight players would compete in Saturday's 36-hole finish, all within 11 shots of the lead. Besides the leaders, they included Byron Nelson, Frank Stranahan, Fred Hawkins, Doug Ford, Billy Maxwell, and Shelley Mayfield at 151; Bud Holscher, Mike Souchak, Bud Ward, Chick Harbert, and Bob Rosburg at 152; Arnold Palmer and Elmer Reed at 153; and Cary Middlecoff at 154. Ten made it into the final two rounds on the cutline, including defending champion Ed Furgol, Dow Finsterwald, and Errie Ball.

Only two of the twenty-seven amateurs in the field qualified for the final two rounds: the coleader, Harvie Ward, and nineteen-year-old Bill Thornton, a private first class in the U.S. Army from Jupiter, Florida, who stood at 154.

Several tour winners and name players failed to make the cut: Al Besselink, Lew Worsham, Jerry Barber, Dick Mayer, Claude Harmon, Ted Kroll, and Lawson Little. Fleck and Inman's friend Mike Krak also missed the cutline with rounds of 82 and 81, while Larry Tomasino fell 10 shots short with scores of 84 and 81. The highest 36-hole score was 184 by a California amateur named Gene McNulty, who failed to break 90 in either round, carding 90 and 94.

Many of the pros who missed the cut would empty their lockers, pack their automobiles, and drive 650 miles north to Portland, site of the Western Open, the next stop on the circuit. A couple of extra days for travel, rest, and practice after the horror of Olympic would do them good. At least one player who failed to qualify for the final two rounds would stick around until the conclusion of the championship—Johnny Bulla, the man who signed an incorrect scorecard and was disqualified.

"Johnny was always interested in things like that," Rosburg later said about Bulla's impulse to stay.

It was a decision Bulla would not regret.

—14—

SATURDAY: ROUND 3

The U.S. Open had spilled onto Saturday's front page of the *San Francisco Chronicle*. BOLT, HARVIE WARD TIED AT 144. The large headline appeared just below a banner headline announcing the acquittal of a local cop who had been tried on burglary and grand theft charges. Bay Area favorite Ward had won the allegiance of the large galleries while grabbing a share of the lead and newspaper headlines. Based on his reception at the 18th green on Friday afternoon, "you'd have thought he won the championship," reported Rosenbaum. The prospects of an amateur winning the National Open looked better than ever, and the golden boy of the San Francisco Golf Club appeared to be just the man to get the job done. The job was far from finished, though. Ward and the other fifty-seven competitors faced another 36 grueling holes on Saturday. The third and fourth rounds lay ahead, the most difficult half of the pressure-filled task.

Fifty-eight players in twenty-nine groups of two would begin teeing off at 8:00 A.M. in the double-round finish. How the USGA determined pairings—that is, who played together—for the third and fourth rounds remained a mystery, just as it had been at previous national championships. One thing was certain: Third- and fourth-round pairings weren't determined strictly by score, as became customary in the modern era. Nor were the leaders the last players to start and finish their rounds as they are today. Another feature of the now-extinct 36-hole finale: Pairings didn't change after the third round was completed. No matter what a player shot, he went the distance with the same playing partner during Saturday's 36-hole marathon.

When asked for an explanation of U.S. Open pairings fifty-five years later, Doug Ford had no answer. All Ford recalled was that for several years in the 1950s he always found himself in the final pairing for the third and fourth rounds of the National Open. That Saturday at Olympic, paired with Chick Harbert, Ford would bring up the rear of the small army of golfers. The Ford-Harbert pairing's morning round would begin at 10:48; their afternoon round was set for 3:18. Unless they shot their way into contention, their finish on the 18th green would be a mere formality and signal the official completion of the tournament.

With the other fifty-six players within 11 shots of Bolt and Ward's lead, anything was possible. A hot third round could vault a player up the leaderboard. Two strong rounds could steal the tournament right out from under Bolt, Ward, or Hogan. Earlier players, who often faced more benign course conditions—especially on the greens, where players' spikes roughed up the surfaces, particularly around the cups—could post a score that put pressure on later players to beat or match it. Starting and finishing early could be a definite advantage.

Coleading with Bolt, Ward would begin his quest to win the Open as an amateur at 8:30 A.M., the sixth of twenty-nine pairings on the golf course. Ward's playing partner would be Walker Inman, just 1 shot off

Ward's pace. It was a good pairing for both men. Besides the bonus of an early start, the two players were friends, their paths having crossed in collegiate and amateur golf.

Reflecting upon the pairing decades later, Inman said, "They [the USGA] would love to have an amateur win the tournament, and he [Ward] had as good a shot at it as anybody'd ever had, so they put us on the golf course first. We would have been able to put a score up a long time before anybody else finished that had a chance to win. I think they were definitely favoring him. I don't know that for sure, but I think so."

The pairing also favored Inman. He could keep a close watch on his fellow competitor while playing the last two loops of the Lake Course. Yet the tour rookie wasn't concerned about Ward or being crowned national champion—at least not early on that Saturday morning.

"My goal was to get into the Masters," he said. "I remember teeing off the last day and I thought, 'Just don't shoot any big numbers and you'll make it.'"

In its infancy in terms of golf telecasts, television probably influenced at least two of the pairings. The two warhorses, Ben Hogan and Sam Snead, were likely to finish their final rounds within the one hour allotted for national TV coverage by NBC. Snead graced a KRON-TV newspaper advertisement that announced the station's broadcast of "golf's biggest annual event" beginning at 5:00 P.M. Part of national radio coverage, KNBC would air tournament action starting at 5:05 P.M.

Snead, playing with Julius Boros in the day's 11th pairing, would tee off thirty minutes before Hogan. Paired with Bob Harris, Hogan would go off in the sixteenth twosome. The longtime rivals were lodged in the middle of the pack.

A pattern is evident in the final-day pairings. The top ten players on the leaderboard were paired together, although not from lowest to highest score, which later became the custom and would have put Bolt with Ward, Boros with Hogan, and so on. Rather, the five pairings of leaders departed at half hour intervals:

SATURDAY PAIRINGS

Morning and afternoon tee times, with 36-hole totals in parentheses

8:30–1:00: Ward (144) and Inman (145)
9:00–1:30: Boros (145) and Snead (148)
9:30–2:00: Hogan (145) and Harris (148)
10:00–2:30: Bolt (144) and Burke (148)
10:30–3:00: Fleck (145) and Littler (149)

With the first morning tee time at 8:00 and the last at 10:48, the leaders were evenly interspersed throughout the field. Why Ward got a ninety-minute jump on fellow leader Bolt was anybody's guess. Maybe Inman was right. Had the modern method of pairing by score been utilized, he and Fleck, posting their 145s after Boros and Hogan, would have been paired on Saturday and had the rare distinction of playing all four rounds together. As it was, among the leaders, Fleck would go out last with Gene Littler, which had no particular significance early on Saturday morning.

Yet after his 69 that tied him for low round on Friday with Boros and Snead, Fleck was slipping out of the shadows. As with his friend the day before, the newspapermen were piecing together a few details about the Davenport golfer, whom Rosenbaum described as having "a nice personality." The *New York Times*'s Lincoln Werden briefly mentioned Fleck along with Inman under a subheadline that read THE UNKNOWNS AT 145. In Iowa, though, Fleck's emergence was more than noteworthy; it was headline news in the *Des Moines Register*: BOLT, WARD LEAD AT 144; IOWAN'S 145 TIES HOGAN FOR THIRD, read the banner headline on the sports page. "Jack Fleck of Davenport, Ia., came out of nowhere Friday to tie for third place in the National Open golf tournament," read the lead. "The 34-year-old Iowa professional, a darkhorse of the blackest hue, came in with a late afternoon 69 to tie four-time champion Ben Hogan." The newspapers—even his home-state newspaper—habitually misreported Fleck's age. He was, in fact, thirty-three. The story went on to fill in a few biographical details about Fleck's career such as his former assistant pro job under Joe Brown at the Des Moines Golf and Country Club. Whether or not he gave it a thought, Fleck was no longer playing solely for himself, Lynn, and Craig. In a small midwestern state with no major professional sports teams, any Iowa native's appearance and success on a national sports stage was a big deal and source of statewide pride. While caddie Emil Schroder carried his clubs, Jack Fleck now carried the hopes of the Hawkeye State.

• • •

Bob Rosburg carried Fleck's Saturday playing partner in his automobile on the forty-mile drive to the Olympic Club from Rosburg's Palo Alto home, where Littler was bunking for the week. "Gene was a very good friend of mine," Rossie later said. "We rode to the course every day."

The route was the same early on Saturday morning, but the weather had taken a definite turn. As Rosburg and Littler sped north, a low gray ceiling hovered above. It was shaping up as one of those foggy San Francisco days. The players would need sweaters and patience. Enveloped in sub-60-degree cool and dampness, the Lake Course would play longer and wetter on the final day of the championship.

The pair arrived early at Olympic to accommodate Rosburg's 8:42 tee time with Charles Rotar, a club pro from San Bernardino, California. Littler would wait a few hours for his appointment with the Iowa pro. He needed a low third round to gain on the leaders and position himself to win the prestigious championship that had narrowly eluded him the year before in New Jersey. Instead, his host for the week would be the one to post a sensational third-round score in the morning fog. Rossie's finest hour was about to begin.

.   .   .

The San Francisco chill and damp were not welcome news for Ben Hogan, whose stiff, aching joints needed to carry the aging champion across 36 demanding holes on rolling, dew-saturated terrain. It added difficulty to an already grueling physical challenge for the gimpy forty-two-year-old. Hogan faced both an eight-hour day and the opportunity of a lifetime. All the early struggles, all the long practice, and all the persistent aches would be more than worth it if at the end of this Saturday he once again hoisted the silver trophy.

After each of the first two rounds, Hogan had returned to the St. Francis Hotel as soon as possible, showered, eaten dinner, and climbed into bed, where he would replay his round shot by shot and plan the next round hole by hole. Shot selection and course management were his keys to major championship golf. Anybody could build a nice golf swing, he later observed. As he prepped his lower torso in the early-morning quiet of his hotel suite, his wife, Valerie, nearby, Hogan knew his plan was as solid as his work ethic. Just 1 shot off the lead, he could play patiently and let others make mistakes, folding under the intense pressure of the final day of the National Open on a severe championship layout. It was a Hogan trademark. Unlike so many other tour pros, the man rarely beat himself. If his legs and putter cooperated, it was quite probable that Ben Hogan would be retired from tournament golf by nightfall.

.   .   .

The pins were set, the bunkers were raked, and the caddies' numbers were in place on their backs. At the practice tee, around the putting green, and near the 1st tee, the crowd gathered in anticipation of the opening shots on the final day of the National Open. For them, it was not a routine Saturday in San Francisco. Chores, yard work, shopping, errands, and other sports such as baseball, America's pastime, would have to wait.

The Saturday galleries at the Olympic Club would reach an official total of 10,700, exceeding the Thursday and Friday spectator counts. Men wore suits, sport coats, ties, light jackets, and sweaters. Many sported brimmed hats of all shapes and sizes. Women were smartly outfitted in suits, skirts, culottes, sweaters, and scarves. Servicemen were also in attendance, an occasional sailor's hat visible in the gathered masses. As they sat in the temporary bleachers and pressed in close behind the gallery ropes, some spectators carried binoculars or one-dollar cardboard periscopes. Still other onlookers stood, sat, stretched, crouched, and leaned to get a better look at the action. Some in the large final-day galleries even perched themselves in the course's abundant trees. The U.S. Open was a national spectacle, and Saturday was the closing act of the show. Olympic was electric.

The golf course was an eerie, mist-shrouded landscape as the first few pairings launched their opening tee shots into the gray sky. Beginning at 8:00 A.M., tee times were spaced at six-minute intervals. Shortly before 8:30, the caddie wearing 60 on his back arrived at the 1st tee. Few in the gallery needed to use the numbering system to check his player's name on a pairings sheet. It was the great amateur and local hope Harvie Ward, handsome and hatless in the morning mist, a player Inman called "a dapper guy." Four years younger and a shade taller than Ward, the slender Inman looked out on the first of 36 holes, the Masters in the recesses of his mind. Ward hit first; then Inman drilled one down the fairway.

By 9:30 A.M., Hogan's tee time, more than half of the fifty-eight players were on the golf course. Boros and Snead departed at 9:00 sharp. Byron
Nelson teed off with a pro named Pete Cooper directly ahead of Hogan
and his playing partner, Bob Harris. Off at 8:42 with Rotar, Rosburg had
started birdie, par, birdie. Hogan wore a dark V-neck sweater with a long-
sleeve shirt underneath, gray pleated trousers, and his signature white flat
cap. It was his work uniform, and he had punched the clock. He would
block out all distractions and get down to business. He took his stance,
waggled his driver, and swept the ball from the wooden tee. Ben Hogan's
final march for the record books had begun.

· · ·

In the next hour, nine pairings streamed onto the course: Dow Finsterwald, Cary Middlecoff, Bo Wininger, and Fred Hawkins among them.
Coleader Bolt and Hogan's fellow Texan Burke also set out on the opening
hole, their hopes running high. Twenty-four minutes later Ed Furgol and
Shelley Mayfield teed off in the pairing in front of two of the leaders: phenom Littler and the obscure club pro named Fleck.

Shortly before 10:30 A.M., Littler stepped to the first tee and shook the
hand of the tall, slim Iowa pro. Littler wouldn't say much to Fleck, but not
because of unfriendliness, or gamesmanship, or the probability that he
didn't know him. Shy, unassuming, and quiet, he never said much of anything to anybody. The two men would tour the Lake Course in virtual
silence. Both men wore light-colored V-neck sweaters. Littler favored a
white baseball-style cap, while Fleck sported a flat cap in the style of Hogan. He normally wore a visor on the golf course, but he opted for warmer
headgear in the cool weather. Fleck teed a shiny new Spalding Dot and
struck his drive down the fairway of the 1st hole, one of two par 5s on the

Lake Course. Then the smooth-swinging San Diegan, owner of three titles that season, smacked his driver. He picked up his wooden peg and started down the fairway, trailing behind the long-striding Iowan.

•　　•　　•

The night before had been quiet for Fleck, which was the way he liked it. Because of his midafternoon round and time with a curious press corps after his surprising 69, he ate a later dinner than usual before retiring for the night. There was no revelry at the El Camino Motel. It was just Fleck, alone with his thoughts, and the inspiring and melodic sounds of tenor Mario Lanza filling the small motel room.

Fleck had come a long way in a year's time. After the confidence-shaking frustration of not qualifying for the 1954 U.S. Open, he had slipped into the elite 1955 field at Olympic and now had survived the tournament's 36-hole cut. These were noteworthy accomplishments in themselves, but there was much more to consider on the eve of the championship finale. To the surprise of the national press, who hardly knew him, Fleck was in contention heading into the final day, tied for third with three others— one of them named Hogan. His prediction of a top-ten finish to the hometown sports editor did not seem far-fetched. Curtains drawn, his head pointing north toward the bright lights of San Francisco, he settled into bed. Saturday would be a long and demanding day at the Lake Course. There were 36 holes to go, a huge opportunity for Fleck in his quest to prove himself as a tournament player. He said his prayers and turned out the lights, falling asleep quickly in the darkness.

Saturday morning was like any other tournament morning for Fleck— until he picked up his razor. He awoke early feeling well rested. He stretched his body, assuming the yoga positions that aided his flexibility.

He turned on his Motorola record player and went into the bathroom to shower. However, when he stepped to the lavatory to shave, his morning routine was abruptly interrupted by something that defied an earthly explanation.

"A voice," he later said, "came out of the mirror, saying, 'Jack, you are going to win the Open.'"

Startled, Fleck glanced around the room. He was alone. Or was he? Mario Lanza was singing "I'll Walk with God" on the phonograph, but that wasn't what he had heard. There were no lyrics about anyone winning a golf tournament. In the few moments that he tried to comprehend what had happened, he again heard the voice as clear as anything.

"Jack, you are going to win the Open."

Goose bumps. Tingles. He later said it was "as if electricity was going through my body." He resumed shaving. The record kept spinning. Lanza kept singing. The golfer's body slowly relaxed, and he soon left his room in search of breakfast. It was an audible voice that spoke twice, as he recalled more than half a century later—not something he heard in his mind. He hadn't heard anything like it before or since, off or on the golf course. There was absolute certainty.

"It just came out and I heard it. I felt the Lord must have been talking to me."

Nonetheless, on that Saturday of the National Open, he told no one about those unfathomable moments in his motel room. Nor would he publicly speak about it for weeks, months, or years to come. How does a person explain a disembodied voice? What would people think?

Fleck tried to put the strange episode out of his mind as he arrived at the Olympic Club around 9:30 A.M. to warm up for the third and fourth rounds. He had to bear down and play golf.

"I never thought about that on the golf course," he said.

It wasn't until forty-four years later in a televised interview with

Peter Kessler on the Golf Channel that Jack Fleck publicly disclosed what he heard in that motel bathroom.

"I wouldn't have ever said it," he said. "He pulled it out of me."

*   *   *

By 11:00 A.M., all twenty-nine pairings were making their way around the damp course. Few players were making a move of any kind, although playing par or near-par golf was a small victory that improved a player's position in the standings.

Rosburg was an exception. With birdies at 1 and 3 and the rest pars, Rossie had fired a 2-under 33 on the first 9. It was a promising start to a long day. Not much of a factor through 36 holes, if Rosburg could keep it going he would surely make up ground on the leaders. He promptly birdied the par-4 10th to go 3 under for the round and 9 over for the championship. The Rosburg-Rotar pairing was collecting new spectators on each hole.

"We started out with about four people," Rossie later said. "By the time we got to 18, we had a pretty big gallery because people heard I was going real good."

Rotar was working on an 80, but it was no drag on Rosburg as he sailed through the back 9. He notched pars at 11, 12, and 13. Then he sank another birdie on the par-4 14th, moving to 4 under for the round. If he could hold steady in the tough closing stretch, he would put the lowest round of the championship on the scoreboard. He'd also have momentum and a hometown gallery on his side when he teed it up early that afternoon for the final 18.

Two groups ahead of Rosburg, amateur sensation Ward was struggling. Harvie bogeyed the par-5 1st, the easiest hole on the Lake Course, bogeyed the par-3 3rd, and came to the 8th hole 2 over for his round.

That's where the golf gods dealt a vicious blow and the jovial amateur lost his groove. His tee shot on the short par 3 landed in a 100-foot cypress tree and never returned to earth, resulting in a double bogey. It was a lousy bit of luck, but ol' Harv wasn't the only golfer to leave a ball in one of Olympic's thirty thousand trees. Lawson Little hit his golf ball into a towering cypress during the first round, never to see it again. A spectator shinnied up the tree and gave it a healthy shake. Out dropped three golf balls, none of them Little's. The fan kept the souvenirs, and Little made the loneliest walk in golf, returning to the tee to hit again after a stroke and distance penalty.

The usually unflappable Ward was upset. A par at the 9th gave him a 4-over 39 on the outgoing 9, a disappointing start. A steady but unspectacular 37 on the incoming 9 added up to 76, 10 over for the championship. Ward needed a sandwich and a fourth-round comeback if he was going to be the first amateur in more than two decades to win the National Open. One shot off the lead when the third round started, Harvie's playing partner had an opportunity to catch both leaders, but, like Ward, Inman carded a 76. The course was playing damp, long, and hard, and nerves were running high as Saturday wore on.

Despite the growing pressure, the 9:00 A.M. pairing whistled along the 6,700-yard layout. Boros put together 9s of 38 and 35 for a respectable 73. Snead was even better. Out in 34 and in with 36, Sam shot an even-par 70. He was striking the ball superbly. After beginning the tournament with a dismal 79, he had stormed back with rounds of 69 and 70 on the devilish Lake Course. The aging campaigner had his first U.S. Open title in his sights. Displacing Ward at the top of the leaderboard, and with Bolt still finishing up his morning round, Boros and Snead were coleaders in the clubhouse with a total of 218—but their lead would not last through the lunch break.

Rosburg also had surpassed fellow local favorite Ward. After his birdie at 14, Rossie parred 15, 16, and, for the third consecutive time, the beastly 17th. A routine tee shot, short-iron approach, and 2 putts at the finishing hole was all he needed for a dizzying 66 and low round of the championship. Although he remembered few details about his third round, Rossie did recall that last hole, the only blemish on his scorecard. "Eighteen is not a really hard hole, but I managed to make a 5 there."

Nonetheless, tying Bolt's opening 67, Rosburg was threatening the lead after shooting only the fifth round in the 60s. At 219, the San Francisco native had improved with each tournament round at his home course: 78, 74, and the remarkable 67.

"When you open up with 78," he later said, "and come back with 74 and then after you shoot one good round you have a chance to win—I think that just shows how hard it was."

Rossie's feat was more impressive in light of another barrage of high scores in the third round. The course was unmercifully beating up most of the fifty-eight golfers. Practice and two tournament rounds had not helped players gain confidence or control of their games at the Lake Course. Trips around Olympic had the opposite effect. Twenty-eight players, nearly half of the postcut survivors, shot 78 or higher in the third round. Fourteen of them had scores in the 80s, including Lord Byron, who started the day one stroke ahead of Rosburg.

There were a few bright spots among players who trailed the lead pack. Bud Holscher shot a 1-over 71. Mike Souchak, Al Mengert, and Art Wall carded 72s. There were a handful of 74s: Cary Middlecoff, Arnold Palmer, Dow Finsterwald, Smiley Quick, and Doug Ford.

Hogan's playing partner, Bob Harris, slid to a 78. The San Jose State grad had a front-row seat for what could be history in the making. Harris and the gallery watched as the Hawk methodically worked his way around the unforgiving layout. With a lone bogey at the 3rd and the rest pars, Hogan was out in 1-over 36. Then he spurted. Birdie at 10. Four consecutive pars. Another birdie at the 144-yard par-3 15th hole. Hogan was 1 under for his round and 4 over for the championship. The nine-time major champion had taken charge. With 21 holes remaining in the U.S. Open, Hogan led by 4 shots, but even the Open par machine could fall out of calibration on the last leg of the trip. *Golf World* called the third round "another Hogan calculated masterpiece until he ran smack into bogeys on Olympic's wearing final three." The disappointing finish turned a 69 or 70 into another 72.

As the Hawk departed for the short break between rounds, the main scoreboard told the story. With rounds of 72, 73, and 72 for a total of 217, Ben Hogan led Sam Snead and Julius Boros by a shot after 54 holes of the U.S. Open. For all the banter about players' chances, both up-and-comers and veterans, a familiar name had once again risen above them all with one round to play. "In a way," later wrote Herb Graffis, "the 55th National Open was like many that have gone before. This time it was the field against Hogan."

Bolt and Burke arrived on the 18th green a half hour later. Bolt, still trying to regain his Thursday magic, holed out for a 75 and total of 219, 2 behind Hogan. Burke was 1 under for his round until he recorded a double-bogey, bogey, par finish to shoot 72. Those last three holes were like neighborhood toughs, Lake Course bullies who mugged and bloodied golfers nearing the safety of the clubhouse, stealing their good scores and daring them to return. At 220, Burke trailed by 3 shots.

Playing alongside Mayfield, the defending champion who had been an inspiration to so many at Baltusrol was deflated at Olympic. Furgol continued his backward slide with an 80. Mayfield followed his 75 and 76 with another 75.

Directly behind the Mayfield-Furgol pairing, Littler and Fleck made their way up the 18th fairway to the small green tucked into the hillside. Moments earlier, wielding an 8-iron and swinging with all his might from 140 yards away, Fleck slashed out of the haylike rough left of the fairway, his ball flying over the front bunker and coming to rest on the edge of the putting surface. Advancing the ball from that jailed position had appeared to be impossible to him and the witnesses who cheered loudly after the near-miracle recovery. He putted his ball to within inches of the cup and tapped in for a hard-earned par. Fleck's 75 put him at 220 after 54 holes, placing him in a tie for sixth with Ward and Burke.

"I was fortunate to score as well as I did on this third round," he told reporters. "I chipped well, but did not putt well."

Behind by just 1 stroke when the day began, Fleck now trailed the new leader, Hogan, by 3. On the positive side, he remained in the top ten. If he could hold his position, he would be exempted into the 1956 U.S. Open and avoid the qualifying juggernaut. Playing partner Littler was 5 shots off the lead after a 73. Nothing was happening for either golfer, and gallery interest in the Fleck-Littler pairing waned as the duo signed their scorecards and headed off to lunch.

"There was no reason to figure Fleck," Rosenbaum wrote. "The slaloming crowd . . . saw his 75 for the morning round and gave up on him."

54-HOLE LEADERS

Hogan	72-73-72—217
Boros	76-69-73—218
Snead	79-69-70—218
Rosburg	78-74-67—219
Bolt	67-77-75—219
H. Ward	74-70-76—220

181

Burke	71-77-72—220
Fleck	76-69-75—220
Inman	70-75-76—221
Littler	76-73-73—222

Executing his game plan and playing solid Open golf, the Hawk had risen to the top of the leaderboard with 18 holes to go. It was textbook Ben Hogan.

"Everybody thought Hogan was kind of finished," Rosburg later said about the legend's 1955 campaign. "They were wrong."

To not win the National Open, Hogan would have to beat himself or someone would have to take it away from him. Or, another possibility, he would have to succumb to the sheer physical strain as he hiked the four miles of fairways along Lake Merced. The second scenario was the most likely of the three. Several able players were giving chase. Snead was charging. Boros was just 1 back. Rosburg, possessing local knowledge, was putting like a demon. Still other worthy opponents such as Bolt and Ward were lurking. No one could realistically expect the Hawk to beat himself or wearily lay down his weapons. To wrestle the lead and U.S. Open title away from Ben Hogan, someone would have to outplay him.

—15—

SATURDAY: ROUND 4

Ed Miller was stationed on the long platform that fronted an immense blackboard that ran the length of the pressroom. As the official scorekeeper for the USGA, Miller had spent three days in the clubhouse of the Olympic Club on the exacting and consuming task of recording the scores of 162 golfers. He was a chalk master who traveled the country to man the scoreboard at important golf tournaments. On this occasion, America's most prestigious golf championship, Miller had an assistant, a nattily attired man named Mel Hulling. Hulling looked more like an English lord dressed for a fox hunt than a scoreboard assistant at the U.S. Open. He wore a red hunting jacket as he chalked graceful numbers on the large blackboard. The first-timer at the scoreboard took special pleasure in keeping sharp points on the supply of white and red chalk pencils. The press corps marveled at the legibility and artistry of the numbers, remarking about the similarity of the two men's writing. Miller looked forward to the day when he could watch the players' shots instead of record their scores. One more round to go. Still more chalk to expend. Later that evening, Miller believed, the blackboard would render the final verdict on the 1955 U.S. Open.

While newspapermen studied the board and ground cigarette butts into ashtrays, Jack Fleck grabbed a half sandwich and bowl of soup. He only had forty minutes between rounds. He also loaded a glass of iced tea with sugar and gulped it down. It was the 1950s version of an energy drink. Sugar was recommended by his close friend Dr. Paul Barton. The good doctor would pass sugar cubes to the Iowa golfer on every few holes throughout the final round. "I never came close to getting tired," he later said. As 3:00 P.M. approached, Fleck walked to the 1st tee for the last loop with Gene Littler. Fifty of the fifty-eight players were already on the Lake Course for the final 18. Nine of those players were within 5 shots of the lead, but most eyes were focused on the two men at the top of the leaderboard, Ben Hogan and Sam Snead.

Despite the difficulty of the course and final-round pressure, play moved along at a brisk pace on Saturday, not unusual during an era long before multimillion-dollar purses and poky play by logo-adorned tour pros. First out in the morning and afternoon, Ralph Evans and Zell Eaton completed *both* rounds in five hours and twelve minutes. Nor were the leaders dallying. With Bob Harris along, Hogan was en route to a fourth round lasting just three hours and two minutes. The final pairing of Doug Ford and Chick Harbert would clock three hours and thirteen minutes for their fourth round. By just after 6:30 P.M. Pacific Time, play would be complete and the 72-hole totals of all fifty-eight players would be carefully marked in chalk on the pressroom blackboard.

By the time Fleck and Littler had struck their opening tee shots, Hogan was deep into his first nine. The Hawk started with a bang, striking a wedge to within two feet of the hole for a birdie at the 1st. He tapped in for a par at the par-4 2nd hole after staring at a 10-foot birdie putt that finished wide right. Then came a 3-putt bogey at the par-3 3rd, only his second 3-putt of the championship. Hogan bounced back at the 4th hole, a tricky 433-yard par 4 that doglegged left and featured a blind second shot to a small green. A 5-iron approach shot left him a 20-footer for birdie. Hunched over the ball gripping his blade putter, he rapped it home. The 5th was a long par 4 that curved right, an ideal hole for the famous Hogan fade. The Hawk overcooked it, depositing his drive into the right rough among a stand of trees. Another bogey. He then reeled off four consecutive pars to complete the outgoing 9 in even-par 35.

Up ahead, Hogan's pursuers were losing ground. Although there was no true real-time scoring—only the Motorola walkie-talkie system—it became apparent that Hogan's 1-shot lead at the beginning of the fourth round had grown to at least a 3-shot margin with 9 holes to play. Par golf, so difficult for his challengers on the deceptively long course, was Hogan's best friend. Nine more holes of par or near-par golf and the trophy would likely be his.

• • •

Twenty-eight hundred miles away, President Eisenhower was spending the day at his family farm in Gettysburg, Pennsylvania. He would soon be bound for San Francisco. Ike took time away from his official presidential duties for an 18-hole round in the Pennsylvania countryside. The thirty-fourth president proudly bagged a pair of birdies along the way. They were birdies that Hogan's challengers could have used as they trudged the Lake Course in their last attempt to catch the legend.

• • •

In the 1:12 pairing, Charles Rotar was playing better than his morning 80. Unfortunately, playing partner Bob Rosburg, the local favorite who had sprung into contention with a 67, had gone off the tracks. He bogeyed two of the first three holes. Although he held on for a 2-over 37 on the front side, he would continue to slip backward, no longer a factor in the championship.

"I didn't hit the ball very well. It wasn't that I putted bad. I just didn't play very well," he later said.

Rossie wasn't alone. One by one, the closest pursuers fell farther off Hogan's pace. Playing an hour ahead of Hogan, Harvie Ward had never recovered from his dull morning round of 76. Ward went out in 40 and was too far back with too few holes left. Low amateur was a lock, but Harvie aspired to much more. It would be a disappointing finish to a promising week for the world's best amateur golfer.

Ward's playing partner, Walker Inman, was going along nicely in the final round until disaster struck on the closing 9. Well ahead of Hogan and other leaders, it was difficult to ascertain positions in relation to others.

"We just kind of sensed it based on the scores guys were shooting," Inman later said.

Ward's sense was that his playing partner had a serious chance—and he said so as the two men approached the finishing holes.

"Standing on the 15th tee—I was about 5 shots ahead of him [Ward]," Inman said. "He said, 'You're going to win the Open.'"

Inman didn't want to think about winning. In his mind, he had 4 tough holes to play to secure a trip to the Masters. Then his round unraveled at 16, Olympic's longest hole.

"I made 8 on that par-5 hole and never missed a shot."

His triple bogey could serve as exhibit A on how one bad bounce or misplayed shot could lead to disastrous consequences on the treacherous course. It began with a drive that hooked "just a little bit" and kicked into the first cut of rough. He swung a 4-iron in the hope of advancing the ball far enough up the fairway to have a reasonable third shot into the green on the 603-yard hole. Instead, the 4-inch Italian rye grabbed the shank of his club, sending the ball left of his target and only about 100 yards. He was still in the sticky first cut of rough near a pine tree. The sensible option was to hack his ball out of the long grass and back into the fairway. He made the green with his fifth shot and hit an aggressive putt hoping to salvage a bogey. He missed, and then missed again, 3-putting for a horrid 8.

"That's what happens in Opens," he said.

Inman's 8 was one of nine triple bogeys on the 16th, a par 5 that produced more double bogeys (49) than birdies (31) during the championship. By the time he had reached the safety of the locker room, a good round had ballooned to a 78. Ward posted another 76.

Now Inman would have to wait a few hours to see if he would tee it up at Augusta National the following spring. "When I made that 8, boy, it was tough playing the next two holes, because I knew I was on the borderline."

One shot behind when they began their final round thirty minutes before Hogan, Julius Boros and Sam Snead retreated on the first 9. After taking an early double bogey followed by bogeys at 4 and 7, Boros needed a birdie on the 9th to escape with a 3-over 38. Snead, still unable to decipher the greens, was 1 shot better. He would need a second-9 rally if he was going to catch Hogan and win the National Open.

As Rosburg recalled, however, the man who had won more pro titles than anyone else in the field had no confidence on the small, sloping greens. "He said, 'Nobody can win the Open that has missed as many putts as I have.'"

Rosburg felt differently. "I thought he had a great chance to win. I was sort of sitting and talking with him before he went out to play the last round. It seemed to me that he should have had a little better attitude because he was playing great."

A half hour behind Hogan, any hopes Jack Burke had of winning the National Open had died in the first seventy-five minutes of his final round when he carded a double bogey and three bogeys in a five-hole stretch. Burke's playing partner, however, was within striking distance of the lead. Tommy Bolt played par golf until a bogey at the 9th hole gave him a 1-over 36. Only 3 shots behind, Bolt, along with Snead, was Hogan's closest pursuer. In sizing up the challengers, the Hawk would not have been surprised to see a pair of the game's best ball strikers on his heels. As he passed by the auxiliary scoreboards and got scoring updates from marshals carrying walkie-talkies, he would surely keep tabs on Snead up ahead and Bolt following behind.

On the other hand, there was no reason to keep an eye on the Fleck-Littler pairing, the last two on the course that started the final round within a few shots of the lead. Trailing an hour behind Hogan, the San Diegan and Iowan were midway through their opening 9 as the Hawk started down the 10th fairway. Littler was not having a good afternoon, and Fleck got off to the same start as the morning round: par, bogey, par, par, par. After a 3-putt bogey at the 2nd hole, he trailed Hogan by 4 shots with 13 holes to play. Few spectators were following Fleck and Littler as galleries gathered up ahead to witness Hogan's finish. Fleck's small support team soldiered on, with Dr. Barton supplying sugar cubes to boost the golfer's energy. Although there was a long way to go, Fleck felt calm and relaxed.

• • •

With holes running out and 3 strokes behind, Snead put on a shotmaking exhibition. There was only one surefire way to catch the steady Hogan, and that was to bag some birdies on the stingy course and apply some pressure. If anyone could find the narrow fairways and hidden pins, it was Snead, whose long game was dropping jaws inside and outside the ropes.

"You just can't hit a golf ball any better than Sam was hitting it," reported Herbert Warren Wind.

He made up a shot with a birdie at the par-4 10th and then immediately gave it back with a bogey at the 11th. On the next three holes, Snead put on a clinic. At the 387-yard par-4 12th, he struck an 8-iron that spun to 9 feet past the hole—and missed the birdie putt. He nearly holed his 4-iron shot for an ace at the par-3 13th, the ball stopping 5 feet behind the hole. Fearing his shaky putter, Snead's faithful were uncomfortable as he stood over another short birdie putt. They had good reason to be. Another jab, another miss. Two prime birdie opportunities gone. At the par-4 14th hole, Snead again struck a sublime approach shot, this one a 5-iron that landed 7 feet left of the hole. Predictably, his birdie putt did not fall. Hitting the ball that close on three successive holes in the final round of the U.S. Open was a colossal achievement. Missing all three birdie putts was a colossal failure. After parring the short par-3 15th, an exasperated Snead still trailed Hogan by 3 shots.

∗　　∗　　∗

In the meantime, Hogan was carding pars at 10, 11, and 12, a streak of seven straight. He was even par for his round and in command of the championship when he arrived at the par-3 13th, but he miscued with a long iron, landing his tee shot in a trap. A superb bunker player, on this occasion he failed to get his ball up and in, taking his second bogey of the round. His lead over Snead had shrunk to 2 shots.

It was getting late in the championship, and few had any hope of catching Hogan. Rosburg was finishing up a 76. Boros was no longer a factor, on his way to a 77. After a front-9 40, Burke was also out of the running. Behind Hogan, Bolt still had a chance, although it was the Hogan-Snead drama that fans and the press found most captivating as the Hawk walked stiffly to his 68th hole of the tournament.

The 14th hole was a 410-yard par 4 that doglegged to the left. A dangerous gully flanked the left-hand side of the fairway. The left side was the most favorable position off the tee since it opened up the second shot to the green, but it also posed the greatest risk. Hogan, author of a fade that slid 5 or so yards from left to right, would not chance anything down the left side. It didn't fit his shot shape, nor was it a safe play with a 2-shot lead on the final holes of the U.S. Open. Whether overguarding against the left side or a rare mishit, Hogan's tee shot veered right of the fairway and landed in the 5-inch rough. He had over 200 yards out of thick grass to a green flanked by a large bunker to the right and a smaller one on the left. The right side was no good. He had a bad angle to the green for his long approach shot. A second straight bogey was a real possibility. With Hogan in serious trouble at the 14th, with 4 challenging holes ahead, the final outcome appeared to be less certain.

•   •   •

Beginning at the par-4 6th hole, not unlike Snead ahead of him, Fleck got dialed in with his iron game. His second shot on the 437-yard par 4 snuggled up within 5 feet of the flag. Unlike the snakebit Snead, Fleck rolled the short putt into the cup. Birdie. At the 266-yard 7th, he wedged his approach to 8 feet from the hole. Wasting no time, he dropped the putt. Birdie. At the par-3 8th hole, he struck another accurate iron, this one a little farther away. It made no difference. He stepped up with his now trusty blade and banged home the 10-footer. *Birdie.* Three holes, three birdies, on an Open course that was eating up and spitting out the game's best. Fleck was the hottest player at Olympic and arrived at the 9th tee 2 under for his round. He didn't know it at the time, but he had pulled within a stroke of (or was tied for) the lead. With Hogan an hour ahead, their exact relative positions on the golf course and real-time scores were unclear. What was clear was that Fleck had put together an astonishing three-hole rally that had lifted him into contention with 10 holes to play.

*   *   *

The Hawk wasn't thinking about Fleck. His undivided attention was on the job at hand, the long second shot from the rough to the 14th green. Hogan inspected the lie and reached for his 4-wood. He stepped in and swatted the ball out of the tall grass. The shot came cleanly off the wooden face and curved slightly from left to right, hitting on the upslope in front of the green and tracking through the opening between the two flanking bunkers. The ball rolled onto the undulating green and stopped 20 feet from the hole. It was a phenomenal recovery, his finest shot of the day. Word soon arrived that Snead had bogeyed 16 and 17. Two putts and Hogan escaped the 14th with another cherished par, one hole closer to his goal.

*   *   *

Fleck dropped a stroke at the par-4 9th after driving into the rough and landing his second shot short of the green. The bogey gave him a 1-under 34 on the first 9. Out in 36 and with pars on 10, 11, and 12, Bolt was still battling, but Snead had run out of holes. The late back-to-back bogeys killed any hope Snead had, and he walked up the 72nd fairway knowing another opportunity to win the Open had vanished like the morning mist. It was a tragic injustice that a man with his talent and one of the game's greatest champions could reach the age of forty-three without winning the national crown.

"He had a phobia about the Open," Rosburg later said, "and I think that's why he never won. It was like a curse to him."

Short of the 18th green in 2, Snead flipped a little pitch onto the green that rolled to within 4 inches of the cup. The thousands seated on the slopes around the final green jumped to their feet and gave him a standing ovation. The 4-incher was a putt he could handle, and he tapped in for a 74 and a total of 292, 12 over par. Sam retrieved his ball from the cup and slung it sidearm high into the gallery on the grassy slope to the left of the green. After the opening 79, Snead averaged 71 for his final three rounds, an impressive display that once again fell short.

"The man shot wonderfully long golf," the *Chronicle*'s Will Connolly wrote. "The three-footers beat him."

•   •   •

The tee shot at the tightly bunkered par-3 15th hole was no more than a 7-iron to an islandlike green. Hogan's iron found the putting surface but left him with a lengthy putt. He surveyed the 35-footer and gave the putt a solid rap. The ball rolled on line and dropped into the cup for a birdie. A tremendous roar blasted through the trees and across adjoining fairways. The Hawk was back to even par for his final round with 3 holes to go. With his challengers falling away, par golf, as planned and hoped, was winning the day.

Back on the par-4 10th, Fleck drove his ball into the rough on the second consecutive hole. There was now more than a vague awareness the Iowan had spurted and was inching closer to Hogan's lead. In the pairing ahead of Fleck and Littler, Mayfield and Furgol witnessed many of Fleck's shots during the Open's late stages. Decades later, Mayfield recalled some better than others, such as Fleck's second out of the rough at the 10th. Fleck struck a 7-iron that landed 20 yards short and bounded toward the opening to the green. Skirting the sand trap on the right, his ball rolled onto the putting surface and stopped within a foot of the cup for a tap-in birdie. Instead of losing a shot, he had gained one with his fortuitous recovery. Fleck was 1 stroke behind Hogan.

The Hawk was on the home stretch, the final three holes the course doctor admired so much, and also the round wreckers for Inman, Snead, and so many others. He parred his 70th hole of the championship, the 603-yard par-5 16th. Hogan then faced the long par-4 17th, the only hole on the Lake Course he had failed to par during the championship. In fact, he had not reached the green in 2 shots in any of his rounds while recording three consecutive bogeys. This time he summoned the reserve to blast two mighty woods up the hill and onto the green. Two putts and he had his 4, a clutch par if ever there was one. Back on the 14th where Hogan had flirted with disaster, Bolt took an ugly double bogey to fall 5 shots off the pace and extinguish his chances of winning the championship. Noticeably limping at times, his left knee sore and legs heavy beneath him, Hogan had nearly completed the 72-hole journey.

"The more I walk," he said, "the more painful it becomes. I know every hill and every rise on that course."

Down to a small valley and up one more slope to the final green ringed by thousands of fans. There were fewer than 400 yards between him and the finish that, he hoped, would earn him the Open title.

. . .

It's unclear where Fleck was on the Lake Course's incoming 9 as Hogan completed the 72nd hole. Accounts in the following day's newspapers differed, as did stories in the years to come. However, based on Fleck's final-round tee time and a pace of play that got him to the clubhouse in about three hours and fifteen minutes—or seventy-three minutes after Hogan—

it's reasonable to assume he was on the 11th, as Rosenbaum reported, or perhaps was playing the par-4 12th, as Wind later wrote. George Tompkins, Fleck's new friend and a roving red-coated marshal, approached as he stepped to the 11th tee, a straightaway 429-yard par 4. Loud cheers had emanated from the direction of the 18th, four fairways distant, and Tompkins thought they signaled Hogan's finish. Would Fleck like Tompkins to confirm by walkie-talkie the finishing scores of Hogan and the other leaders? Yes, Fleck replied. While Tompkins slipped back into the growing gallery and transmitted his message to the official scorekeepers, Fleck reeled off pars at 11, 12, and 13.

·　　·　　·

The Hawk sent his tee shot on the last hole far down the right side of the fairway, leaving himself no more than a pitch up the slope to the 18th green. As a photographer and five others crouched a short distance behind him, Hogan struck his approach shot with a three-quarters swing and short follow-through. The ball cleared the fronting bunker and landed softly to the left of the front-right pin position, drawing back a shade and stopping 15 feet from the cup. It was a safe and well-judged play, exactly what one would expect from a four-time national champion. With an uphill putt that broke slightly from left to right, birdie was a possibility and par was a virtual lock. Hogan took his putting stance. Then, as was his putting ritual and a common routine of the era, he placed his blade directly in front of the ball for a brief moment before returning the putter head to its original position behind the ball. The putt rolled straight for the hole before losing steam and trailing off to the right. There was one last flash from the fierce competitor as he mock-swung his putter in frustration as if to say, "Get it there, Ben!" From about the same spot where his rival Snead had stroked his final putt a half hour earlier, Hogan tapped in for his par and a final-round 70, the first time he matched par on the Lake Course. Of those who had finished, it was the lowest score of the afternoon. He had saved his best for last and was all but assured of winning the title.

Roars, cheers, and applause engulfed Hogan as he removed his white linen cap and strode to the side of the green. He nodded his head in acknowledgment of the gallery's appreciative outburst. After handing his putter to Zitelli, Ben raised his arms to quiet the boisterous crowd while Bob Harris putted out for his 77. A nearby official also waved his arms to restore a semblance of order to the triumphant scene. Harris finished, and a second wave of cheers cascaded down from the crowded slopes.

"He walked off of the 72nd green," Wind wrote, "the apparent victor to one of the greatest and most honestly earned acclamations in the history of a game which will go a long time indeed before it knows another champion of his stature."

It was a few minutes after 5:00 P.M. NBC had just come on the air for its hour-long live telecast from San Francisco. Millions who had tuned in on their black-and-white television sets saw commentator Gene Sarazen intercept Ben Hogan before he exited the stage.

After congratulating him on winning a record fifth U.S. Open, Sarazen asked, "Ben, would you do everybody a favor and put up five fingers?"

Hogan complied before fully comprehending the request.

"It's not over yet, Gene," he said, even though Sarazen and thousands surrounding the finishing hole disagreed.

Hogan then handed his golf ball to USGA executive director Joe Dey, a historic souvenir for the game's national museum at USGA headquarters.

"This is for Golf House," Hogan said before disappearing into a sea of people and lumbering up the steep slope to the three-story clubhouse adorned with half-circle strips of red, white, and blue bunting.

. . .

"It's final," Tompkins said as Fleck came off the 13th green. "Hogan 287."

The marshal also reported that Snead had finished at 292, 5 shots back. He was excited about Fleck's prospects, telling the Iowan all he needed to do was make one more birdie to tie Hogan.

Fleck's silent playing partner could not resist a comment. "He'll need a few pars, too," Littler offered.

With Hogan finished and Fleck 1 off the lead with 5 holes to play, word raced throughout the grounds that there was one man on the course who had a chance to deny the Texan his fifth U.S. Open. Fleck? The name did not register with many of the assembled masses. While Hogan talked to reporters and sipped a Scotch and water in the locker room, curious golf fans streamed onto Olympic's back 9 to get a look at the Iowa club pro. Watch him fold like the Sunday newspaper was more like it. No one, it seemed, thought Fleck could catch Hogan, especially on Olympic's take-no-prisoners finishing stretch. Many accomplished players had failed under similar circumstances. It was the norm when the U.S. Open was on the line. The *Chronicle*'s Goethals went so far as to list odds, giving Fleck no better than an 8,000 to 1 chance of tying Hogan and forcing a playoff.

Reaching the 14th tee, Fleck decided he would not play for second, not after coming so far.

"I played boldly," he later told reporters. "There was no other way."

On the same hole where Hogan launched his decisive 4-wood shot from the rough to secure a crucial par, Fleck, adrenaline pumping through his system, smashed one of his longest drives of the day. He bombed it so far that he could not bring himself to hit a 7-iron, even though he was within range. He instead swung a 6-iron and pulled the shot, his tendency when he eased off a club. The ball landed in the thick collar and hopped into the left-hand bunker. He blasted out nicely but missed the 8-foot par putt, tapping in for bogey. He was now 2 strokes behind with 4 holes to play and noticed that many in the gallery were motionless as he walked off the 14th green. Picking up fifty or so spectators per hole since the 10th, the crowd following Fleck's twosome had grown to about four hundred. Now they stood their ground, not rushing into position to watch him play the 15th.

"I thought to myself, 'They think I'm through,'" he recalled.

It was a reasonable conclusion. Fleck needed two birdies and two pars on a finishing stretch that had punished every player in the field. There was no evidence or precedent to suggest that he could exploit Olympic's final gauntlet when so many others had failed to escape with pars.

*   *   *

Up at the clubhouse, reporters congregated in the men's locker room as Hogan waited for the championship to conclude. The Hawk took the scribes through a club-by-club recap of his afternoon round. The National Open crown appeared to be a mere formality, but he wasn't one to take such things for granted. He refused to enter the pressroom until it was official.

"What's this guy Fleck doing?" he asked.

Hogan was informed that the Iowa pro needed two birdies on the last four holes to tie—and, as Littler was inclined to say, a couple of pars, too.

An early finisher, Rosburg was sitting in the clubhouse having a beer with friends. He was set to leave when Hogan finished but changed his mind since Fleck had a chance. At the time, Fleck was a mystery man to Rossie. "I had met him, but I didn't really know him," he said.

Arnold Palmer knew Fleck, having played with him several times prior to the Open. "All of us gave him credit for being a really good player,"

Palmer later said. Like other players, though, he hadn't seen enough of Fleck to consider him a serious Open contender.

The pin was set on the back of the 15th green, so Fleck selected a 6-iron instead of the usual 7-iron for his tee shot on the par 3. He needed the extra distance to maneuver his ball to the rear portion of the green and have a go at what would be his fifth birdie of the round. The putting surface was flanked on three sides by bunkers. Missing long would put him in a bunker. This time his 6-iron shot, a full swing rather than the easy one he attempted at 14, was on the mark. His ball touched down on the narrow green and skidded to a stop 8 feet from the flag. With the long 16th and 17th ahead—where the field would only manage 36 birdies in four rounds—it was, for all practical purposes, a must-make situation. He sank it. The gallery erupted. Now hundreds of spectators were running ahead to find a spot behind the ropes as Fleck walked to the 16th tee. He was 1 shot behind with 3 holes to play.

•   •   •

Seated on the bench in front of his locker, a spent Hogan told those within earshot that he was all but through with tournament golf. The preparation was too hard on the fierce old competitor. "This one doggone near killed me." Asked about his leg, he said only his left knee bothered him. At the end of the row of lockers, an attendant shouted an update: Jack Fleck is on 16 and needs one birdie to tie.

"Good for him," Hogan replied with a thin smile.

•   •   •

The back 9's only par 5, the 16th was unreachable in 2 shots. A sweeping curve to the left, Olympic's beast of a par 5 had surrendered few birdies and was no cinch par. With adrenaline and the doc's sugar cubes flowing through his bloodstream, Fleck swung his Tommy Armour driver with added force. His rocketing golf ball flew slightly left and appeared as if it might catch the thick rough at the corner of the dogleg. "Oh, no," he cried, but the ball remained airborne until it reached the distant fairway.

He then ripped a solid 3-wood up the fairway, leaving himself a short-iron shot to the green. Fleck was astonished by how far he had struck his two woods, making it difficult to comprehend his remaining yardage. He settled on a 9-iron and arched his third shot high and left of the flag, landing on the collar of the green 25 feet from the hole. That was fortunate—he could putt the ball from the apron. Had his golf ball hopped into the wiry rough edging the green, he would have needed to finesse a chip shot from the long grass and sink a par-saving putt. As the gallery held its collective breath, Fleck nearly holed the 25-foot birdie putt and tapped in for his par. He was still 1 behind.

The Hawk scowled when a reporter asked on which hole he won the championship. It wasn't quite over. "You don't win tournaments on just one hole," Hogan said. "There's 72 holes."

Fleck arrived at the 71st hole, the hardest one of the bunch. After a par in the first round, he had made two bogeys on the 17th. Now he needed at least a par. He also needed a birdie, but that seemed too much to ask on a stingy par 4 that would give up only five birdies for the entire championship. In addition to its upward slant, the 17th fairway tilted from left to right in the landing area. Guarded right and left by bunkers, the green was large by Lake Course standards. The air was cool, and a course that had never dried out on the overcast day was getting damper in the late afternoon. It made the 17th play even longer. Fleck cracked another big drive that flew down the left center of the fairway. Although he was in ideal position, he would need to wring every last yard out of his Ben Hogan 3-wood to reach the green in two shots on the converted par 5. He slammed into his Spalding Dot with the spoon and followed the flight of the golf ball as it screamed up the slope toward the green.

Perched on a platform on the hillside behind and to the left of the 17th green, announcer Harry von Zell and U.S. Open champion Lawson Little were calling the action for a national radio audience. The two men watched Fleck's second shot touch down on the putting surface and roll to a stop 20 feet wide of the hole. Few players had reached the 17th in two swings. About an hour earlier, Hogan had performed the feat for the first time in nine tries. An excited Little blurted that Fleck's long second shot "was the greatest 3-wood on the 71st hole in an Open championship when it was needed!"

The hole was cut toward the left-center section of the green. Fleck, whose ball was long and right of the flag, had a downhill putt that would break sharply from right to left. It was a speed putt with 3 or 4 feet of break, depending on how hard he hit it. He judged it well. The ball started out far to the right as it worked its way toward the hole. As the putt lost momentum, it took a final dive left toward the cup. Those in the green-side gallery with the best vantage point watched in anticipation, expecting it to drop. The ball hit the hole and rimmed out, a near birdie on a nearly impossible birdie hole. The crowd exhaled a mixture of groans and cheers. Fleck tapped in for his par. To tie Hogan, he would have to birdie the final hole.

•   •   •

It was 9:00 P.M. in the East—6:00 P.M. at Olympic—and NBC's allotted hour of TV coverage of the National Open was over. As the network switched to other programming, millions of viewers across the country assumed Ben Hogan was the winner and new record holder, the only man to win five U.S. Opens.

"Actually, they kind of gave the trophy to Hogan before they went off the air," Rosburg later said.

Hogan handed out souvenirs in the locker room: practice balls, two books of food and drink tickets, and his white flat cap. Another messenger arrived and announced that Fleck parred 17 and needed a birdie at the last to tie. Hogan stood up, removed his trousers, and headed to the shower. Small talk faded into silence.

Tom Gallery was uneasy. The NBC television sports director approached announcer Lindsey Nelson after Nelson climbed down from the TV platform on the slope behind the 18th green.

"Do you think this fellow Fleck can get that last birdie?" Gallery asked.

"I don't think so, Tom," Nelson replied. "There's too much pressure on him."

The sportscaster would soon board a plane to New York City to accept an award on *The Ed Sullivan Show*. The network had declined its option to televise a playoff.

.　　.　　.

As he approached the 18th tee, Jack Fleck paused to marvel at the incredible view. He saw as many as ten thousand golf fans, two thick walls of spectators lining the short par 4 from the tee to the green, with six thousand of them jammed on the hillside overlooking the putting surface. The large clubhouse sat atop the slope in the distance, and a few shafts of golden sunlight broke through the clouds above. For a brief moment, Fleck took it all in, and it looked heavenly to him. With the chance to tie Hogan and force an 18-hole playoff—and with the eyes of thousands of spectators fixed on him—Fleck wasn't nervous. He was keyed up, but he wasn't scared. It didn't square with conventional wisdom about pressure situations in major golf championships, especially when faced by an unheralded player.

Herb Graffis noticed an uncommon composure. "I've seen Fleck in minor tournaments and on practice tees looking far more concerned than he seemed to be with his dream either just about to come true or turn into a terrible nightmare."

Meanwhile, Littler left Fleck alone, intent on not being any kind of distraction to the Iowa golfer as the tension escalated. "He didn't get into the act in any way," Fleck later said. "He just played."

The tee shot at 18 was a poke down into a small valley that set up a pitch or short-iron shot up the slope to a small, tilted green protected in front and on both sides by four traps. Stray tee shots found serious trouble, either heavy rough on the left or, to the right, thick trees and trampled rough where the spectators had trod. As was the case throughout the tight Olympic layout, the tee shot set up the hole and was usually an accurate predictor of success or failure. More interested in control than distance on the 337-yard closing hole, Fleck had hit his 3-wood every day and reached for it once again. He teed his ball, waggled the spoon, and let it fly. Countless pairs of eyes strained to follow the flight of the ball as it rose into the sun-streaked sky.

·　　·　　·

Sitting alone in the clubhouse, Valerie Hogan waited for her husband. She was ready to start home for Fort Worth. The U.S. Open had strained his body and her nerves to the absolute limit. Moments earlier the building's public address system had announced a long distance telephone call for Mrs. Ben Hogan. Perhaps it was someone calling to offer congratulations for Ben's historic victory. She would never know, refusing to take the call. She sat motionless, eyes shut for long stretches, keeping vigil while her husband got dressed in the players' locker room below.

Hogan slipped on his pants and tasseled leather shoes. He managed a grin as he scanned the locker room. Another messenger burst in. Fleck was in the rough on 18! Everyone turned toward Hogan, who reached into his locker for his silk necktie and began knotting it. A nervous reporter broke the uncomfortable silence, asking if he used his Hogan-manufactured clubs in the tournament. "Of course I did!" he snapped. "Are you kidding?"

. . .

Fleck's tee shot landed on the fairway but trickled into the first cut of rough, a mere 6 inches off the left edge of the fairway. The crowd groaned. What might have seemed to the large gallery like an unfortunate break would instead work to the Iowa pro's advantage. The hole was cut on the front right of the narrow green, with a large bunker wrapping around the right and front sides of the putting surface. There was little room for error in going directly at the flag, Fleck's only option since he had to make a birdie. With his ball sitting up nicely in the 2-inch rough, the lie and the angle were ideal for attacking a tight right-hand pin position. The distance—about 125 yards—dictated a club choice of an 8-iron or 9-iron. In fact, neither club was under consideration, for Fleck had a different shot in mind, an easy, towering 7-iron.

"That was my plan," he later said. "Hit it real high so it comes down dead."

By "dead," he meant virtually no spin, the ball dropping straight out of the sky and landing on the green with a soft thud like a small stone. He reasoned that a full 8- or 9-iron shot would create a lot of backspin and be hard to control. The ball could fly the proper distance but spin way back,

203

perhaps off the front of the green that sloped rather severely from back to front. Fleck's low-spin 7-iron was a shot born from hours of practice with Ted Kroll and others. He would make a big shoulder turn, creating a wide arc and keeping his hands quiet, not flipping them at the ball as one might on a full short-iron shot or wedge. As much as anything, it was a feel shot played with imagination and instinct.

There is scarce film footage of the 1955 U.S. Open. Only a handful of shots would survive through the years, and Fleck's dramatic approach from the edge of the short rough on the 72nd hole was one of them. "But fate and a cool unheralded professional by the name of Jack Fleck arrive on the scene," intoned the narrator as the camera showed Fleck from the vantage point of the 18th green. Schroder stood 10 yards away in the fairway as Fleck took his stance. He waggled twice and swung. The backswing was short, the follow-through high and full. The ball climbed high in the air as it flew toward the small target 125 yards up the slope.

·　　·　　·

Hogan sat in front of his locker with his head down and arms resting on his knees. He hoped Fleck took a 2 or a 4 at the last. An 18-hole playoff was the last thing he wanted. He lit a cigarette and exchanged forced banter with players as they arrived, waited, and departed. Burke reported that he had driven in the rough all day. Bolt came in and gave Hogan the business, as he was prone to do. Tommy was the rare person who could good-naturedly swear at Ben and produce a smile and a chuckle.

"I said, you little SOB," Bolt recalled a few months before his death in 2008. "We always cussed one another out and were jabbering all over the place."

On his way out of the locker room, Cary Middlecoff approached the legend with typical deference and extended his right hand, offering congratulations. Fred Hawkins was also there, waiting those interminable final minutes.

Hogan slipped into his sport coat and pulled his clubs from his locker. A head cover fell to the floor, and he jokingly asked if anyone wanted it. A blast of cheers from the direction of the 18th green drowned out the nervous chatter in the locker room. The guy holed out from the rough, reacted the tightly wound Bolt. A reliable update from a courier followed seconds later: Fleck had a 7-foot putt to tie.

       .   .   .

Fleck's ball cleared the fronting bunker and floated lazily to earth, landing softly between the flagstick and the right-hand edge of the green. He had taken dead aim and struck the ball a shade right of his target—a makeable birdie distance.

"Never have I seen a finer shot under such tremendous mental pressure," wrote a British correspondent.

Only 7 feet of grainy *Poa annua* stood between Fleck and a head-to-head duel with his idol. With Schroder leading the way, he walked up the slope between the fronting bunkers and onto the final green. Littler and his caddie followed. Fleck's demeanor betrayed nothing that indicated the moment had arrived, the biggest opportunity of his professional life, a pressure situation on golf's foremost stage that few face, much less overcome. His dream and future were riding on a 7-foot putt to tie Ben Hogan, although those thoughts never entered his mind. He simply knew he had a chance to win—if he could sink that putt. More than a half century later, Fleck insisted he felt no added pressure.

"I wasn't nervous," he said. "How or why? Ask the Lord."

In fact, it was a monumental putt for two men: Fleck and the weary champion in the players' locker room who could do nothing but wait and listen.

Littler putted out for his 78 to clear the way for the Iowa club pro, a disappointing finish to a week that had begun with so much promise. All eyes were on Fleck as he crouched behind the ball off the edge of the green to get a line on his birdie putt. He would not take long. Graffis later reported that Fleck took only twenty-four seconds to line up and stroke the putt. There wasn't much to see. The slightly downhill putt would break perhaps an inch from right to left. Littler was crouching on the back of the green like a baseball catcher. His caddie was kneeling at the front of the green, the closest person to Fleck as he prepared to putt. Schroder was sitting in a reclined posture at the side of the green as if enjoying an evening picnic. Packing the hillside and slopes that surrounded the green area, the thousands of spectators were deathly still and quiet as Fleck took his stance. Bill Callan, the scorecard runner, was there. Recalling the scene decades later, the incredible silence of the moment stood out in Callan's mind. An adventurous few stood motionless on low-hanging limbs of large trees.

Fleck took two practice strokes. Then he placed the Bulls Eye blade in front and behind the ball, glanced twice at the hole, and stroked the putt. It came off the putter dead on line and at a perfect pace. His head was still down as the ball dropped into the left-center portion of the cup.

•   •   •

Topics of conversation and patience were wearing thin in the locker room. A man asked another question about Hogan's golf club company. Hogan said his company could make 460 sets of golf clubs in a month's time. When asked if he scrapped $100,000 worth of clubs, Hogan nodded. He again took a seat in front of his locker. "Nobody stirred," noted the

Chronicle's Goethals, who was there with *Sports Illustrated*'s Wind, the *Times*'s Werden, Stan Wood of the *Los Angeles Daily Mirror-News*, and several other reporters. The silence didn't last long. A thunderous roar penetrated the clubhouse walls. "The kid's sunk it!" exclaimed a reporter. Hogan's head dropped and he cursed under his breath.

The news soon reached Mrs. Hogan in the clubhouse. It was not a surprise. She had heard the roar and knew what it meant. There was no visible reaction. She remained silent and frozen as she stared out the clubhouse window at the evening sky. It was a crushing blow. Hogan later said he had been watching the scoreboards all day and was sure he had won by at least 2 shots when he finished. He hadn't accounted for Jack Fleck. No one had.

Playing in the last pairing on the course, Doug Ford was on the 17th hole when he heard an incredible roar up ahead. Someone must have holed out, Ford remarked to playing partner Chick Harbert. No, Harbert replied, somebody must have made a putt to tie.

•   •   •

The sound that arose when Fleck's ball fell into the cup was like a small, rumbling earthquake.

"It was just deafening," recalled Wood, one of the reporters with Hogan in the locker room. "The building practically shook."

Excitement rippled from the 18th green: Spectators jumped to their feet and cheered wildly, punched the air with their fists, waved their arms, and applauded with abandon. A most unexpected result had elicited pandemonium.

When the ball disappeared into the hole, Fleck slowly raised his arms, his putter extending from his gloved left hand and pointing skyward. He removed his flat cap as he stepped to the hole to retrieve his ball. It was long before the days of fist pumps, leaps, hugs, and other player celebrations. His reaction was subdued and in keeping with the times. If anything, Fleck, managing a slight grin, appeared to be dazed by his accomplishment. Littler strolled up and was the first to offer his hand in congratulations. Schroder hovered nearby to replace the flagstick. Three more groups had yet to finish. An excited, arm-waving official swept in and patted Fleck four times on the left shoulder before ushering him from the green to sign his scorecard.

Hogan's 70 was the best score of the final round until Fleck walked off the 72nd green. The Iowa club pro had caught the Hawk by shooting a 3-under 67, tying the lowest score of the tournament carded by just two other men, Bolt and Rosburg. Fleck's rally and victory from a 9-shot deficit still stands as a U.S. Open record.

There would be an 18-hole playoff on Sunday at 2:00 P.M. to decide the winner of the U.S. Open. The 18-hole playoff was the norm for breaking tournament ties on the 1950s PGA Tour. Later on, television coverage dictated shorter sudden-death playoffs, although the U.S. Open still employs an 18-hole playoff, if necessary, to determine its champion.

With grim faces surrounding him, Hogan turned to caddie Tony Zitelli and asked him to unpack his gear. Then he stood up and walked out to join his wife upstairs. "See you fellows tomorrow." Mr. and Mrs. Hogan left the Olympic Club arm in arm. All were quiet in the locker room, except for Burke, who deemed the ending "the unluckiest thing I've ever heard of." It was 6:23 P.M.

•   •   •

Ed Furgol, who had just finished with Shelley Mayfield, graciously stepped in to help Fleck navigate the postround bedlam. It was foreign territory for the shy Iowan. Furgol, the surprise winner the year before at Baltusrol, had recent experience with being thrust into the national spotlight. Furgol walked with Fleck to the pressroom and stood by his side while fifty-plus reporters and photographers heaped attention on the man from Davenport.

The press hardly knew him, so they asked all sorts of questions, some of them silly. No, Fleck had never been a farmer, only a golfer. He had served in the navy. He had a wife and four-year-old son at home in Davenport. Some details of his biography would be misreported and become a part of golf lore. One was that he registered for the National Open from a driving range—he would be known as a driving-range pro for years to come—even though both of the municipal courses he oversaw had 18 holes, and Duck Creek didn't even have a driving range. Excitement about the unknown Iowa pro spawned exaggeration. One example that appeared in the next day's wire-service report: Fleck had skipped lunch, pulling off golf's biggest surprise in decades on an empty stomach. (He had soup and a half sandwich between rounds.) Another: Fleck had collected a little more than $2,700 on the circuit in the '55 season, not enough to cover caddie fees. (Although he wasn't flush with money, Fleck's consistent midteen finishes on tour had earned him enough purse money to cover his caddie fees and other modest expenses on the road.) The questions kept coming for well over an hour. Fleck thought of Dr. and Mrs. Barton as they waited patiently for him to complete his postround odyssey.

The man of the hour finally broke free of the press corps and entered the locker room to change his shoes. He also made arrangements with Inman to drive his Buick to Portland for the Western Open. Doug Ford and Dow Finsterwald would ride along. Inman would leave on Sunday morning and use Fleck's car for the next few tournaments. Win or lose, Fleck was going to fly home to Iowa after Sunday's playoff with Hogan.

By 7:00 P.M., the slope surrounding the 18th green where six thousand astonished fans had cheered wildly forty-five minutes earlier was deserted. The ground was trampled, and the matted grass was strewn with nearly a solid layer of newspapers used to protect the seated masses from dew and grass stains. Many of the animated spectators who streamed out of the gates on Saturday evening would return the next day for the play-off. Elmer Border and his grounds crew would again hustle to clean up the debris and prepare the Lake Course for one more round.

Sarazen had a different kind of mess on his hands. At the Fairmont Hotel that evening, the new TV commentator was inundated with tele-grams from Iowans chastising him for prematurely calling Hogan the winner. So had NBC-TV, for that matter. It was golf's version of DEWEY DEFEATS TRUMAN, the famous incorrect headline on the front page of the *Chicago Tribune* the morning after President Harry Truman won reelec-tion in November 1948.

Sarazen didn't let it bother him much, saying that he was merely twenty-four hours early. Hogan would win on Sunday. It was the prevail-ing view, according to Sarazen's roommate that week, PGA promotions di-rector Fred Corcoran. The steel-willed four-time champion was the clear-cut favorite. How could anyone imagine a different result?

"I think that if we were asked at the time," Palmer later said, "we probably would say that Hogan would have smothered him in the playoff."

Rosburg concurred. "Everybody in the world would have said he [Fleck] had no chance, that he just can't do it."

Sarazen's debut had resulted in some questionable commentary, to say the least. According to reporter Stan Wood, Sarazen said on the national telecast that Littler (Sarazen's pretournament pick) had injured his hand and was playing with only one good hand on the final 9. When later asked repeatedly if he hurt his hand, a bemused Littler emphatically said, "No." The only thing that may have been hurting the San Diegan was his pride. Littler's afternoon trip with Fleck produced his highest round of the tournament and pushed him down the leaderboard to a fifteenth-place finish.

FINAL SCORES: THE TOP TEN PLUS TIES

Ben Hogan	72-73-72-70—287
Jack Fleck	76-69-75-67—287
Sam Snead	79-69-70-74—292
Tommy Bolt	67-77-75-73—292
Julius Boros	76-69-73-77—295
Bob Rosburg	78-74-67-76—295
Harvie Ward	74-70-76-76—296
Bud Holscher	77-75-71-73—296
Doug Ford	74-77-74-71—296
Jack Burke	71-77-72-77—297
Mike Souchak	73-79-72-73—297

Mayfield and Frank Stranahan finished in a tie for twelfth at 298. Hawkins, Middlecoff, and Palmer finished in the top twenty-five despite failing to break 300. In fact, only 14 of 58 players bettered an aggregate score of 300, or 20 over par. The fifty-eight players who qualified for the final two rounds shot a collective 1,440 over par, an average score of a shade over 76. (Defending champion Furgol needed 78 strokes per round and finished forty-fifth.) The par-4 17th was the most difficult hole, averaging close to the members' par of 5. Of 440 rounds played during the championship, only 6 were below the par of 70, and just 3 matched it. Fleck owned two of the subpar rounds; four other players—Bolt, Boros, Snead, and Rosburg—each cracked par once.

There was one other finisher of note—Fleck's good friend and playing partner in the first two rounds. Walker Inman finished alone in fourteenth place at 299. The top-sixteen finish earned the Augusta, Georgia, native his first trip to the Masters, a boyhood dream come true.

—16—

SUNDAY: THE PLAYOFF

Bert McGrane covered golf and college football for the *Des Moines Register.* The fifty-eight-year-old sportswriter had been at the newspaper for thirty years and was so respected as a football writer that he would later have an annual award named for him by the Football Writers Association of America. On Saturday afternoon when Jack Fleck was engineering his shocking back-9 rally to tie Ben Hogan, McGrane was at Wakonda Country Club in Des Moines covering the Trans-Mississippi Golf Tournament, one of the country's prestigious amateur championships.

McGrane was typing away on a story when he received a series of messages by teletype from the office: Jack Fleck has a chance to win the U.S. Open. He needs two birdies and two pars on the last four holes to tie Hogan. Fat chance, thought McGrane. No Iowan is going to win the Open. Fleck wasn't going to get the birdies—not on those finishing holes. McGrane knew Fleck had worked as an assistant pro at the Des Moines Golf and Country Club and was aware of his undistinguished pro career that included minor successes in local and regional tournaments. The reporter kept typing. He had a story to file.

Later that evening McGrane was eating a steak at Vic's Restaurant when the proprietor approached him. What are you doing here? Vic asked McGrane, telling the reporter about Fleck's late surge that tied Hogan. McGrane finished his meal and called the office. The newspaper had made a reservation for him on an 11:00 P.M. flight to San Francisco. You better get moving, they told the man who seemed to be among the last to know about Fleck's stunning finish at the Lake Course.

It was 9:00 P.M., and McGrane had just two dollars in his pocket, so Vic handed the reporter a small wad of twenties to finance his unexpected West Coast trip. McGrane rushed home to grab a clean shirt and say good-bye to his wife, who already knew about the red-eye to San Francisco since the office had called looking for her husband. Then he stopped by the office to wire ahead for a hotel room.

"I thought our gang was nuts," McGrane later wrote about the two-thousand-mile all-night sprint to the coast.

McGrane would be lucky to get a room. With dignitaries arriving for Monday's United Nations meeting and the U.S. Open adding a day, a lodging squeeze had hit San Francisco. The hundred-plus members of the press would stick around one more night, a twenty-four-hour delay to the expected coronation of William Ben Hogan. Local hotel officials were confident that all visitors would be accommodated. As if on cue, President Eisenhower, the First Golfer, would land on Sunday night in advance of the UN gathering. Perhaps Ike would arrange a meeting with the U.S. Open winner while both he and the champion were in town and the dramatic conclusion was fresh in the minds of the nation's sports fans. He was well acquainted with Hogan. The two had enjoyed each other's company during many golf outings. The president knew nothing about Fleck.

While the Hogans were having a quiet dinner, Fleck ate with the

Bartons in the Papagayo Room at the Fairmont Hotel. Earlier he had phoned Lynn and talked at length about his thrilling day at Olympic. "She could hardly talk," he later said about their conversation. After dinner, Dr. Barton presented the golfer with a cartoon drawn by Cal Bailey. The odd sketch showed Fleck with a sickle in his hand saying, "Fore!! Mr. Hogan," while a diminutive Hogan, wearing his flat cap, was neck deep in the Lake Course's tall rough. Little did they know that Bailey's impromptu cartoon was strangely prophetic.

Fleck returned to his room at the El Camino Motel, showered, listened to "I'll Walk with God," said his prayers, and turned in for nine and a half hours of sleep. Sportswriters would later question Fleck on that point, expecting him to say he had a night of tossing and turning in nervous anticipation of an 18-hole playoff against the era's greatest golfer for the national title. That would be the normal scenario for an unproven player, but it wasn't normal for Jack Fleck. Whatever Sunday's outcome, he would be well rested because he slept as peacefully as a baby in its mother's arms.

. . .

There was no rest on Saturday night for McGrane. After collecting what he could find in the office files on Fleck, he drove to the Des Moines airport, boarded his flight, and flew to Omaha, where he had a three-hour layover. At 3:00 A.M., the sportswriter hopped on a plane to Denver. After a short stop in the Mile High City, he flew over the Rockies and landed in Salt Lake City before departing on the final leg to San Francisco. McGrane checked his watch and asked a deadheading pilot seated in front of him about the route from the airport to the Olympic Club. The pilot told him it was fifteen miles across town. Watching the minutes tick by, McGrane wondered how long a cab ride might take in weekend traffic.

⁕   ⁕   ⁕

At 1:00 A.M. in Evansville, Indiana, Bob Hamilton, the 1944 PGA champion and a friend of Fleck's, got up from a poker game to take a phone call from New York Yankees owner Dan Topping and a man named Mike McLaney. Considering a playoff bet with long odds on Fleck, the two men wanted Hamilton's read on the Iowan.

"Hogan is the iceman and doesn't talk," McLaney said.

"I'm not telling you how to bet," Hamilton replied, "but I will say this: Hogan will talk more than Fleck."

They said their good-byes, and Hamilton returned to his cards.

⁕   ⁕   ⁕

On Sunday morning Fleck checked out of the El Camino Motel and walked to the nearby cafeteria, where he had become something of a regular. If anybody had bothered to open the newspaper early that morning and scan the photographs, they might have recognized the slim golfer as he loaded his breakfast plate with eggs, fruits, and dark grains.

Jack called Lynn—he had called every day from California. His wife told him to stay calm. Lynn could have benefited from her own advice after a restless night during which she slept just two hours. Despite the mind-racing excitement from developments in San Francisco and life-changing implications for the Flecks, Lynn opened the Credit Island pro shop at 5:30 A.M. on Sunday in a rainstorm. Joined by a crowd of eager Davenport golfers, Lynn would listen to the hole-by-hole radio account of the playoff while she performed her pro shop duties. Mrs. Fleck would display "remarkable composure during the tense playoff," according to one report. In truth, she was far more nervous than her husband.

Before heading to the golf course, Fleck drove to a nearby beach and

215

took a short walk to soak up the peace and beauty of the coastal surroundings. He prayed for the power and strength to compete, the prayer Ralph
Riley had suggested to him in his Davenport pro shop less than two weeks
earlier. Then he climbed into his Buick and drove the short distance to the
Olympic Club for his 2:00 P.M. playoff with Ben Hogan, golf's greatest
champion and the man who had graciously made a set of clubs for him. It
would be Fleck's third encounter with his idol and the first time they
played golf together—a match that would decide the winner of the national title.

•   •   •

McGrane's plane rolled up to the San Francisco terminal at 12:30 P.M.
The tired, hungry reporter located a snack bar, grabbed a sandwich, and
was chewing his first bite when he heard his name on the intercom. A
young man near the airline counter eyed the sportswriter and his typewriter and asked if he was Mr. McGrane. It was McGrane's driver, who
escorted the weary sportswriter to a parked automobile. McGrane was
humbled that the press committee had sent a car to rush him to the golf
course in time for the playoff. He arrived at the Olympic Club with forty-
five minutes to spare. Handing his bag to an attendant—there was no time
to stop at a hotel—he made a beeline for the pressroom.

•   •   •

Sunday's weather forecast called for a cool and overcast morning followed
by a sunny and slightly warmer afternoon. The day's high would only
reach 58. After numerous practice and tournament rounds under gray skies
and with persistently damp conditions, both players knew what to expect
on the championship layout. With only 3 strokes separating his lowest and

highest tournament rounds, Hogan had played his usual consistent brand of U.S. Open golf.

"He really didn't want to go," Rosburg said of Hogan's attitude about the playoff.

Maybe not, there was no quit in the golf legend. He had miraculously survived a head-on collision with a bus, resumed his tournament career to the surprise of his doctors, and had since won six major championships, including three U.S. Opens. No one could doubt the grim resolve of Ben Hogan.

As the morning newspapers reported, Hogan said he would retire from tournament golf if he won the Open. The preparation had become too much for him. One Hogan authority disagreed—his wife.

"I don't think Ben will ever retire," Valerie said. "I think he will play golf as long as he is able to pull himself out to a golf course. It's in his blood."

If Hogan was Mr. Steady, then Fleck was a wild card who could shoot high or low. The Iowa pro had yo-yoed with first and third rounds in the mid-70s and second and fourth rounds of 69 and 67. Yet he approached the playoff with uncommon confidence considering the incredible pressure and his lack of experience. Upon arrival at Olympic just before noon, Fleck met Walker Inman and Doug Ford to hand over the car keys and say farewell as they departed for Portland.

"I thought he was going to win," Inman said a half century later. "His attitude showed me he was going to win."

Soon after, Fleck came face-to-face with Hogan as the two men approached the three-story clubhouse. They carried on a friendly conversation as they walked down the stairs and entered the locker room. The two players were silent as they sat down in front of their lockers to slip on their golf shoes, not far from one another since the lockers were arranged alphabetically. Fleck got up first and walked the short distance to Hogan's locker.

"Ben," he said, "I was driving from El Paso, Texas, when I saw and heard the two motorcycle police and ambulance coming toward El Paso. I did not know it was you until I read it the next morning in the paper."

He told Hogan he was among the many Americans who prayed for Hogan's recovery. "I want to wish you well today," he added, "so no matter what the outcome is, you'll know what I mean. So good luck and play well."

You'll know what I mean. It was a peculiar statement that Fleck struggled to comprehend. "I don't know how or why that came out," he said decades later.

Fleck certainly felt a connection to Hogan and a deep sense of gratitude for the clubs, encouragement, and kindness. Beyond that there was no available explanation for his spontaneous and heartfelt locker room comments, although he felt Hogan wondered about it later that day.

"He wanted to ask me something, but it just wouldn't come out."

The two men shook hands. Hogan thanked Fleck for his kind words and wished him good luck. Then Fleck headed out the door to the practice tee.

*   *   *

McGrane was greeted like a long-lost friend in the pressroom. "Look who's here," said Francis Powers of the *Chicago Daily News.* McGrane glanced around the room and saw Charlie Bartlett, Al Laney, Lincoln Werden, Will Grimsley, Bob Myers, Pres Sullivan, and many others. There was one notable absence—Fleck's hometown newspaper. Neither sports editor John O'Donnell, to whom Fleck had written before the U.S. Open began, nor any other staff member of the *Davenport Democrat* was in San Francisco to cover the playoff. McGrane may have been unshaven, rumpled, and hungry, but the *Des Moines Register* had its man on the scene and would bring the story home to Iowans.

•   •   •

First on the range, Fleck was striking his practice shots with surprising precision. "I was hitting balls right to the caddie," he recalled.

Hogan soon joined him on the practice tee.

Fleck's routine was to start with the wedge and work his way up the ladder—9, 8, 7, and so on—hitting a few balls with each club. He completed his warm-up sessions by hitting about a half-dozen balls with his Tommy Armour driver.

It was later reported that while on the practice tee Fleck turned to a friend and asked if the playoff format was match play or stroke play. That never happened, he emphasized years later. He said he knew the format was stroke play, which meant he would have to shoot a lower score than Hogan to win the playoff. If the two players were tied after 18 holes, the playoff would continue in a sudden-death format. The first player to record a lower score on a hole would be declared the winner.

A short while later, Fleck walked over to the practice putting green to stroke a few putts. A crowd of more than eight thousand was gathering on the Lake Course. The playoff was about to begin.

McGrane grabbed a sandwich while his fellow newspapermen offered to fill him in on anything he needed to know. Then the press men climbed the steps to exit the clubhouse and walk to the 1st tee. Bob Myers of the local Associated Press bureau asked McGrane if he had an armband to walk inside the ropes during the playoff. McGrane didn't, so Myers removed his armband and handed it to the Iowa reporter. McGrane had endured a long night en route to the coast, but now he was in the company of colleagues who were coming to his aid in small but important ways.

Fleck had made his way to the back of the 1st tee and was awaiting the announcement for the playoff to begin when he heard a loud whisper.

"Jack, Jack." It was Olympic head pro Johnny Battini speaking through a small window in the nearby pro shop. "Chops is on the phone. He wants to talk to you."

It was Ed "Porky" Oliver, one of Fleck's occasional practice-round partners and a man with multiple nicknames. Oliver had lost too many golf balls in the Lake Course rough and missed the cut. Fleck walked over to Battini and took the receiver.

"You beat him," Oliver said, "or I will kick your ass up to your shoulders. Good luck and good-bye!"

HOLE 1/PAR 5/530 YARDS

Moments later the players were called to the tee by a USGA official and drew numbers. Hogan drew the number 1 and would tee off first. Dressed for the cool, overcast weather, both players wore similar clothing: pleated trousers, long-sleeve V-neck sweaters over buttoned polo shirts, and flat caps covering their heads. They were also both playing Hogan clubs, the only two professionals to wield them. That's where the similarities ended. The playoff pitted a forty-two-year-old nine-time major champion against a thirty-three-year-old obscure Iowa club pro. The players' competitive experience, golf swings, and physical attributes were in stark contrast, and the hundreds of spectators, officials, and media members surrounding the 1st tee watched in rapt curiosity as the four-time Open champion prepared to strike the first shot of the playoff. With his golf ball teed near the right-hand tee marker, the Hawk set his feet, waggled twice, and cracked his trademark fade down the middle of the fairway.

Fleck teed his ball halfway between the two tee markers and wasted no time in getting his first shot airborne, a semiskied drive that plopped down 15 yards behind Hogan's ball in the center of the fairway. Of the handful of shots from the playoff captured on film, two of them were the players' opening tee shots. The footage of Fleck's first swing shows the ball launching high into the air off the clubface.

In the years and decades that followed, Fleck's state of mind and degree of nervousness at the start of and during the playoff would be a subject of interest in various accounts.

"I may have been a little nervous," Fleck later said about his opening tee shot, but he gave no indication that he was quaking in his golf spikes.

A violent case of the jitters would have been expected. What was far stranger, according to press reports and other eyewitness accounts, was Fleck's unusual calm during the 18-hole playoff against his idol. From tournament officials to reporters to spectators, they seemed to speak with one voice.

"He never once appeared flustered in the playoff," wrote USGA executive director Joe Dey a few weeks after the playoff.

"He's in another world," said tournament chairman Robert Roos Jr. during the playoff. "You could stick a six-inch needle in his back and he'd never know the difference."

The Olympic Club's Frank Herman later wrote that Fleck "seemed to have ice water coursing through his veins."

Reporters overheard comments from the playoff gallery that appeared in wire-service reports printed in the nation's newspapers the following day, including the *Des Moines Register.*

"He looks like he was strung together like a doll. I never saw anyone so relaxed," said one woman.

"This man is more like Hogan than Hogan himself," said another spectator.

Fleck's demeanor also made a lasting impression on fellow players such as Fred Hawkins, who decades later said, "Nothing seemed to bother him. Normal people would have been a little upset about having a playoff against him [Hogan]."

As Hogan and Fleck entered the 1st fairway to begin the four-hour duel that would determine the national champion, two women followed close behind. Marge Colvin, president of the Women's Northern California Golf Association, and Kay Sorensen, cocaptain of the Women's Olympic Club committee, were the honorary scorekeepers who would count the strokes and record them on the official scorecards.

Playing first, Fleck sent his 3-wood second shot into the right-hand rough. Hogan's 3-wood found a bunker short and right of the green, setting up a long awkward pitch from the sand, neither a short blast nor a full shot. Fleck hit a pitch shot that skidded to a stop 12 feet from the hole cut in the center-right portion of the green. Then Hogan pitched out of the sand to within 17 feet of the cup. Both players missed their birdie putts, Fleck's stopping 4 inches short of the hole. Colvin and Sorensen marked 5s on the scorecards.

Hogan 5, Fleck 5
Playoff tied

HOLE 2/PAR 4/423 YARDS

The 2nd was one of the Lake Course's more difficult par 4s, especially the tee shot. The fairway sloped from right to left, and a thick stand of trees blocked the path to a well-bunkered green if tee shots strayed too far right. Favoring the right side was the ideal play. Hogan hit a perfect drive in the right center of the fairway. Fleck pulled his drive, and his ball bounced into the rough 6 yards off the fairway. His poor position was compounded by a poor lie. He chose an 8-iron and swatted his Spalding Dot up the slope to a spot just shy of two greenside bunkers, leaving himself short of the green for a pitch and putt for par. Hogan tossed his cigarette to the ground and struck a middle-iron approach shot onto the green 20 feet beyond the hole. Fleck's delicate pitch was a good one. The ball rolled to within 3½ feet of the hole. The Hawk missed his birdie putt and tapped in for his par. Fleck stood over his first crucial putt of the playoff, a knee-knocker to save par and an early test of his nerves. He knocked it in the jar.

Hogan 4, Fleck 4
Playoff tied

HOLE 3/PAR 3/220 YARDS

At 220 yards, the 3rd hole was the longest and most challenging of Olympic's four par 3s, a 2-iron or 4-wood from an elevated tee to a putting surface with treacherous ripples and slopes. Hogan reached for his 2-iron and was about to address his golf ball when a rabbit scampered in front of him. The Hawk stopped and looked up as the frightened bunny was shooed away. He started over. The interruption might have flustered other players. Not Hogan. He lashed a 2-iron that tracked to the back-right pin position. The ball landed on the front of the green, bounced, and rolled to a stop 4 feet short of the hole.

"He hit a great shot," Fleck later said.

Birdies were rare at the 3rd. In three rounds there had been a total of 19 deuces on the long par 3. It was a masterful stroke that could turn things in Hogan's favor. Fleck, too, chose his Ben Hogan Precision 2-iron. Struck solidly, his tee shot was a slight pull, landing on the left front fringe of the green and rolling to a stop 20 feet wide of the flagstick.

Hogan was staring at what looked like a certain birdie. Fleck faced the prospect of falling behind early. From the left side of the green, Fleck putted up close and tapped in for a routine par. If there was an early turning point, it was what happened next on the 3rd green. The Hawk's 4-footer for birdie hit the right edge of the cup and rimmed out. The gallery groaned. An opportunity to jump ahead of the inexperienced club pro and gain momentum was lost.

Hogan 3, Fleck 3
Playoff tied

HOLE 4/PAR 4/433 YARDS

The Hawk again drove first, a 260-yard beauty that split the fairway of the dogleg to the left. Fleck teed off with his 3-wood, one of two holes on which he used his spoon for control. "I hit my 3-wood perfect," he said.

Jack's tee shot landed on a slope down the left side and kicked to the right into the fairway. The tee shot had been well rehearsed. "I hit a lot of practice balls there just to make sure."

Fleck struck a middle-iron approach shot 24 feet past the hole, which was located on the front third of the green. Hogan's 6-iron was also long, but closer, 16 feet away. Fleck cozied his birdie putt to within a foot of the hole and tapped in for par. Hogan's birdie effort came up 3 feet short. Perhaps thinking of his short lip-out at the 3rd, he nearly missed his par putt.

Hogan 4, Fleck 4
Playoff tied

* * *

Fleck's competitive history had not prepared him for this day—or had it?

One of the benefits of caddieing at the Davenport Country Club was the chance to play in the annual caddies' tournament in August. Since they usually didn't have a set of their own, caddies would request permission to use members' clubs. Fleck had the use of Mr. C. E. Lapham's clubs, a fine set of Kenneth Smith woods and Bobby Jones irons, the top of the line in the 1930s. In the Monday qualifying round, a caddie in his group warned Fleck not to play too well or else he might end up in the championship flight. Fleck told the boy he would do his best. He shot a respectable 89 on the course that hosted the 1936 Western Open. Not only did he land in the championship flight, he won his first two matches against caddies who expected to beat him handily.

In the quarterfinals Fleck met Vic Siegel, a fine golfer and star athlete who went on to captain the University of Iowa basketball team. Fleck was 4 down to Siegel after 6 holes but fought back to even the match by the time they arrived at the par-5 12th hole. He hit a solid drive that put the green within reach if he could strike a good second shot. Standing in the fairway, Fleck was rattled by the thought of tying Siegel. He stabbed the turf 4 inches behind the ball, barely making contact. The ball crawled 5 yards along the ground. Fleck claimed that he never felt nervous hitting a golf ball from that point on. He went on to beat Siegel 1-up but lost in the semifinals.

Had Siegel and tournament competition in the years since prepared Fleck for meeting Hogan on this stage? If any situation could cause a man to crumble under pressure, it was this one.

HOLE 5/PAR 4/457 YARDS

The 5th was a lengthy par 4 that doglegged right. It set up perfectly for Hogan's fade—a solid left-to-right drive that trimmed the corner of the dogleg would position him for the approach to a small green fronted by a dip and flanked by bunkers. Uncoiling his sturdy upper torso from the elevated tee, the Hawk made his first bad swing of the day. His tee ball flew into the tall trees to the right of the fairway and dropped into the gnarly Italian rye. Hogan was well back from where a normal drive would be, his path to the green obstructed by cypress trees. Swinging his 44¼-inch Tommy Armour driver with easy rocking-chair tempo, Fleck blasted his tee ball across the corner of the dogleg. He caught it so well that the ball rolled through the fairway and into the short left-hand rough.

Puffing on a Chesterfield, Hogan surveyed his predicament in the long grass. It wasn't pretty. With low-hanging trees 25 yards away, he had no shot at the green. His only play was back into the fairway, a near-sideways shot that would leave him a long third. He hit onto the fairway short of the dogleg and then struck a long iron that cleared the dip and landed on the putting surface, leaving a lengthy putt to save par. Fleck inspected his lie in the short rough. It was decent. He could get his club on the ball. He carved a 5-iron shot out of the thick grass that made the green, about the same distance away from the hole as Hogan. In a playoff during which most observers expected the four-time champion to dominate from the outset, Fleck had an opportunity to take the first lead. He hunched over the birdie putt and gave it a popping stroke. It missed, but left him easy work for his fifth consecutive par. The pressure was on Hogan to answer. His 28-foot par putt looked like it had a chance, but the ball failed to graze the cup—bogey. Murmurs arose from the gallery. Colvin and Sorensen marked down a 5 for Hogan and a 4 for Fleck.

Fleck 4, Hogan 5
Fleck leads by 1 stroke

HOLE 6/PAR 4/437 YARDS

Standing on the 6th tee, a par 4 that featured a fairway bunker 240 yards away, Jack had the honors for the first time in the playoff. His rhythm and timing in perfect sync, he rifled a long drive that rolled beyond the bunker straight down the middle of the gently curving fairway. Hogan followed with a good drive of his own but was 25 yards behind the pumped-up Iowan.

Fleck was sneaky long off the tee, and with adrenaline working in his favor he could outdrive players who matched or outhit him in practice rounds.

The hole was cut near the center of the pancake-shaped green.

Hogan's iron from the heart of the fairway stopped 11 feet past the flag, setting up a good birdie chance. Fleck's long drive placed doubt in his mind about club choice. Concerned about going long, he eased up on a short iron and pulled the approach shot. The ball bounced off the left edge of the green and dropped into the bunker. Hogan now had an advantage as Fleck wriggled his feet into the sand below the level of the green. A good bunker player, he blasted the ball nicely, but the putting surface didn't cooperate.

"It's almost like I could hear it now," he later said. "That thing is grinding with backspin and it kept going. I couldn't believe it went by that far."

Fleck had work to do. Eighteen feet stood between him and a sixth consecutive par. Putting from near the green's edge, he stroked the ball and looked up in time to see it disappear into the cup.

"That was a big putt," Fleck said.

He had escaped with a par. Still, Hogan was within close range for a birdie that could tie Fleck. He missed, and the Iowa pro held on to his slim lead as they headed to the 7th.

"Would Fleck never crack?" wondered the *Chronicle*'s Rosenbaum.

Fleck 4, Hogan 4
Fleck leads by 1 stroke

HOLE 7/PAR 4/266 YARDS

The short 7th looked easy on the scorecard. The little par 4 had given up more birdies than any other hole in the championship, a total of 66. Nevertheless, trouble lurked for those who missed the Dewdrop landing area situated in front of a green with a crown contour that produced devilish putts. Heavy rough surrounded the Dewdrop, and trapping extended across the entire face of the green. Threes were possible, but so were 5s and 6s, of which there had been more than a hundred. The course doctor had reached deep into his bag of design gimmicks to make the runt of a golf hole as tough as possible.

In practice, Fleck determined he couldn't reach the green-fronting bunkers with his driver. Teeing off first, he landed his ball in the small patch of fairway just short of the bunkers, perfect position. Hogan then did something he had spent much of his career guarding against: He hooked his drive into a small jungle of rough and vines near the trunk of a large tree. From where Fleck waited near the green, it looked like his opponent was in jail.

"I thought as heavy as it was he was going to play short of the bunkers by the green," Fleck said.

Hogan took a long time sizing up his options. Finally, after determining he could make a full swing without being hindered by the tree, he chopped his ball out of the tangle of vegetation and onto the back of the green, a Houdini-like escape.

"He hit a helluva shot to get out of there," Fleck remembered.

The pin was near the front of the green, and Fleck lobbed a short pitch over the bunkers and onto the putting surface eight feet right of the hole. From the back of the green, Hogan lagged his long birdie putt to within inches of the cup for an easy 4. It was a tremendous par after confronting the possibility of a bogey or worse. Fleck lined up his birdie opportunity, a slanting 8-footer that could increase his lead. His putt slid by the hole. Somewhere in the gallery Johnny Bulla, who had stuck around for the playoff, might have been shaking his head. Fleck had missed another of those makeable putts.

Fleck 4, Hogan 4
Fleck leads by 1 stroke

HOLE 8/PAR 3/139 YARDS

The 8th was the short par 3 that finished near the clubhouse, a prime viewing spot for thousands of spectators who wondered how long the Iowa club pro could hold off the great Ben Hogan. The hole played slightly uphill—the green was 20 feet above the tee. The flag was just beyond a large bunker in the front-right portion of the green. Fleck decided to hit a towering, easy 7-iron instead of a hard 8-iron, not unlike the dramatic shot he played to the 72nd green twenty-four hours earlier. It was a beauty. His ball landed softly and spun to a stop 7 feet to the left of the hole.

If Hogan felt pressure, he didn't show it. He teed his ball and peered at the green. He then sent his short-iron shot toward the rear of the deep green. He faced a long putt, a 35-foot breaker from left to right, downhill much of the way. It was at this moment that Hogan, a player known to struggle over short putts but often uncanny from long range, did something heroic: He sank it. It was the first birdie of the playoff. The large gallery surrounding the green and seated on the slope erupted.

The Hawk was circling, yet there were no signs of alarm in Fleck. His birdie putt was about the same length as the one he missed on the previous hole. He took measure of it and brushed it into the cup for a deuce. Fleck had matched Hogan's amazing birdie, and applause and cheers showered both players as they departed the 8th green.

Fleck 2, Hogan 2
Fleck leads by 1 stroke

. . .

Powers turned to McGrane and said, "Wish I could stay with 'em, but I got to go file a story."

McGrane asked Powers to check on a room at the Sir Francis Drake Hotel. As Powers headed for the clubhouse, McGrane followed the mass of people to the 9th hole. The playoff drama was tightening its grip on the excited crowd.

HOLE 9/PAR 4/420 YARDS

Fleck still clung to a 1-stroke lead as the players and their caddies reached the 9th tee. The improbable birdie had gotten Hogan back to even par for his round. Both players hit superb drives onto the 9th fairway, a par 4 that was downhill from the tee to a landing area that tilted slightly from right to left. It was still overcast, and Hogan, clad in his dark sweater, was the first to play his second shot. His middle-iron approach shot landed on the putting surface and rolled 15 feet past the hole, which was cut near the center of the green. Fleck followed with a solid iron that stopped beyond the flagstick.

The players appeared to be the same distance away from the hole, so a USGA official determined the order of play. Fleck was away and would putt first. The pace of his putts had been nearly perfect on the Lake Course greens through 8 holes. It was a matter of determining the correct line and noting any subtle influences in the grainy putting surfaces. He settled into his stance and stroked the putt. The shiny Spalding Dot came squarely off his garage-built John Rueter Jr. blade, rolled on line, and tumbled into the cup. Fleck had holed back-to-back birdies, and the thousands of amazed witnesses burst into applause as they wondered what he might do next.

Hogan exhaled. Slightly closer than Fleck's, his putt was definitely makeable. He rapped it and stared at the ball as it rolled to a stop 15 inches shy of the hole. Frustrated, he tapped in for his par. He had tallied an even-par 35, tying his best 9-hole score, yet trailed by 2 shots. Fleck had carded his second consecutive 2-under 33, the other on the incoming 9 of

Saturday's final round. It was hard to fathom how such an inexperienced player could be outplaying one of the all-time greats.

Fleck 3, Hogan 4
Fleck leads by 2 strokes
First 9: Fleck 33, Hogan 35

HOLE 10/PAR 4/417 YARDS

The opening hole on the inward 9 was a dogleg right that terminated at a small, heavily bunkered green with a bank behind it. The temptation was to cut too much of the dogleg. Thick rough at the bend in the fairway tormented players whose drives strayed too far right.

Leading off for the fifth straight hole, Fleck fired another bullet far down the right center of the fairway. Hogan's tee shot found the fairway, short of Fleck's drive. His next shot landed on the front of the green and rolled to the back, 40 feet from the front-right pin. The flagstick was tucked behind a mound, so Fleck chose a line left of the hole and struck another high, soft 7-iron that stopped 13 feet from the cup. Everything was working for the underdog. He had even made a few putts.

Hogan, on the other hand, was in the uncustomary position of playing catch-up. It didn't help that he faced a long putt while the man he was chasing had another good look at a birdie. The Hawk crouched over his ball and knocked it across the green, an excellent lag that slid 17 inches past the hole. He holed his par putt and walked to the side of the green to watch the nerveless Iowan take aim at a third consecutive birdie. Fleck gave it a firm stroke and stared as the ball drifted slightly to the right and plopped into the cup. Birdie. Birdie. *Birdie.*

The spellbound gallery again rewarded his bold play with hearty claps and loud cheers. Fleck was 3 strokes up on the four-time Open champion, who was not exactly hacking it around the course. The game was coming easily to him, and it didn't appear to matter who he was playing or what they were playing for.

"The garland of the hero," observed Rosenbaum, "seemed to sprout from his temples."

Fleck 3, Hogan 4
Fleck leads by 3 strokes

* * *

Hogan, a reluctant warrior in overtime, had lost his share of playoffs, but there were no Flecks in his past. The defeats had come at the hands of proven opponents such as Byron Nelson and Sam Snead at the Masters and Jimmy Demaret at Phoenix. Yet this was the U.S. Open, the province of Hogan since 1948 when he won the first of four titles in six tries. The last U.S. Open playoff had been in 1950, and everyone knew how that one turned out. It was the stuff of legend. After narrowly surviving the head-on crash on a foggy Texas highway sixteen months earlier, Hogan went 18 extra holes to defeat Lloyd Mangrum and George Fazio at Merion, a mythic victory that loosed soft sobs of joy from Valerie on the club's porch and stunned a nation of adoring fans. Although he trailed on Sunday afternoon at Olympic, Hogan would not give up. That was unthinkable. As long as he could walk and swing a club, he would battle on. It would be foolish to count him out.

HOLE 11/PAR 4/429 YARDS

Gallery control had broken down. The ropes were still in place, but many spectators were no longer treating them as boundary lines. Fans had been roaming the fairways of the Lake Course since the 6th hole. The USGA's

Dey and tournament chairman Roos suspended play for five minutes while the 11th fairway was cleared.

Up a gentle slope to an elevated, two-tiered green, the 11th played long and tough. As if to demonstrate why 3 strokes was not a comfortable margin, Fleck sprayed his tee shot to the right in the second cut of rough. His fate depended on the lie. Hogan surely saw it as an opening, and he split the fairway with his drive. Fleck walked to his ball and got the news: It had settled into a deep patch of Italian rye. Going at the green was not a sane option. It was a layup shot, and he hit a hard 8-iron to a small swale short of the green. Long iron in hand, Hogan flicked his cigarette to the ground and pulled his approach shot into a bunker left and short of the green. Worse, the ball was buried in the sand. Both players faced making bogey, for getting up and down on the undulating 11th green was a difficult business.

Fleck flipped his pitch shot dead at the flag.

"I thought I hit it stiff," he said.

The ball landed on a crown in the green and spun back, rolling down the slope 18 feet from the hole. Hogan dug into the bunker and tore the ball loose from a buried lie. The ball danced across the green and halted 6 feet from the hole.

"He played an impossible trap shot to a tight pin," Fleck said.

Unable to sink a fourth consecutive putt, Fleck tapped in for his first bogey of the playoff. The Hawk took advantage. He dropped the putt for a hard-earned par, trimming a stroke off the challenger's lead.

Hogan 4, Fleck 5
Fleck leads by 2 strokes

HOLE 12/PAR 4/387 YARDS

Hogan had regained the honors for the first time since the 5th hole and immediately struck a regrettable drive, hooking his ball into the eucalyptus trees. The 12th was a tight-driving hole to a green that sat 15 feet below the landing area. Position was the key, length a bonus, and Jack got both with a long drive down the right side of the fairway. Looking oblivious to the highly charged atmosphere, the two players strolled side by side down the fairway, a phalanx of officials and fans tromping close behind.

When he got to his ball, Fleck looked over and saw Hogan in the trees more than 200 yards away from the green. Further, it looked like the rough was up over his ankles. Fleck thought there was no way Hogan could do much with his second shot. He was wrong. The Hawk slashed a long iron out of the tree line that landed far short of the green and darted like a gray squirrel through the opening between the two giant flanking bunkers. The ball skirted onto the putting surface and hurried to the back 45 feet from the hole. Because the pin was tucked near the left-hand bunker toward the front of the green, Fleck lofted his 8-iron right of the target. The ball landed 9 feet from the flagstick, another superb approach shot.

Hogan lagged his long putt to within 3 feet of the hole. Fleck missed his birdie. His putter had cooled off. Still, it was an easy par. The Hawk faced a troubling distance. He had reached the point in his career where short putts tormented him, and the little one on the 12th green to secure his par didn't fall. Hogan was again 3 strokes behind and running out of holes.

Fleck 4, Hogan 5
Fleck leads by 3 strokes

•   •   •

The switchboard at the *San Francisco Chronicle* was lighting up like Times Square. Caller after caller wanted to know the result of the playoff between Hogan and Fleck. From the 2:00 P.M. start to the 6:00 P.M. conclusion of the playoff, the *Chronicle* was deluged with 1,500 calls. The newspaper called it "unprecedented," exceeding the number of calls on national election night.

HOLE 13/PAR 3/187 YARDS

The 13th hole featured a long, skinny green well guarded by bunkers and bordered by cypress trees. Distance could be hard to judge from the long tee box to a deep green that was concealed by filtering afternoon light. First to play, Fleck hit a 3-iron onto the green 12 feet to the left of the back-right hole location, a bold shot for a player with a 3-shot lead. A reputed long-iron player, Hogan rifled his tee shot toward the green but with a very different result. The ball drifted right and lodged in a heavy-limbed tree for a few seconds before falling into the giant front-right bunker. Any advantage Fleck appeared to have was tempered by Hogan's brilliant bunker play. The Hawk blasted out of the sand to within 6 feet of the cup. Fleck could add another stroke to his lead if he could coax home the 12-foot birdie putt. Instead, he rolled it 3 feet past the cup and sank the comebacker. This time Hogan drained his par putt, another great sand save. There was no sign of surrender in the champion, even though his faulty gait was noticeable to Fleck and others.

"He had a little catch in his walk," Fleck said. "You could tell he was limping a little bit."

Fleck 3, Hogan 3
Fleck leads by 3 strokes

HOLE 14/PAR 4/410 YARDS

Both players drove in the fairway at the dogleg-left 14th. Hogan squinted at the green as he measured the approach shot in his mind. The flag was tucked behind a bunker on the front-right portion of the green. He selected

235

a middle iron and struck the shot crisply toward the center of the kidney-shaped green. The ball landed on target and spun to a stop 15 feet from the hole. Fleck's second, a 6-iron, drifted too far right and buried in the right-hand bunker six inches from the lip.

A shot from a buried lie is difficult to control. It was compounded by the fact that the green sloped away from Fleck. His next swing defied those sobering realities. He thumped the ball from the sand and watched his explosion shot nestle up to within 3 feet of the cup. The two men who both played Hogan wedges were putting on a clinic from the Lake Course's bunkers. Fleck had not missed any short putts, so Hogan could assume his opponent would make his par. The only way to cut into the lead was to sink a putt, which the Hawk did with his next stroke, a clutch birdie that trimmed the lead to 2 shots with 4 holes to play. It wasn't over, and Fleck knew it.

Hogan 3, Fleck 4
Fleck leads by 2 strokes

•   •   •

McGrane was walking inside the ropes and wondering about the story he would write. It was 5:00 P.M.—7:00 P.M. in Des Moines—and the direct wire to the office had just opened. With 4 holes to go, another hour of golf, the answer was obvious. McGrane had to stay with Fleck and Hogan to the conclusion of the playoff and bang out the story when he got back to the pressroom. The time difference on the West Coast was a killer for deadline-driven sportswriters. McGrane was still in need of a hotel room—the United Nations influx had exhausted lodging options—but Powers was going to make one more try on his colleague's behalf.

HOLE 15/PAR 3/144 YARDS

The par-3 15th was a pesky short hole that had yielded just twenty-seven birdies during the championship. Bunkers surrounded the green, a small island with the flag toward the back. Hogan had made two of the birdies at the 15th and was determined to make another one. Time was running out, the fifth Open crown in doubt. As he inhaled a burning Chesterfield, onlookers wondered if the gritty champion could summon the shots to overtake the surprising Iowan. No one had expected Hogan to be chasing at this late stage. The birdies in the third and fourth rounds were reassuring memories as he sized up his tee shot. He would have a good chance to make it three in a row after he clipped a short iron to within 16 feet of the hole. The unflappable Fleck answered with a 7-iron that edged inside of Hogan by a foot.

Hole by hole, spectators crowded into every available spot to watch the two men battle. One boy, desperate for a vantage point near the 15th green, scaled a tree. As Hogan was studying his birdie putt, the youngster slipped and crashed to the ground along with a tree limb, an abrupt and brief interruption to the tense duel. The Hawk resumed his routine and failed to can a second consecutive birdie, tapping in for par. Fleck also missed, and the playoff moved to the longest hole on the Lake Course.

Hogan 3, Fleck 3
Fleck leads by 2 strokes

HOLE 16/PAR 5/603 YARDS

Hogan desperately needed another birdie. Matching pars with Fleck on Olympic's closing holes spelled certain defeat. Hitting solid drives and 3-woods, the two competitors played up the long, double-dogleg fairway and wedged onto the heavily trapped green, about 25 feet from the cup.

237

The hole was cut in the front-right section of the putting surface, making it difficult to get their third shots close without landing in a bunker or the clumpy grass on the green's edge. Neither player could afford such an error at this late juncture.

Hogan would have to make a sizable putt to narrow the margin, and he came close on the 16th green, sliding his birdie bid 4 inches by the cup. Fleck left himself a 3-footer for par but calmly stroked it in to retain a two-stroke lead with two holes to play. He was 800 yards away from winning the U.S. Open and defeating golf's greatest champion, a tough, unknowable man who sometimes performed acts of kindness, such as gifting him with a custom set of golf clubs seven weeks earlier.

Hogan 5, Fleck 5
Fleck leads by 2 strokes

.　　.　　.

Two thousand miles away in the Credit Island pro shop, Lynn listened to the animated voices on the radio as the final holes of the playoff unfolded in San Francisco. Earlier that day she had told her husband to keep his composure. He was as cool and calm as a mountain lake. She was not.

HOLE 17/PAR 4/461 YARDS

With only five 3s recorded in 72 holes, no one would mistake the 17th for a birdie hole. For many, it wasn't even a par hole. Hogan had managed just one par in four rounds. Fleck had made two. The 17th's length and difficulty could crush the spirit of a golfer as he neared the clubhouse. Somehow the Hawk reached down for a little extra to produce his longest drive of the day, a bullet fade that split the right-tilting fairway. Fleck had driven well all day and cracked his Spalding Dot far up the right center of the fairway beyond where Hogan's ball lay. Hogan would attempt to do what he had accomplished once in four previous tournament rounds and a half-dozen practice sessions—reach the 17th in 2 shots. It would take everything in his bag and every ounce of strength in his weary forty-two-year-old body. He lashed the ball with his 3-wood and stared into the distance as the dimpled sphere rocketed toward the giant green. Fifty-five years later, Hogan's shotmaking at the 17th still shined bright in Fleck's mind.

"He hit his best two woods . . . in the playoff," he said. "He had been playing all day with these bad legs. How did he knock it that far?"

The wire-service account reported that Hogan was on in 2. As Fleck remembered, Hogan was on the fringe of the green. No matter; the brave champion had struck two tremendous blows when he needed them most and was in position to putt for a rare birdie. Fleck also reached for his 3-wood, but was concerned about going too far. The previous afternoon he had made the green in 2 shots and drifted beyond the hole.

"I eased up on it," he said of his pushed 3-wood that settled into the four-inch rough to the right of the green.

Fleck inspected the lie. It wasn't good. The ball was sitting down in a patch of heavy grass, so he stepped away and took practice swings with his wedge to gauge the feel and resistance of the greenside rough. Then, wasting no time, he stepped up and chopped down on the ball. It popped out of the thick grass, landed in the fringe, and trickled onto the green, stopping 4 feet from the hole.

Hogan's medium-range birdie putt needed to go down to trim at least one stroke off Fleck's lead. He rolled it close and tapped in for his second par in five tries on the 17th. If Fleck could ease in his 4-footer, he would walk to the 18th tee with a 2-shot cushion, not an insurmountable lead but a safe one if he stayed away from the rough and trees.

Hogan waited at the side of the green. He had played 89 holes of steady championship golf, but if things didn't quickly turn in his favor he would return to Fort Worth with bitter memories of how the fifth Open slipped from his grasp. Then a break. Knowing firsthand the fickle nature of 4-footers, Hogan watched Fleck miss his first short putt of the day. The crowd groaned, a reflex reaction even for those rooting for the four-time champion. The throng of excited spectators streamed ahead to stake out position on the deciding hole of the playoff. Colvin and Sorensen recorded a 4 for Hogan and a 5 for Fleck. The Hawk had cut the deficit to 1.

Hogan 4, Fleck 5

Fleck leads by 1 stroke

HOLE 18/PAR 4/337 YARDS

Upwards of six thousand expectant fans jammed the hillside and bowl-like 18th green area beneath the large stucco clubhouse. Young Bill Callan was seated on the slope. His older brother, Hogan's forecaddie during the play-off, and his father, captain of the marshals, were also on the scene. Another two thousand spectators stretched along both sides of the fairway back to the elevated tee where Ben Hogan reached for his driver. He needed a birdie. He couldn't expect the Iowan to make another bogey as he prepared to hit his tee ball down the sloping 18th fairway.

The Hawk set his feet, eyed the target, waggled the club, and swung with characteristic force, but something had upset the machinelike chore-ography of Hogan's famous swing. His right foot slipped on the damp turf that was top-dressed with sand. The ball screamed left, headed for the deep rough 20 yards off the fairway. To the astonishment of eight thousand witnesses, the misdirected ball dove into the shin-high Italian rye. Many would report that Hogan's errant tee shot on the final hole of the playoff was a dreaded hook, the nasty rattlesnake that had returned to bite him as he was on the cusp of a dramatic comeback. In fact, the ball came off the neck of the driver and went straight left from the moment it flew off the clubface. Fans and reporters were not immediately aware that Hogan slipped, and some wondered how the golf great could hit such a poor shot at that crucial moment.

Hogan wasn't the only player to lose his footing on the 18th tee, which had been lengthened for the national championship. "My right foot slipped from under me," Errie Ball recalled a half century later, "and I hooked it right into the rough almost where Ben Hogan put his shot."

The 18th was one of two holes on the Lake Course on which Fleck used his 3-wood from the tee. "I practiced with a lot of balls in every practice round. I definitely knew I would never use a driver on that hole," he said.

Fleck valued accuracy more than distance on the short par-4 finishing hole. Behind by a stroke and desperate for a birdie, Hogan went for both.

While spectators were still absorbing the shock of Hogan's wild drive, Fleck stuck a tee into the ground and sent his ball down the middle of the fairway.

If the Hawk's predicament looked bad from the 18th tee, then it was all but hopeless when he arrived on the scene. "We had a hard time just finding the ball," he later said.

Cal Bailey's strange cartoon from the night before was playing out on the final hole. Hogan had no choice but to try to come out sideways and get his ball back into the fairway. Fleck, his caddie, and officials moved back 20 yards to clear a path for Hogan's recovery shot. Although he would have been better served with the sickle in Bailey's odd cartoon, Hogan gripped his sand wedge and took a mighty slash at the jungle that concealed his ball. A patch of thick grass clung to the club as he completed his vicious swing. Perhaps moving a foot, the ball was still at his feet. Again he ripped into the rough, and again the ball failed to escape the tall grass. On his third try, the ball broke free and flew to the safety of the fairway. Hogan lay 4. Unless an epic collapse awaited Fleck, the cause was lost. Any remaining hope of a historic victory had been buried in the Olympic rough. There would be no coronation.

The hole was positioned toward the front-third of the long, steep green. All Fleck needed to do was put his ball on the putting surface. He chose an 8-iron and hit a high, soft shot that stopped 20 feet below the hole. Hogan's fifth swing was a wedge to the back of the green, some 35 feet away. The two players broke through the crowd that had spilled into the playing area and walked onto the 18th green amid a loud, prolonged ovation.

The Hawk was first to putt. The ball took nearly six seconds to roll down the slick green before falling into the heart of the cup for a 6. It typified Hogan's competitive spirit. He had finished like a champion. Caddie Tony Zitelli retrieved his employer's ball from the hole as Hogan stepped to the edge of the green.

Fleck fought back tears. He could take four putts and win the U.S. Open. He only needed two. The first one stopped less than 2 feet short of the hole. Not hurrying, he walked up, placed his Bulls Eye blade in front and behind the ball, and tapped it into the hole for a 1-under 69 and a 3-stroke victory over Ben Hogan, who carded his third 72 in five trips around the Lake Course. An unknown entrant on Thursday, Fleck had rallied to tie the era's greatest player late on Saturday and beaten him head-to-head on Sunday to win the national crown.

"It defied everything anybody knew about golf," Rosburg later said.

The Iowa club pro had crossed the wide chasm from obscurity to fame in four days. His life would never be the same.

Fleck 4, Hogan 6
Totals: Fleck 33-36—69, Hogan 35-37—72

As another ovation filled the cool evening air and photographers, officials, and police officers rushed onto the green, Hogan walked 50 feet to where Fleck stood near the hole and offered his heartfelt congratulations. At the moment of his greatest disappointment in golf, Ben Hogan displayed a kind of grace in defeat that Jack Fleck would remember for the rest of his life.

Photographers swarmed and snapped pictures of the two combatants. Someone asked Hogan to have some fun with it, so, being a good sport, he removed his white linen flat cap and fanned Fleck's Bulls Eye putter while Fleck grinned at his idol. The fans loved the gesture, and the playful photograph would appear in the nation's newspapers the next day and in other publications for months and years to come. Later on the hot-putter image would be a painful reminder to Fleck as he defended his win over Hogan on the merits of fine shotmaking as well as good putting.

. . .

In Davenport, whoops of joy rang out in the Credit Island pro shop after Fleck holed his final putt. Brad Wilson of the *Des Moines Register* had been on hand all afternoon to witness the roller coaster of emotions for the twenty-six-year-old Mrs. Fleck and a group of area golfers.

"I don't think I could have stood it another minute if the match hadn't ended then," Lynn said. "My, it's really wonderful."

. . .

Moments later police officers ushered the two players from the green. Fleck and Hogan signed their scorecards and retired to the locker room for fifteen minutes to wash up and slip into sport coats for the trophy presentation on the 8th green, where a red carpet, microphones, wooden folding chairs, and a table with floral arrangements had been set up. Low amateur Harvie Ward was already waiting when the two players emerged from the clubhouse and walked onto the 8th green. The fair-haired Ward wore a dark suit and tie and took a seat beside Hogan. Always the consummate professional at trophy ceremonies, Hogan had slipped into a dress shirt, knotted a necktie, and put on a dark sport coat that complemented his pleated trousers. It made quite an impression on teenager Callan, who remembered that Hogan looked as sharp as a businessman and gave an impressive speech to boot. Fleck was tieless but had long been following Horton Smith's advice to carry a sport coat on the road. Donning a light-colored jacket that looked a little long in the sleeves, he was sufficiently prepared for his first professional victory.

Thousands of lingering fans listened as a USGA official made introductory remarks and then awarded local hero Ward the medal for low amateur. Runner-up Hogan was recognized next, and he made an announcement that stunned the large crowd.

"I'm through with competitive golf," he said with a catch in his voice. He went on to say he had worked harder than ever before in preparation for the U.S. Open and had played to win. As Herman noted, "The four-day ordeal was written all over his countenance." The lost opportunity at Olympic would haunt Hogan for the rest of his days.

"From now on," he concluded, "I'm a weekend golfer."

The ornate silver two-handled trophy and USGA check number 1486 for $6,000 were then presented to Jack Fleck, an unpretentious thirty-three-year-old club pro who had stolen the crown from the reigning king of golf. He had even used the king's weapons, the Hogan Precision irons and fairway woods that had been in his canvas golf bag for less than two months. Fleck eyed the trophy. It was sterling silver and measured eighteen inches tall and six inches in diameter with a winged victory figure perched on the lid. Engraved on one side were the words UNITED STATES GOLF ASSOCIATION OPEN CHAMPIONSHIP. Underneath the words was a rendering of early golfers surrounded by a laurel wreath. The other side contained the names of all the U.S. Open champions since the tournament's inception in 1895.

A reluctant public speaker since his school days, he kept his remarks short. "I thank God for giving me the strength. I thank my father and mother, my wife, and my little boy." He also expressed gratitude to the USGA, the Olympic Club, volunteers, and fans.

McGrane didn't hear a word. The *Des Moines Register* sportswriter was in the pressroom bearing down on his story, so jumpy that he repeatedly jammed the typewriter keys. An Iowan had won the U.S. Open. A meteor dropping out of the sky and landing at the foot of the state capitol on Grand Avenue in downtown Des Moines would not have been more surprising. Myers stopped by and asked if McGrane had attended the trophy ceremony. The Associated Press bureau man handed his notes to McGrane, another act of collegial kindness, and McGrane incorporated them into his lengthy article. Rod Ryan, the man directing the Western Union operators, helped get McGrane's copy on the wire to the Des Moines office in time to make the newspaper's first edition. (During the 1955 National Open, Western Union wired an estimated 350,000 words, more than in any other golf championship.)

McGrane realized he still hadn't spoken to Fleck, so he wandered out of the pressroom in search of the new champion. After checking the locker room, he spotted Fleck surrounded by policemen, well-wishers, and autograph seekers on the 8th green. McGrane walked down the clubhouse steps and over to where Fleck was patiently acknowledging the fans. The two made eye contact, and Fleck threw his arm around the Iowa sportswriter. McGrane followed along as Fleck walked into the clubhouse and entered the pressroom, where he remained for ninety minutes.

"I was never nervous," Fleck told reporters. "I simply kept playing as hard as I could and the putts dropped in for me."

Hogan also obliged the reporters but slipped away from the press gathering before Fleck. "I want to congratulate Fleck," he said. "His was a marvelous demonstration of superb golf. It was guts and fortitude." Hogan said he had never seen an inexperienced player perform so well and commented on Fleck's composure.

At some point in the aftermath of the playoff, a thirteen-year-old boy approached Hogan and asked for an autograph. Callan later lost the cherished signature, but the sweet memory of his brush with the great Ben Hogan would linger well into the twenty-first century.

In Davenport, Lynn was sitting by the phone awaiting Jack's call. Beside her was the list of things her husband had promised when he won the National Open. The family joke had come true. Mrs. Fleck was overjoyed. Four-year-old Craig said he was rooting for his daddy but was unhappy that Hogan lost.

Word would soon get around that Topping and McLaney, the late-night callers to Hamilton, won $89,000 betting on Fleck.

A tournament car was waiting to transport Fleck to the Stewart Hotel in Union Square, his hastily arranged accommodations for the night. McGrane also hopped in, along with Dr. and Mrs. Barton. The four of them joined another Iowan, Dr. Bob McFarlane, for a late dinner. They ordered champagne and toasted the new champion. Upon their return to the hotel, a clerk handed Fleck a thick stack of telegrams that took two hands to carry. He did not fall asleep until well after midnight.

The Iowa sportswriter who hadn't shaved, hadn't put on a clean shirt, or hardly slept for two days, finally had a room. It was the room next to the new U.S. Open champion.

PART

III

—17—

HOMECOMING

As Jack Fleck slept at the Stewart Hotel on Union Square, the morning editions of the nation's newspapers that would trumpet his extraordinary achievement to the world were going to press. The shy Iowan would awake in the glaring light of instant fame. He had leaped onto the front page of the *San Francisco Chronicle*. The headline FLECK WINS, HOGAN RETIRES was positioned just below a banner headline about Juan Perón's anticipated ouster as Argentine president and dictator. Underneath was this: IKE HERE—HIS SPEECH TODAY OPENS U.N.'S 10TH ANNIVERSARY. He had eclipsed the president's visit—at least in newsprint.

The nation's sportswriters had chiseled their leads to deliver the dramatic news of Fleck's stunning victory and Hogan's tragic defeat. The *Chronicle*'s Art Rosenbaum captured the remarkable outcome in his twelve-word opening: "Mr. Unknown defeated Mr. Golf to win the National Open championship yesterday," he wrote. "Mr. Unknown is a nerveless, lean-jawed Jack Louis Fleck. . . . In an 18-hole playoff over the Lake Course of the

Olympic Country Club, his calm was the calm and his ice was the ice of a—well, of a Hogan."

There were many more, ranging from the staid *New York Times*—whose reporter was the only man to not remove his coat in the pressroom—to the excited declarations of the press services.

Will Grimsley (the Associated Press), "Jack Fleck, an obscure son of a one-time Iowa truck farmer, crushed Ben Hogan's bid for his fifth title Sunday in an 18-hole playoff which brought a Cinderella climax to the fifty-fifth National Open golf tournament."

Hal Wood (United Press International), "Jack Fleck, a bronzed Iowan with a nondescript golfing background, wrote a new Cinderella chapter into the sports record Sunday as he whipped the supposedly invincible bantam Ben Hogan in the play-off to win the National Open Golf championship."

Fleck was also front page news in Monday morning's *Des Moines Register.* FLECK'S 69 BEATS HOGAN BY 3 read the banner headline over a large headshot photograph of a wide-eyed Fleck. "Jack Fleck," read McGrane's lead, "the unheralded man from Iowa, put an end to the Ben Hogan era in golf here Sunday by winning the United States Open Championship."

The monumental upset called for historical context, and Herbert Warren Wind provided it. In a *Sports Illustrated* feature titled "Jack the Giant Killer," Wind wrote, "Perhaps all of us who saw this playoff can appreciate a bit better now how it felt to be at Brookline in 1913 when another complete unknown—the name was something like Ouimet—defeated the peerless Harry Vardon, and that other contemporary giant, Ted Ray, in that historic Open play-off."

Rosenbaum and others in Olympic's pressroom agreed that Fleck's shocker resembled the magical victory of Francis Ouimet. The son of immigrants, Ouimet was a twenty-year-old amateur who lived across the street from Brookline Country Club, where he beat the great Vardon and

Ray, a stunning win that gave rise to the game of golf in America. Although a professional, Fleck was also the product of a working-class family and, like Ouimet, had beaten the greatest player of his era and arguably the best to grace the fairways since the legendary Bobby Jones. Henceforth, many would regard Fleck's triumph as the greatest golf upset since Ouimet's, the two standing alone in the annals of major championship golf.

• • • •

Life as the new U.S. Open champion began early on Monday morning. Fleck departed the hotel at 4:00 A.M. for KRON-TV to appear along with his caddie on NBC's *Today* show with Dave Garroway. He received an appearance fee of $1,000, the first of many monetary perks. It was estimated the Open title would bring between $50,000 and $75,000 in endorsements, exhibition fees, and other off-course income. The unanticipated boon for Jack and Lynn Fleck meant the days of stretching dollars at home and on the tournament circuit were behind them. Lynn could buy a new dress or two, as well as a few other things on her cherished list.

After the *Today* show, Fleck's small entourage took a taxi to the Cliff House for breakfast, followed by a short drive along the coast. A sudden celebrity, he was unaccustomed to the royal treatment he received at the restaurant, the hotel, and elsewhere. It was odd to be recognized and asked for an autograph everywhere he went.

There were, however, two men who had combed the city since Sunday evening without spotting the new U.S. Open champion. They had scoured the hotels, restaurants, the airport, and bus terminals. (Fleck was difficult to find because he was an unregistered guest at the Stewart Hotel, having taken the room occupied by the Bartons' son.) They were imposing-looking fellows in suits whom Fleck might have mistaken for Mafia men had they not said they were with the United States Secret Service. They had important business when they finally located him at the Stewart Hotel. President Eisenhower wanted to meet the new U.S. Open champion.

• • •

The numbers were in, and by most every measure the National Open championship had been a grand success. San Franciscans had supported the event with both their attendance and their wallets. Attendance and gate receipts ranked second best for a U.S. Open, trailing the previous year's championship in New Jersey by a slim margin. The total estimated gross receipts for tickets, food and drink, advertising, radio and television, entry fees, parking, and incidentals exceeded $400,000, a healthy boost to the local economy. The *Chronicle*'s Goethals reported that the spectators at the Olympic Club were "big spenders," doling out fifty cents on average for food and drink. The USGA was pleased. The decision to conduct the second National Open on the West Coast had been rewarded with a terrific venue, a thrilling tournament, and a surprise winner, as well as the usual grief from players about the extreme difficulty of a course setup on which only fourteen men broke an aggregate score of 300. Players would long remember Olympic's tall rough.

"In every way, it was a memorable tournament," executive director Joe Dey wrote in the July issue of the USGA's journal.

It was the first of several USGA trips to the Olympic Club to conduct championships.

• • •

Emil Schroder, Fleck's caddie who was nearly fired on the first day of practice, enjoyed his fifteen minutes of fame. In addition to his appearance with Fleck on *Today*, for which he received $600, the caddie was interviewed by the local newspaper.

"Jack never broke 80 during a practice round," Schroder said, adding that his player did his homework on the Lake Course during their long practice sessions. Still, the caddie had known Fleck would play well and predicted he would "go a long way."

With the "Jack never broke 80," the caddie sounded a refrain that would become a part of the tournament's lore. It was true. Fleck hadn't paid much attention to his practice-round scores, which he admitted weren't good. His game suddenly came together as the tournament got under way. He drove superbly on the tight Lake Course, and his usual lackluster putter came alive on the small greens.

Partnered with Fleck on the losing end of a bet against Walker Inman and Mike Krak in the Wednesday practice round, Al Mengert would be among those who reminded Fleck and golf writers over the ensuing years that the Iowan couldn't break 80 before Thursday's first round. Nor did a lot of players, for that matter, including Mengert and Inman. That was different, though. The man who couldn't hold up his end in a practice-round wager had four days later felled the great Hogan in an 18-hole playoff to win the National Open. It was incomprehensible, spurring stories, explanations, and theories that would later put Fleck on the defensive.

"We were really shocked to see how well he [Fleck] played," Krak later said, "but he was that type of individual. The way he hit the ball you could never tell how he was going to score because he was a real grinder."

In the immediate aftermath, Fleck's play and composure were admired from near and far. McGrane, the fellow Iowan who was familiar with Fleck's undistinguished career in professional golf, marveled at the transformation.

"It was a strange new Jack Fleck who moved to the top of golf," he wrote in his last dispatch from San Francisco. "There was never a suggestion of nervousness as he outsteadied Ben Hogan, supposedly the coldest-blooded golfer of them all. Fleck matched anything Hogan did and, in the clutch, did it better."

Schroder, meanwhile, had gotten his face on national television, his name in the newspaper, and a fat check in his wallet. The nine-day player-caddie partnership had worked out well for both men. It was Fleck's first and last brush with the Olympic Club caddie, except on an occasion when Schroder was low on funds and rang up his former employer.

⸻ • • • ⸻

Facing Ben Hogan might not have spooked Fleck, but the thought of meeting the president of the United States certainly did. In a few minutes, he would meet the leader of the free world. Major championship golf was easy compared to this. He cleaned up and wondered about his attire. Should he wear a sport shirt? A coat? He turned to McGrane. Do you call him Mr. President?

At 5:00 P.M. Fleck walked across the street to the St. Francis Hotel and was escorted by the Secret Service to a service elevator at the far end of the lobby. The elevator operator took him to the sixth floor, where he strolled past foreign dignitaries and arrived at the door of the president's suite. An attendant slipped into the room.

"Mr. President, the U.S. Open champion is here."

A familiar voice said, "Send him in."

Fleck walked into the room and clasped hands with the president.

"Congratulations on a great win," Ike said. "Come in and sit down and tell me about it."

Feet up, the president was relaxed and friendly, putting Fleck at ease.

The two golfers talked about the championship a short while until a telephone call from a general interrupted their conversation. As the president stepped away, his press secretary, James Hagerty, picked up a stack of newspapers on the large coffee table and good-naturedly pointed out that Fleck had leapfrogged the president in the headlines. Eisenhower returned, and the two talked for a few more minutes. Ike wondered if Fleck was nervous during the playoff. He mentioned his friendship with Hogan and Byron Nelson and asked if Fleck had ever played in the Masters. Fleck learned that a wire had been sent to his home to invite him to a sportsmen's luncheon at the White House in July. A game of golf was in their future, promised the president, who also had called Hogan to offer his regrets. The ten-minute meeting ended, and the president walked Fleck down the hall with his hand on Fleck's arm.

Fleck returned to his hotel, where he ate a late lunch and packed for a red-eye flight to Chicago. What a day. The telephone in his hotel room never stopped ringing. Offers were piling up as fast as telegrams.

At 8:45 P.M., a chauffeur-driven Cadillac was waiting at the front of the Stewart Hotel to whisk Fleck, McGrane, and the Bartons to San Francisco International Airport. A male employee of Trans World Airlines whispered to McGrane that his party was getting the red carpet treatment. Indeed, an actual red carpet extended to the steps of the Lockheed Super Constellation airliner. The flight they were about to board was the "Champagne Special," the airline's plush transcontinental service. Not long after, the sportswriter soaked up the luxury as the large plane climbed into the dark sky, speeding away from the site of the greatest sports story he had covered in his long career. His one regret was not bringing an extra shirt.

．　　　．　　　．

Lynn and Craig arrived early on Tuesday morning at Chicago's Midway Airport to meet the conquering hero. Herb Elliott, operator of a Davenport air charter service, flew the Flecks in his twin-engine Beechcraft airplane. After picking up Fleck, McGrane, and the Bartons, Elliott would fly the merry band to Davenport's Mount Joy Airport for a welcome-home celebration, followed by a parade through the streets of Davenport and Bettendorf.

While her husband was signing autographs, answering phone calls, and meeting the president in San Francisco, Lynn tried to have a normal Monday at the Credit Island golf shop, but it was anything but normal. On the way to work, she couldn't "beg, borrow, or steal" the morning edition of the *Des Moines Register.* She took calls all day from people arranging the welcome celebration for her husband. It had been a hectic few days, and Lynn was both excited and bone tired.

The Chicago press was on hand to meet Fleck at daybreak, swarming the new Open champion in the airport terminal when he arrived from San Francisco. After accommodating the reporters and photographers with good-natured patience, Fleck and company boarded the small plane for the short flight home. It had been twelve days since he loaded his clubs and record player into the Buick and left Davenport on the solo trip to the coast. Now Fleck was flying in more ways than one.

En route to Mount Joy Airport, pilot Elliott invited a nearby aircraft to fly alongside the new National Open golf champion. Tell him all of Tulsa was rooting for him on Sunday, came the reply. Fleck finalized arrangements for his first exhibition by radio as the plane neared Davenport. He would play at Rock Island Arsenal Golf Club on Saturday at 2:00 P.M. with a group that included a local golf professional. Terms were set. Fleck would receive half of the gate. The plane descended and swung around for a view of area golf courses, including Duck Creek and Credit Island. As the plane

256

circled for landing, locals hoped Fleck would see the forty-foot banner that read in four-foot-high letters, WELCOME, CHAMP.

The small aircraft touched down and rolled to a stop near a hangar just north of the airport terminal. A banner strung to the hangar proclaimed, CONGRATULATIONS, WE'RE PROUD OF YOU, JACK. Below it was a twenty-foot-high cardboard putter. A thousand well-wishers, including the mayors of Davenport and Bettendorf and other dignitaries, cheered as Jack, wearing a white sweater and blue slacks, stepped out of the plane with Lynn and Craig. For the most part, he had kept his emotions in check since winning the Open. Now, standing on the plane's wing with his wife and son by his side, Fleck's eyes blurred with tears as he looked out on a large crowd that included his father, brothers, sisters, and friends. Many speeches followed until the man of honor was invited to say a few words. Holding Craig in his arms, with tears in his eyes, Jack thanked God, his family, everyone. As he stepped from the platform, he spotted his father, who was crying.

"I thought you forgot about me," Louis Fleck told his son.

"I love you, Dad," Jack said. The two embraced. "I could never forget you."

Then Jack and Lynn, pretty and prim in a dress, necklace, and hat, climbed into a two-door white Cadillac convertible, the lead car in a police-escorted motor caravan that cruised through the business districts of Davenport and Bettendorf. Banners that read WELCOME HOME JACK FLECK NATIONAL OPEN CHAMPION were draped on both sides of the sedan. Mr. and Mrs. Fleck perched themselves on top of the rear bench seat and waved to the men, women, and children gathered on the city sidewalks. The day was bright and the mood buoyant as the motorcade rolled toward its final stop on the homecoming tour, Credit Island Golf Course, where Fleck arrived to more cheers and signed autographs for the youth.

Later that day Fleck entered his house on East Street. He picked through a two-foot-high stack of telegrams. Overwhelmed with offers, he called Fred Corcoran and asked the PGA publicity man to help him with the crush of business and publicity opportunities. At 10:00 P.M. he fell into bed. He was home at last and looked forward to a sound night's sleep. His return would be brief. Jack and Lynn were leaving in the morning for New York City.

—18—

BANQUETS AND DEALS

Twenty-four hours after arriving home, Jack Fleck boarded a private plane to Chicago, where he would catch a flight to the Big Apple for a two-day business trip. He was a red-hot property. As a man of humble origins who had never earned more than a modest sum from golf, he was determined to cash in on the U.S. Open windfall and secure his family's immediate future. The afterglow of his stunning victory over Ben Hogan would soon fade.

On the Chicago–New York leg of the flight, a sportswriter approached Fleck and requested an interview. It wasn't a lucky coincidence. The New York scribe knew Fleck would be on the plane and asked the new champion about his life and golf career. When they landed at LaGuardia Field in New York City, the sportswriter asked Fleck to sign his name to authenticate the story. The sportswriter didn't want his boss to think he made it up—at least that's what he told Fleck.

Fleck's first meeting was with Vinnie Richards, president of Dunlop

Sport. He signed with the sporting goods maker and became its newest staff member. Richards would oversee most of Fleck's early business contracts, including exhibitions and charity events. The next day he and Richards entered the offices of the *Saturday Evening Post*. The popular weekly magazine was prepared to pay Fleck $10,000 to run a six-part life story about the new U.S. Open champion. There was a problem, however. They wanted an exclusive, a vice president explained, as he held up the morning newspaper. There was Fleck's life story and signature. There would be no lucrative deal with the magazine. He had been duped, later explaining that the *Saturday Evening Post* opportunity was common knowledge in journalism circles. Fleck confronted the sportswriter at a tournament soon after. "He just laughed," Fleck remembered, "and I said, 'You will be pushing up daisies before me!'" They were words he regretted because the man died within three months.

Fleck attended a large gala banquet of sports stars and other dignitaries put on by Dunlop Sport at Toots Shor's Restaurant, an establishment made famous by the celebrity in-crowd such as retired New York Yankees great Joe DiMaggio and show-business luminaries Frank Sinatra and Judy Garland. He enjoyed conversing with other golf pros and fielded questions from a gaggle of sportswriters. Dinner was served at 10:30 P.M., an hour at which he was normally asleep. He had unknowingly embarked on a long-running banquet schedule that would have an adverse effect on his well-ingrained eating and sleeping routines.

Fleck's instant fame thrust him into the limelight. In his two-day gallop through New York, he appeared on *The Ed Sullivan Show* and was a guest contestant on the new TV quiz show *The $64,000 Question*. He was DiMaggio's guest at Yankee Stadium as the Bronx Bombers marched toward another American League pennant. He also visited the USGA's Golf House to present his putter to the association's museum, although he planned to use it for the near future. A replica would be exhibited in its place. Featured later that year in a gift section of *Sports Illustrated*, the Bulls Eye model putter would be a hot item in golf pro shops thanks to Fleck's victory.

The *New Yorker* reported details of Fleck's visit in its "Talk of the Town" column, comparing him to movie star Gary Cooper—tall, slender, and soft-spoken. A magazine staffer was at the office of Endorsements Inc. on Forty-second Street and Fifth Avenue when Fleck, with Fred Corcoran at his side, signed one deal after another. Fleck asked the vice president of an advertising agency representing American Airlines what was required of him. Fleck looked at Corcoran, who nodded, and then signed the paperwork and shook hands with the advertising executive. An account executive for McGregor Drizzler jackets and slacks explained that Fleck would be the seventh U.S. Open champion to endorse the colorful line of jackets that required little or no ironing. The total deal came to $4,000: a $1,000 honorarium and ten exhibition matches at $300 apiece. Fleck said he didn't want the exhibitions to impede his preparation for next year's Open. About to sign, he leaned back in his chair and asked about "conservative" colors. Drizzlers come in all colors, he was told. What if he wanted to wear something besides a Drizzler jacket? Wear them or don't wear them, as you please. Fleck picked up the ballpoint pen and signed his name.

More people representing golf balls, golf gloves, and other products waited in the wings, but there were no cigarette or spirits makers since Fleck didn't smoke or drink.

"All this sure is a long way from playing golf," he remarked.

The words could have served as a headline for Fleck's next three years. Only a few days removed from his life-changing win, it was too soon to recognize how the new distractions and associated fame would put his golf game on a long downward slide.

•   •   •

That summer and fall Ben Hogan appeared in two major magazine stories. In the August 8 issue of *Life* that featured Hogan on the cover, the first was a story about his famous swing secret. A previous "secret" article, for which Hogan received the sum of $10,000, had been published in *Life* in April 1954. On this occasion, Hogan revealed the "mysterious maneuver that made him a champion." As Curt Sampson explained, there were three keys: a weakened left-hand grip, an open clubface on the backswing, and a cupped left wrist. All three were designed to prevent a hook, Hogan's curse on the long, practice-obsessed road to championship golf. The secret sold magazines but did little to help the majority of the nation's golfers, who desperately wanted to cure a slice, the opposite of a hook.

Hogan had gotten a lot of mileage from his secret, but it was the next major feature in the November 1 issue of *Look* that covered the equally compelling subject of why the nine-time major champion was hanging up the sticks. As told to Seth Kantor, Hogan summed up his career and disappointment at the Olympic Club in a piece titled "Why I Quit Tournament Golf." He covered the many sacrifices made on the way to the top of the golf world and paid homage to his wife, Valerie, who encouraged him when others told him to quit. The Hawk talked about his four-month preparation for the National Open—his single golf goal in 1955—and the deep disappointment when Fleck caught him to force the 18-hole playoff. Hogan admitted he thought he had won the tournament in regulation, adding that "a play off is always somewhat of a letdown." Of the pulled drive into the left-hand rough on the 18th, he said, "I accepted defeat with that shot."

Ben concluded that out of fairness to his friends and Valerie he would no longer play tournament golf. Despite the long bylined explanation—in essence Hogan's self-penned golf epitaph—Mrs. Hogan had been right when she told reporters in San Francisco that she couldn't imagine her husband leaving the game. The Hawk wasn't through.

. . .

The whirlwind continued when Fleck returned home. He played in back-to-back exhibitions at Rock Island Arsenal Golf Club across the river in Illinois and Hyperion Field Club in Des Moines. In Des Moines, he was paid a fee to hit golf balls from behind home plate at a night baseball game. Fans cheered as Fleck's 7-iron shots soared over the center-field fence. The following week he was feted at a civic banquet in the ballroom of the Hotel Blackhawk in downtown Davenport. Franklin "Whitey" Barnard, Fleck's boyhood friend and golf teammate at Davenport High, was among the honored guests as Fleck was presented with a new Cadillac, luggage, silverware, and other gifts from local citizens and the city's two newspapers. All of Iowa, it seemed, was proud of their fellow Hawk-eye who had won the land's most prestigious golf trophy. The *Des Moines Register* took the opportunity to laud Fleck on its editorial page, writing, "He came out of nowhere (as far as golfing fame is concerned) but played with a cool precision and perfection that it had taken almost twenty years of hard work, determination, and doing without to develop."

One week following his victory, the newspaper also published an expansive story titled HOW I WON THE OPEN—BY JACK FLECK. As told to Bert McGrane, Fleck talked about his shotmaking and the sudden putting transformation. He expressed regret that Hogan hit into the rough on the last hole of the playoff, beginning a half century of ambivalence about denying his idol a record-breaking fifth Open. He also alluded to the spiritual aspect of his amazing triumph. "There's no doubt about it. I had other help—Power—to carry me through to the win." However, there was no mention of the voice in the motel room. That would remain a secret for decades.

On July 11, Fleck, along with other sports stars such as baseball's Willie Mays and golf's Bobby Jones, arrived at the White House for a luncheon that marked the beginning of the President's Council on Physical Fitness and Sports. Arranged by an Iowa congressional representative, Fleck met with Vice President Richard Nixon prior to the luncheon. The golfer shared an idea with the vice president: The federal government could allow local and state governments to borrow funds to build and promote golf courses to increase recreational opportunities and enhance communities. Nixon said the idea would be a political disaster at the polls. In an ironic twist, more than fifteen years later Fleck began the design for a small golf course at President Nixon's western White House in San Clemente, California. Watergate later halted the project.

Fleck was seated two chairs to the right of President Eisenhower during the luncheon. On his left sat Bobby Jones. Two other golfers were in attendance: Lloyd Mangrum and amateur sensation Billy Joe Patton, who nearly won the Masters in 1954. Fleck would continue to cross paths with the president in the years to come.

One occasion would be a source of embarrassment. At the inaugural Palm Springs Golf Classic in 1960, later known as the Bob Hope Classic, Fleck had just completed play with Arnold Palmer and Gene Littler when a man wearing a fedora poked his head through the crowd.

"Hi, Jack!"

Startled while checking his scorecard, Fleck looked up and blurted, "Hi, Ike!"

The president was on hand to award the Eisenhower Trophy to the tournament winner. Fleck realized his breach of etiquette. The proper greeting was "Mr. President." Residing in Southern California at the time, he drove home, wrote a letter of apology, and mailed it to the president's winter home at the Eldorado Country Club in Palm Desert. He soon received a personal response from the president: Don't worry about it, Jack—I've been called a lot worse names.

Fleck returned from the nation's capitol in time to play in his first event since winning the U.S. Open, the Miller High Life Open in Milwaukee, Wisconsin. While he had been occupied with celebrations and business opportunities, his Buick in the care of Walker Inman had rolled to another victory. Dow Finsterwald, one of Inman's two car mates, won the British Columbia Open, his second title in five weeks. Finsterwald was moving up. Fleck, on the other hand, was in the early stages of a post-Open freefall. Rustiness from lack of practice and tournament competition can set in quickly, and it showed in Fleck's game as he missed the cut in Milwaukee. Cary Middlecoff won, one of six 1955 victories, arguably his finest season in a Hall of Fame career. A week later, Doug Ford, the other rider in Fleck's Buick, defeated Middlecoff in the 36-hole final to win the PGA Championship in Detroit. Fleck made it into the final sixteen before losing a match that would have put him into the quarterfinals.

* * *

Not long after winning the U.S. Open, Fleck signed a lucrative contract with the Nadco Sporting Goods Company to be the first player representative for golf equipment. Nadco was new in the golf business, and although Fleck cherished his Hogan clubs, he also wanted to benefit financially while his stardom peaked. Nadco gave him a base salary and would match all monies he won on the PGA Tour, including bonuses for high finishes at the majors. He also would receive a percentage of all purchases made by club professionals, amounting to a cut of all sales since Nadco clubs were only sold in golf pro shops.

Despite the financial upside and excitement of representing a new company, Nadco turned into a fiasco. The big four equipment companies—Wilson, MacGregor, Spalding, and Hillerich & Bradsby—were not eager to welcome a newcomer to the party. In addition, True Temper Company, makers of golf's best club shafts, would not do business with Nadco, a devastating blow since no other shafts on the market matched True Temper's quality. The inferior shafts in Nadco's clubs would bend after a short while, forcing Fleck to abandon the new sticks and return to his Hogan clubs prior to the 1956 U.S. Open. Nadco soon closed its doors and brought a multimillion-dollar lawsuit against the big four and True Temper. An out-of-court settlement was reached a few years later. After the Nadco disaster, Fleck signed with Spalding.

.   .   .

There was one last banquet to attend in 1955, a December sports gala put on by the *Los Angeles Times* during which Fleck was honored as the professional golfer of the year. The banquet room of the Hollywood Palladium was filled to capacity as Fleck and other award recipients from the world of sports sat at a long table on the dais. Fleck and pole vaulter Bob Richards, an Olympic gold medal winner at the 1952 Helsinki games, would be the last athletes to receive their awards. Then came the part that petrified the man who as a boy loathed standing at the front of the class: Their short acceptance speeches would be seen on television. The eyes of hundreds of banquet attendees and countless TV viewers would be fixed on the shy Iowan who abhorred speech giving.

"I died a thousand deaths that night," he recalled, although others said he did fine delivering his brief remarks.

The U.S. Open crown that had brought so many good things into Fleck's life and assured his place in golf was also an uncomfortable fit. He was a quiet, solitary man who didn't enjoy making small talk or eating late dinners in revolving social settings. Fame came with the new territory, but it was an alien land in which he had lost his bearings. The intense routine of practice, diet, yoga, and rest that had made the major breakthrough possible was broken. The putting touch that helped carry him to victory had left him. There was also an invisible burden that would grow heavier as his game sagged. Fleck hadn't just won the Open; he had beaten a legend. With his historic win over the great Ben Hogan came a world of expectations that would be impossible for the Iowa pro to fulfill.

— 19 —

CHERRY HILLS

Jack Fleck, it seemed, had left his golf game in San Francisco. With his attention diverted to the bounty of outings, exhibitions, and other money opportunities, his tournament golf floundered for much of the next three seasons. The luster of his phenomenal U.S. Open triumph faded and was replaced by criticism of his poor play. Some in the media resented him for beating Ben Hogan, and his worthiness as a national champion became a topic of discussion in the golf world.

"Although he won the tournament and beat everybody, they were not really for it too much," said ninety-two-year-old Tommy Bolt a few months before his death in 2008. "The sportswriters didn't like it too much."

If it was hard to beat a legend, Fleck was learning it was harder still to earn credit for the monumental win.

"No one ever beat another man—a man who had cheated death and become an icon—so many other people were rooting for," later wrote *Golf World*'s Bill Fields.

For understandable reasons, the 1955 U.S. Open would be characterized as Hogan's tragedy, the historic one that got away. It was Hogan's loss, not Fleck's win, regarded by some as a fluke. It would dog Fleck for years to come.

After the post–U.S. Open honeymoon ended, Fleck's relationship with the press soured. "Fleck wasn't the easiest guy to be around," later said Stan Wood, the *Los Angeles Mirror-News* reporter who was with Hogan in the locker room at Olympic when Fleck sank the tying putt. "He was a very quiet guy and he didn't get too much publicity—none of which was exceptionally pleasing to him."

Mike Krak and Walker Inman, two of the players closest to Fleck, were well aware of the champion's uneasy relationship with the ink slingers.

"In all fairness," Krak said in recent years, "Jack's personality killed him." Krak suggested that Fleck could have bought the sportswriters champagne and called himself "the luckiest guy in the world" like Tony Lema did after winning the 1964 British Open. "He got to where he could not stand the press because they disliked him for beating Hogan."

Inman had a more sympathetic view, saying, "He was a good player.... They never gave him credit for that. I think Jack, over the years, never liked the press very much. He just thought they never gave him credit for being as good a player as he really was."

"I think he has kind of gotten knocked for a lot of things," Bob Rosburg said not long before his death in 2009. "He was the guy who beat Hogan, and everybody wanted Hogan to win. I think Jack took a pretty tough time about that."

. . .

In April of 1956, along with his friend Walker Inman, Fleck made his first trip to Augusta National Golf Club for the Masters. He finished in a tie for forty-third and broke his trusty Tommy Armour driver in the process, a bad omen for a golf game already in decline. It would take him a year to find a suitable replacement. Jack Burke Jr. won the Green Jacket, making up 7 shots with a 71 in a final round during which the wind gusted up to 50 mph through the Georgia pines. Just as he had every year since the automobile accident, Ben Hogan turned up at Augusta, finishing in a tie for eighth. It had been a short retirement.

For Fleck, reigning U.S. Open champion, playing in the Masters for the first time was an honor. For Inman, the first Augusta native to play in the Masters, it was the pilgrimage of his short lifetime. He worshipped Bobby Jones and the course and tournament Jones had created. Now twenty-six-year-old Inman had the privilege to tee it up with golf's best players on Augusta's hallowed ground. His head was swimming as he approached the first tee and saw a few thousand fans.

"It was like teeing off in front of everybody I knew," he later said.

So nervous was Inman that he had a modest wish as he bent over to stick his tee in the ground. Don't miss the ball. Hit it anywhere on the clubface. He exceeded his goal, sending a solid drive 270 yards down the middle of the lush fairway. He followed with a 6-iron to the middle of the large green and sank a 30-foot putt for a birdie. The nerves left him.

"Shoot, there's nothing to this," he thought. "I thought this was going to be hard."

As he stepped through the ropes and onto the 2nd tee, there sat Jones and Masters Tournament chairman Clifford Roberts in a golf cart. Roberts stepped out of the cart and walked over to Inman.

"Walker," Roberts said, "Mr. Jones and I are very happy to have an

Augusta boy playing in our tournament for the first time. Mr. Jones would like to watch you play a few holes. Do you mind?"

Inman wasn't about to say no to his father's fraternity brother, the great man who made it possible to fulfill his long-held dream of playing in the Masters. He would have to play under the gaze of the golf legend, a realization that sent his nervous system into overdrive.

"Now all of a sudden my nervousness comes back and I've got to perform for the best player that's ever walked around."

Roberts and Jones watched on several holes of the opening 9, and Inman went on to card a respectable 1-over 73. Conditions toughened, and Inman finished in a tie for twenty-ninth after 3-putting numerous times in howling winds during the final round. A finish in the top twenty-five would have earned him a return invitation.

"I thought I'd be there many more times," he said. "Of course, it never happened anymore, but . . . that's a memory I'll always have."

.   .   .

For the first time in his career, Fleck didn't have to qualify for the National Open. The 1956 U.S. Open was set to be played at Oak Hill Country Club in Rochester, New York, the club's first of several U.S. Opens and PGA Championships. As he prepared to defend his title, Fleck put away the Nadco clubs with the unreliable shafts and reached for his Hogans. Oak Hill wasn't Olympic, and he couldn't find the groove that had vaulted him to the top of the golf world in San Francisco. He missed the 36-hole cut by a stroke.

After completing his final round of 70, Cary Middlecoff was a nervous leader in the clubhouse at 1-over 281. An all too familiar player was stalking him—the Hawk. Tied for the lead on the 71st hole, Hogan, using a new blade putter, stepped away from a 3-foot par putt. Although he had made a number of lengthy putts on Oak Hill's undulating greens, the short ones bedeviled him. He returned to his ball on the 17th green and missed another one. With a par at the final hole, Hogan's bid for the record Open title fell 1 stroke short, a runner-up finish for the second consecutive year. Thirteen thousand fans applauded Ben Hogan as he walked to the clubhouse, wondering if there would be another chance at history for the aging great.

Promising signs reappeared for Fleck at the Motor City Open played near Detroit later that summer. A Donald Ross design, the Western Golf and Country Club was a tough track that yielded few sub-70 scores. Julius Boros withdrew after rounds of 76 and 75. Arnold Palmer left a day earlier after opening with 77. Fleck had a penchant for tight championship courses, and his 70-71-72 placed him among the leaders going into the final round. He played steady golf and came to the final green needing to hole a 4-foot putt to gain a spot in a playoff. He missed it. Bob Rosburg beat Ed Furgol on the first hole of sudden death. Fleck finished alone in third. It was the last time anyone would see Jack Fleck in contention for a long while.

During the 1959 season, nearly four years after his remarkable playoff victory over Hogan, Fleck's name reappeared on leaderboards. The post-Open circus was over, and his focus had returned to his golf game. He was enjoying practice and competition again, and good results followed. Fleck shot a 12-under total of 276 to finish third behind winner Ernie Vossler and runner-up John McMullin at the Tijuana Open in January. He posted his best finish at the Masters, a tie for eighteenth, and tied for nineteenth at the U.S. Open at Winged Foot, where short-game wizard Billy Casper won. That fall Fleck made noise in Southern California. At the Hesperia Open in mid-October, he was the first-round leader with a 66 and went on to tie for second, finishing ahead of Casper and Gene Littler. The following week he posted another runner-up finish at the Orange County Open won by Jay Hebert.

Good scores and high finishes had restored Fleck's confidence. His ball striking was back, but he continued to struggle with the putter. He dared to think about winning. Another victory would prove he wasn't a one-hit wonder and perhaps silence the disturbing comments he had heard in the years since his stunning breakthrough at the Olympic Club.

*　　*　　*

Busy running his golf equipment company and building a sprawling white brick home near Shady Oaks Country Club, the creation of long-time friend and business mogul Marvin Leonard, Hogan still played a limited schedule on the PGA Tour. At the beginning of 1959, after two substandard seasons, Hogan didn't look like his old self. He just looked old. Players noticed and were surprised to see the man they had measured their games against for more than a decade struggle on the fairways. At the Masters where Art Wall Jr. won by making up a 6-shot deficit with a 66 in the final round, the Hawk finished a distant thirtieth. He hadn't won a tournament since 1953, the immortalizing three-major season that ended with a ticker-tape parade on Broadway in New York City. That spring there was no reason to believe he would ever win again.

A few weeks later Hogan shot a course-record 63 at Colonial Country Club in a practice round. Sounding his return as a serious contender, the four-time winner of the Colonial National Invitational opened with rounds of 69 and 67 in his hometown tournament. Three-putting five times, the forty-six-year-old champion wobbled to a 77 in the third round. This was Colonial, though, and a Texas-sized wind was blowing. No one was tearing it up. Hogan rebounded with a 72 in the final round to tie Fred Hawkins at 5-over 285. The two men met in an 18-hole playoff and 40 mph winds the next day.

"I shot 73," Hawkins later said, "which is a pretty good score."

It wasn't good enough to beat Hogan's 69.

"He said it was the best round he ever played under those conditions," Hawkins added.

•   •   •

Site of the 1960 U.S. Open, Cherry Hills Country Club, located in the Denver suburbs, had hosted the national championship once before. It was in 1938 when Ralph Guldahl won his second consecutive Open during a three-year span of brilliance that saw him collect two National Opens, two Western Opens, and a Masters. Playing to a par of 71, Cherry Hills measured 7,004 yards but would play a few hundred yards shorter due to the mile-high altitude. Long hitters in the field of 150 professionals and amateurs hoped to take advantage of Cherry Hills, but, as with all Open courses, trouble lurked for those who strayed from the fairways.

The tournament favorite at 4–1 was Arnold Palmer. Palmer had won seventeen tournaments since his first victory at the 1955 Canadian Open, including the 1958 and 1960 Masters. He had already notched five wins that season in Palm Springs, San Antonio, Baton Rouge, Pensacola, and Augusta. His all-American good looks and pants-hitching go-for-broke style of play had elevated golf's popularity during a period when the number of household televisions and hours of television coverage were on a steady rise. After the second win at Augusta, *Life* magazine declared that Arnold Palmer had replaced Ben Hogan and Sam Snead as golf's biggest star. Palmer's charisma and star power put him in the same company as sports heroes like baseball's Mickey Mantle and Willie Mays and football's Johnny Unitas. Not only was Arnold good and good-looking, he was rich and famous. He had signed with Mark McCormack, a Cleveland lawyer turned sports agent, and was on his way to becoming one of sports' greatest pitch men.

Palmer had yet to win a U.S. Open, something he had dreamed of since he was a young boy roaming the fairways of Latrobe Country Club in western Pennsylvania, where his father was head pro and greens-keeper. So Arnold took the measure of Cherry Hills, rifling drives and irons through the thin Colorado air with his muscular, slashing swing in preparation for another national title bid. He had something to prove.

The man whose record and game still garnered Palmer's deep respect arrived outside of Denver just two months shy of his forty-eighth birthday. Five years after his throat-catching retirement announcement on the 8th green at the Olympic Club, Ben Hogan remained on the hunt for the elusive fifth U.S. Open. As Palmer slipped into his second green jacket that April, Hogan returned to Fort Worth after a sixth-place finish at the Masters. At the Memphis Open Invitational, in a final tune-up before the Open, Hogan caught Tommy Bolt and Gene Littler with a clutch birdie on the final hole and narrowly lost the next day to Bolt in an 18-hole playoff. The old man's ball striking was still splendid; his short putting was still suspect. Putting aside, Cherry Hills would present another challenge for the limping, chain-smoking golf legend. The high altitude would rob his body of oxygen, causing shortness of breath and giving him headaches. The USGA set up temporary facilities around the course where players could receive oxygen. Nearly one in three players used them. It was just one more in a long list of things the Hawk had to endure to play major championship golf. Nothing had stopped him, for golf itself was like oxygen to Ben Hogan.

The era of top amateurs contending at majors was fading from view. Amateur stalwarts such as Harvie Ward, Ken Venturi, and Billy Joe Patton—the latter two of whom nearly won the Masters—were now a rarity. There was, however, one exceptional amateur at Cherry Hills, a chubby twenty-year-old man-child from Columbus, Ohio, named Jack Nicklaus who idolized Bobby Jones and feared no one on a golf course. Nicklaus had first competed against professionals at the precocious age of eighteen at the 1958 Rubber City Open. He finished twelfth. The following year he won the U.S. Amateur. While Palmer and others sized up Cherry Hills and the professional competition, the pudgy amateur with a crew cut was launching drives over the practice-range fence. Palmer, Hogan, and everyone else were soon to find out that Jack Nicklaus possessed the raw talent to overpower golf courses and the game's best players. As authors Curt Sampson, James Dodson, and Ian O'Connor duly noted, golf's past, present, and future had assembled on the edge of the Rockies in the persons of Hogan, Palmer, and Nicklaus. An epic Western showdown was about to commence.

•   •   •

Jack Fleck arrived at Cherry Hills with reason for optimism. Nineteen fifty-nine had been the forerunner to what was shaping up as his best season on tour. In January, he rolled into the parking lot of the Phoenix Country Club for the $22,500 Phoenix Open. He would walk off with the trophy and the winner's check for $3,150. Fleck posted an 11-under total of 273, including a 66 in the final round, and then waited as Bill Collins came in to tie him. The two faced off the next day in an 18-hole playoff. Making clutch birdies on the last three holes, Fleck won 68 to 71. The long and often painful wait for a follow-up victory was finally over. He had returned from "semi-oblivion," as one golf sketch artist termed it in a welcome-back cartoon published later that season.

In March at the $15,000 St. Petersburg Open, where five years earlier he had spied the Hogan irons in Skip Alexander's pro shop, Fleck caught George Bayer at the end of regulation play. In the final round, played on Monday because of a weather delay, Fleck's 69 was bested by only one player. Had his putter not failed him—he 3-putted three of the last five greens—he could have won outright. Both players missed the green in 2 shots on the first hole of the sudden-death playoff. Fleck was away and pitched his ball stiff for a certain par. Six feet five inches and 230 pounds, the hulking Bayer delicately pitched over a mound and into the cup for a birdie to claim his third victory on tour. Fleck agonized about his blown opportunity. At thirty-eight, he was playing the best tournament golf of his life and had climbed to second on the money list behind Palmer. His failure to convert short putts was a persistent flaw in an otherwise solid golf game.

After a so-so thirty-fourth-place tie at the Masters, Fleck again threatened at the $35,000 Houston Open. He was tied for the halfway lead with Palmer and Collins after rounds of 68 and 69. He fell 3 shots off leader Collins's pace in a third round that drew a record Texas gallery of thirty thousand. His final-round 72 left him 1 stroke shy of an 18-hole playoff with Collins and Palmer, which Collins won, 69 to 71.

During a practice round at Cherry Hills, Shelley Mayfield witnessed the premium brand of ball striking that was propelling Fleck to the top of leaderboards during the 1960 season. A club professional at the Meadow Brook Club on Long Island who no longer played the tour on a regular basis, Mayfield flew to Denver and arrived at Cherry Hills late on the Monday afternoon before Thursday's opening round. He looked around for a practice partner, and there was Fleck, alone, on the putting green.

"Jack," Mayfield said, "I'm going to go a fast 18. Want to join me?"

"Sure," Fleck replied.

The two men gathered their clubs and caddies, and off they went.

Mayfield recalled the 9th hole of that practice round nearly fifty years later. Measuring 430 yards, the uphill par 4 doglegged right and played long despite the thin air. Both players hit solid drives. Mayfield was the first to play his approach shot, a 2-iron that made the green. Fleck also chose a 2-iron and struck a solid shot that flew straight as a clothesline for the distant green. The ball landed just short of the putting surface and bounced hard and high, flying over the green into a hedge near the clubhouse.

"Jack, did you see that?" Mayfield asked. "What in the world happened?"

"I don't know."

"Drop another one, hit another one."

Fleck reloaded and executed the same shot. The ball landed in the same spot and bounded high into the air and over the green. Mayfield couldn't believe his eyes. When the two players arrived at the front edge of the green, they discovered the sprinkler head that Fleck had hit on consecutive shots.

"That is almost an impossibility," Mayfield later said, "but he did it there two in a row. I know Jack Fleck hit a lot of good shots, no question about that."

After they finished their practice round, Mayfield found USGA executive director Joe Dey and told him about Fleck's two direct hits on the sprinkler head at the 9th green. Soon after, tournament officials laid a small piece of rug over the sprinkler head for the duration of the championship.

.   .   .

As the tournament got under way and a record first-round gallery of more than fourteen thousand streamed onto Cherry Hills, some wondered if Hogan's 72-hole record of 276 set in 1948 would fall. Hogan himself had issued his verdict on the course after his fastidious practice sessions: "Too easy." He didn't believe the par-71 layout's generous fairways and shallow rough were up to Open standards. Maybe so, or maybe the Hawk was up to his old mind games, as Cary Middlecoff suggested with a smile. At least one player agreed with Hogan's assessment—Jack Fleck.

Hogan needed 75 strokes on Thursday. His putting was atrocious. At the par-4 9th hole, he hooked his tee shot into the gallery, striking a man in the stomach. By day's end, he trailed first-round leader Mike Souchak by 7 shots. Big Mike, who had won earlier that season in San Diego, only needed 24 putts on his way to a 68 that gave him a 1-stroke lead on short-game magician Jerry Barber and forty-nine-year-old Henry Ransom. Thanks to a recent putting lesson from Burke, Souchak carried a new stroke and a prayer: The former Duke defensive end tucked a Jesuit prayer in his money clip for good luck. Reigning U.S. Amateur champion Nicklaus matched Cherry Hills's par of 71, as did Dow Finsterwald, Billy Casper, and Ken Venturi. Sam Snead, who skipped his ball across the moat guarding the 17th's island green and made birdie, signed for a 72.

Doug Sanders was not as fortunate with the water. The short-swinging Georgia native needed a par on the final hole to tie Souchak for the lead. Instead, Sanders walked off with a double bogey and a 70 after a fish in the lake bordering the 18th fairway startled him midswing. The fish jumped and Doug jerked, sending his ball into the water.

"I thought for a minute somebody was unloading a truckload of empty beer cans," he quipped.

A jumping fish was no competition for the antics of Tommy Bolt. The 1958 U.S. Open champion was ready to explode when he reached the 18th tee. The fuse had been lit early on the back 9 when Bolt drove out of bounds on the par-5 11th and dunked his ball in the water at the par-3 12th, taking a triple bogey. He had gone out in even-par 35. On the incoming 9, he was en route to a ridiculous 45. At 18, his misery nearly over, Bolt yanked his tee shot into the lake. He teed another ball and again put it into the water. His third tee shot found the fairway. Satisfied he could play that one, Bolt wound up. As he drew back his driver, playing partner Claude Harmon shielded himself as best he could. With a loud cry and mighty sling, Bolt heaved the wooden club into the lake. Soon after, a ten-year-old boy dove into the lake and retrieved the club. The gallery cheered as the dripping boy and amused Bolt approached each other, but the kid gave the golfer a fake and ran off with the prized possession. After signing for an 80, the man known as "Thunder Bolt" withdrew from the tournament.

*   *   *

Fleck was grouped with Palmer and Middlecoff for the first two rounds. Palmer was mad from the start. He attempted to drive the 346-yard par-4 1st hole, a successful strategy in two practice rounds. His first swing of the tournament steered his golf ball into Little Dry Creek to the right of the fairway. After taking a drop and 1-stroke penalty, Palmer hit a tree, flew his next shot over the green, chipped on, and holed a 5-footer for a double bogey. Fumes trailed off him as he left the green barking at his caddie, Bob Blair.

At some point early on, Fleck intervened. "Arnie, it's just the beginning of the tournament. You've got to settle down." Later he said, "Maybe I should have kept my mouth shut."

Palmer got enough of a grip on his emotions and game to shoot a 1-over 72. Fleck shot a 70, tying him with Sanders, Gary Player, and amateur Don Cherry. Two-time Open champion Middlecoff was not on his game, headed for a forty-third-place finish.

His putter still hot, Souchak continued his assault on Cherry Hills with a 67 in the second round. His two-round total of 135 shattered Snead's 36-hole scoring record of 138 set at Riviera in 1948. The long-hitting thirty-three-year-old pro only used his driver six times.

"I played the first two rounds with him," Bob Rosburg later said, "and he was leading by quite a bit. But he should have been leading by more. Mike, when he got going, was a great player."

Souchak would head into Saturday's 36-hole finale with a 3-shot lead over Sanders, who carded a 68 for 138. Three players were 5 shots back at 140: Barber, Dow Finsterwald, and Fleck. Snead, Casper, Cherry, and Ted Kroll were at 141. After another 71, Nicklaus was tied at 142 with Julius Boros and a resurgent Hogan, whose 67 tied him with Souchak and Rex Baxter for low round of the day. No one would go lower at Cherry Hills.

Somehow the Hawk had put together another brilliant round at the U.S. Open. After Thursday's dismal 75, he raced to a 32 on the outgoing 9 and came home in 35 to put himself within shouting distance of Souchak's lead. Even the old man's putting woes disappeared for a day: He needed just 28 putts. Playing partner Finsterwald, who was no slouch with a 69, termed Hogan's performance "one of the best rounds of golf I ever saw." Hogan called Finsterwald "a magician on the greens." Perhaps Finsterwald's best trick was to birdie two of the closing holes after his temperamental caddie quit on the 14th hole following heated words with his employer. A Portland, Oregon, sports broadcaster ducked under the ropes and carried Finsterwald's clubs the rest of the way. In his usual deep trance, the Hawk might have missed the whole thing.

·   ·   ·

Saturday's morning round teed off under a cloudless Colorado sky. An eleven-time winner on tour, Souchak had yet to win a major. His best finish was a third-place tie in the previous year's Open at Winged Foot. Some wondered how big Mike would hold up under the pressure, especially with the added burden of leading the tournament since Thursday.

Rosburg, in fact, approached Fleck at dinner on Friday night and quietly expressed confidence in his chances. "Jack, you're in great position to win another Open."

It caught Fleck off guard. "Souchak's way out there," he replied.

Rossie told Fleck not to worry about Souchak or Sanders. They didn't have what it took to win an Open.

Souchak was going along nicely at even par for his round until he reached the long 18th hole. His lead was 4 shots when he arrived at the tee. It had shrunk to 2 when he walked off the green. Souchak's unraveling began with the tee shot. A spectator had a camera, a no-no, and snapped it at the worst possible moment—in the middle of Mike's backswing. He misfired and finished with a double bogey for a 73. He was so mad he couldn't eat lunch. Carding a 77, Sanders was freefalling to a tie for forty-sixth after starting the day alone in second. Souchak and Sanders were Cherry Hills' tragic couple.

Souchak's flub of the 18th hole brought eight players to within 4 shots of his 54-hole lead. Finsterwald, who was paired with Fleck for the final 36, was 2 back after a 70. Barber and Boros, whose 68 was the lowest third-round score, joined Finsterwald 2 shots off the pace. Nicklaus and Hogan, the day's most interesting pairing, both fashioned 69s and trailed by 3. Another shot back were Fleck, Cherry, and Johnny Pott. Heading into the final round, the U.S. Open was wide open.

After a morning round of 72 that left him 7 shots behind, no one thought Palmer had a chance except Palmer.

"I never ruled out the possibility of winning," he later said. "Until it was figuratively impossible, I always thought I had a shot."

Fourteen players, including three U.S. Open champions, were ahead of Palmer, who was doing math in the locker room between rounds. Nearby were two players, Rosburg and Venturi, and two reporters, Bob

Drum of the *Pittsburgh Press* and Dan Jenkins of the *Fort Worth Star-Telegram*. Palmer reasoned that if he could drive the 1st green, which he had failed to do in the first three rounds, "I might shoot a hell of a score." A 65, he noted, would give him a total of 280.

"Doesn't 280 always win the Open?" Palmer asked.

"Yeah, when Hogan shoots it," Jenkins replied.

Palmer angrily tossed aside his cheeseburger and headed to the range to pound balls.

· · ·

The man to whom Jenkins referred sipped soup and iced tea for lunch. Before his 1:30 P.M. tee time, Hogan washed up, combed his hair, resecured the elastic support wraps on his legs, changed his socks, and took an aspirin. The Hawk had hit all 18 greens in regulation in the morning round, an uncanny shotmaking display that had the large galleries again pondering a fabled fifth Open.

Playing two groups ahead of Palmer, Hogan split the 1st fairway with a 3-wood and proceeded through the front 9 in a machinelike cadence of fairways and greens. The only distraction was a news helicopter that hovered a little too close to the action, which, at Hogan's request, officials shooed away. Hogan made all pars on the outward 9, but he was losing ground to his playing partner. Young Nicklaus was demonstrating supreme talent and the kind of resolve under pressure that would soon catapult him to the top of the golf world. Buoyed by an eagle at the par-5 5th hole, he opened with a 3-under 32 to reach 5 under for the championship. In what would be a dizzying afternoon of lead changes, the Ohio State golfer had pulled even with Souchak.

· · ·

At 1:42 P.M., wearing a white shirt and light gray slacks, a visor atop his head, Palmer gripped his beloved Hogan driver. Paul Harney, a three-time winner on tour, stood to the side of the cherry-shaped tee markers holding the sensible choice, a 2-iron. The 1st hole called for a long iron or fairway wood and a simple pitch. Harney had seen the driver strategy hours earlier in the morning round. It hadn't worked. He thought Palmer was nuts.

Others shared Harney's view as Palmer stepped up to the ball like a strongman preparing to swing the mallet and ring the bell at the county carnival. He ripped into the ball with brute force and desperation. The ball flew on target in a slight right-to-left arc, landed in the rough that fronted the green, and leaped forward, rolling to a stop on the green's fringe 30 feet from the cup. The greenside gallery roared as Palmer charged off the tee and practically ran toward his eagle putt. He missed his bid for a deuce and, rushing, nearly lipped out the short birdie putt. He was off to the races.

At the par-4 2nd hole, he chipped in from 35 feet for a birdie. At the short par-4 3rd, he struck a wedge to within a foot of the cup for another birdie. He then rolled in an 18-footer on the long par-4 4th for his fourth consecutive birdie. Drum, flushed and out of breath, arrived at the 6th tee to see what all the commotion was about. A lightning storm of birdies had jolted the high country. Arnie's Army was enlisting hundreds of new recruits.

"I knew I'd have to do something sensational to get your fat ass out here," Palmer said to Drum.

He then birdied the 6th hole from 25 feet and flipped his visor into the warm mountain air. Another birdie against a lone bogey gave him a 5-under 30 on the front 9. Palmer's pedal-to-the-metal play had brought him to 3 under for the championship and within an eyelash of the lead.

•   •   •

If Palmer was desperate to catch up, then Souchak was anxious to hang on. The Palmer birdie roars seemed to goad him into a strategic blunder. Knowing that Arnold had driven the 1st green, big Mike grabbed his driver on the 1st tee even though he had hit his 4-wood in every round. Souchak's wallop drifted right and landed in the same creek Palmer had visited in round one. Counting the 18th in the morning round, it was Mike's second consecutive double bogey. He had thrown away 4 shots in 2 holes. He rebounded with two birdies, but a bogey at the 9th knocked him out of the lead for the first time since Thursday.

While Nicklaus and Palmer were charging and Souchak was faltering, another pairing was moving up the leaderboard. Finsterwald was among the leaders until he hit his tee shot under a pine tree at the 9th and took a double bogey. He lost another stroke with a 3-putt on the 10th. Meanwhile, his playing partner was spurting. If Arnold and his Army had left the front nine in ruins, then Fleck, playing two groups behind Palmer, had gathered up the spoils, birdieing five of the first 6 holes. At the par-4 7th, he failed from 6 feet to drop another birdie. He bunkered his tee shot at the long par-3 8th and, bothered by a photographer's camera click, blasted out 6 feet from the hole and missed his par putt. Nonetheless, with 10 holes left to play, Fleck was tied for the lead.

•   •   •

On the 13th green, Nicklaus held a 1-stroke lead over Palmer, Boros, and Fleck and was 2 strokes ahead of Hogan. The kid from Columbus stood over a 12-foot birdie putt to go 2 up in his bid to be the first amateur to win the U.S. Open in twenty-seven years. His birdie attempt slipped 18 inches by the hole. The remains of a ball mark were between his ball and the cup, but Nicklaus was too embarrassed to ask Hogan if it was permissible to repair the indentation. Nicklaus feared the golf legend would belittle him for not knowing the rules. He putted and missed. Bogey. Four players were now tied for the lead. Four more, including Hogan, had a chance. Three-putting from 40 feet, Nicklaus made another bogey at the 14th and trailed by a shot. Tied for the lead at 4 under, Palmer was content to make pars as he crept closer to the clubhouse and the growing possibility of his first national title.

Hogan had put on a clinic that day, arguably his finest shotmaking in 19 U.S. Open appearances. Through the 12th hole of the final round, he had hit every green in regulation on Saturday—30 in all. At the 13th, where his inexperienced playing partner missed the 18-inch putt, Hogan hit the flagstick with his approach shot. Instead of being inches away for a certain birdie, the ball caromed off the flagstick and rolled 10 feet from the cup. After freezing over the putt, he pulled the trigger and missed. The Hawk was running out of holes and U.S. Opens. He parred 14, tying Nicklaus, one shot off the lead. Then he struck a long iron onto the green of the 196-yard par-3 15th. His ball was not close—in the 15–20 foot range—yet this time he summoned a stroke that rolled the ball into the hole for a deuce, only his second birdie of the final round. With 3 holes to play, Hogan was tied for the lead with Palmer and the giant killer—Fleck.

. . .

The 13th hole was a relatively short, straightaway par 4 with a sloping postage-stamp green. A ditch crossed the fairway about 270 yards from the tee. After a solid tee shot, Fleck landed his short approach 7 feet beyond the cup, a downhill birdie putt to seize sole possession of the lead. He stroked the slippery putt and watched it slide by the hole. Then, like Nicklaus twenty minutes earlier, he flubbed the tiniest of putts and made a bogey. Now Palmer and Hogan were alone at the top of the leaderboard.

Up ahead, Hogan lined up a 12-foot birdie putt on the par-4 16th hole, where a player named Ray Ainsley took 19 shots in the 1938 U.S. Open. Still battling, Nicklaus was less than 6 feet away. Both players missed their birdies, and Hogan, long demonized with the putting affliction known as the yips, froze over the tap-in before ramming it into the cup. The Hawk still held a share of the lead with Palmer with 2 holes to play. Nicklaus, Boros, and Fleck were one back.

Standing on the 17th tee, puffing on a cigarette, Hogan knew he co-led the Open but was surprised when he learned the identity of the other leader from a spectator. Palmer.

"He's not a contender, is he?" Hogan asked.

It was nearing 5:00 P.M., growing late for the Hawk in more ways than one. For the hobbled, nerve-frayed forty-seven-year-old, it had all the markings of his last hurrah, a fitting last chapter in a mythic career. A tie would mean an 18-hole playoff, an unsatisfactory option for the old man with bad legs and a broken putting stroke. Hogan knew he needed a birdie, and the 548-yard par 5 that stretched out before him was the last realistic opportunity. He drove in the fairway and laid up with a 3-iron, leaving 50 yards to the island green fronted by a 12-foot-wide moat. Nicklaus also laid up. (Going for the green in 2 was beyond bold, but Cherry later tried at a juncture when a birdie would have tied him for the lead. His daring 3-wood shot rolled into the moat. He recorded a double bogey and went on to finish in a tie for ninth.)

The hole was cut 12 feet from the front edge of the green. The hardened putting surface sloped toward the water. It was a dangerous shot, and Nicklaus, in no mood to gamble on getting it close to the pin, hit his pitch 20 feet past the hole. Palmer watched from the 17th tee as Hogan made his final mental calculations and settled over the ball. A hint of a breeze blew against him as the Hawk struck the half-wedge shot exactly as planned. It looked good in the air, and the gallery began applauding before the ball made landfall. Nicklaus later noted he thought Hogan's pitch was going to be perfect. The ball hit short of the green and bounced on, but tremendous backspin abruptly stopped its forward momentum. Like a yo-yo at the end of its string, the ball spun backward. After pausing for an instant on the top of the bank, the ball trickled down the slope and disappeared into the water. On a shot with virtually no margin for error if he wanted to get the ball close enough to the hole for a kick-in birdie, Hogan had hit his wedge shot a fraction short. He stared in disbelief.

"When that happened, Hogan deflated like a balloon," Nicklaus later said.

The gallery gasped and grieved. Standing nearby behind the ropes, Hogan friend Marty Leonard, Marvin's daughter, turned her head and cried, as did other stunned fans. For all intents and purposes, the 71st fairway of the 1960 U.S. Open marked the end of the legend's competitive career.

* * *

After pars at 14 and 15, Fleck struck his approach shot at the par-4 16th to within 15 feet of the hole. It was a level putt, not much to it. If he could sink it, he'd tie Palmer for the lead at 4 under. He missed. Then he missed the next one, too, a 3-putt bogey. The final-round charge that vaulted him into a share of the lead had fizzled.

* * *

A stroke behind Palmer, Hogan's only faint hope was to manufacture a birdie on the 468-yard par-4 finishing hole. He had gamely removed his shoe and sock near the 17th green and splashed his fourth shot out of the moat, but the downhill 12-foot par putt didn't fall. In a bold attempt to set up a shorter approach shot on the long uphill 18th, Hogan took the most direct route across the lake from the tee. The ball curved gently from right to left and splashed down a few feet from the fairway. For 34 holes the Hawk had been perfect, hitting every green in regulation on the final day of the U.S. Open. Then, gambling for a win for the ages, he had steered his ball into the water on the 71st and 72nd holes. It was almost too painful to watch. He took an ignominious triple bogey at the last hole and limped off the stage to prolonged applause. It was over. Hogan would make a few curtain calls but never again threaten to win a National Open.

.   .   .

After seeing Hogan in the moat, Palmer recorded another routine par. "I knew that I had a shot if I didn't screw up the last two holes," he said. He hit a 1-iron off the final tee followed by a 4-iron shot that landed left of the 18th green. Palmer chipped on and sank a 3-foot par putt for a 65 and a 72-hole total of 280, the exact numbers he had envisioned in the locker room. He joyously tossed his visor skyward as the gallery roared its approval.

At the 17th, Fleck hit the perfect pitch over the moat that Hogan had hoped for, stopping his ball 4 feet short of the cup. He missed the birdie putt. Then he missed another short one at the final hole to finish with a bogey and a total of 283, falling into a six-way tie for third with Souchak, Boros, Finsterwald, Kroll, and Dutch Harrison. Nicklaus finished alone in second.

"I gave him that Open," Fleck later said.

At least a half-dozen others felt like Fleck did, although in the years to come the 1960 U.S. Open would be best remembered as the site of the Palmer-Nicklaus-Hogan showdown.

"Perhaps it had to end that way," Curt Sampson wrote about the battle between Arnold, Jack, and Ben. "The present and the future must be served, while the past just fades away."

Jack Fleck had also faded on that late afternoon at Cherry Hills. There was no giant killer. There was the coronation of a new king.

•   •   •

Less than two months later, Fleck once again faced the hard-charging Palmer at the Insurance City Open in Hartford, Connecticut. After rounds of 69, 65, and 65, he was the 54-hole leader, holding a 2-stroke advantage over Bill Collins, but Palmer caught Fleck and Collins by firing a 66 in the last round. Collins dropped out on the first hole of the sudden-death playoff as Palmer and Fleck made birdies. Ted Kroll, who stuck around for the playoff, told Fleck his second shot dipped into the hole and spun out. Fleck tapped in and watched as Palmer holed a 12-foot sidehill putt to stay alive. Fleck missed a 4½-foot birdie putt to win on the second playoff hole. Both players hit 4-irons to within 14 feet on the third playoff hole, a par 3. Fleck 3-putted, and golf's new king walked away with his seventh title of the season.

With the February win in Phoenix, 1960 had begun with great promise for Fleck. It ended after a disappointing string of near wins: two playoff losses at the hands of Bayer and Palmer and a pair of thirds at Houston and the U.S. Open. Fleck's game had crested that season, but his putting had let him down at the crucial moments when tournaments are won or lost. After three more seasons, at the age of forty-one, Jack Fleck would no longer be a regular player on the PGA Tour.

EPILOGUE

Putting is arguably the most baffling aspect of the game of golf. It consists of a golf ball, a putter, a closely mowed grass surface, and a hole that's 4¼ inches in diameter. The object, of course, is to get the ball into the hole in as few strokes as possible. Easy enough. Yet, as anyone who has played the game knows, the simplest-looking part of the game can also be the hardest to master. When putts go in, one after another, confidence soars like a bull market. Everything is right with the world. As odd as it may seem, players in a confident state expect to make *every* putt. Conversely, when putts don't go in, dark clouds form in the minds of golfers, and self-doubts can spread like cancer to other parts of the game.

Gardner Dickinson explained the "uncharitable view" of putting shared by many pros. "To us, putting was like the crazy aunt you keep in the closet and bring out only when you can't avoid it any longer. You just hoped she wouldn't do anything to embarrass you, but you were afraid that she might."

Some players putt well early in their careers and struggle later, as if they exhausted their quota of made putts. Some players never excel on the greens but are competent enough to make a living in the game. Rare is the tour player or major champion who putts consistently well throughout a long career.

Jack Fleck never built lasting confidence on the greens and, despite long hours of practice, never molded himself into what he considered to be a good putter. In later years, he struggled to explain why, as if it were a grand mystery. There was a certain logic to his perplexity, for had he known how to solve the most persistent flaw in his game he would have done it. Searching for an explanation, Fleck said he probably overpracticed. He thought he tried too hard to hole putts instead of freeing himself up to simply stroke the ball and accept the result. He concluded that his mental attitude during his years on the PGA Tour was not conducive to good putting. Fleck branded himself as a poor putter, a belief he never overcame, which inevitably led to more misses that further reinforced the belief.

Some of those closest to Fleck on tour did not agree with his self-assessment.

"He'll tell you today that he has never been a good putter," Walker Inman said in recent years, "but I played enough with him and saw him make putts. He doesn't like to admit that."

Dow Finsterwald, the man paired with Fleck for the final 36 holes at Cherry Hills, noted that players' memories often focus on negative outcomes. "There are a lot of guys like that," Finsterwald said. "They tend to remember the ones they missed and don't, for some reason, want to remember the ones they make."

Mike Krak echoed Inman. "There's no way you can win and be a poor putter. He was a good putter. He might not have thought so. Compared to other guys, I thought he was outstanding."

Bob Rosburg, on the other hand, seemed to agree with Fleck. "He always was a good ball striker," Rosburg said, stating a widely held opinion among Fleck's peers. "Never was a great putter. . . . That's always the way it has been."

Besides his having a long game that drew the admiration of his peers, there was another common view in the locker room: Fleck had a self-critical streak that was detrimental to his tournament golf career. Despite learning how to better manage his emotions and mindset, he continued to struggle with anger and frustrations about his play.

Finsterwald: "He sometimes could get a little down on himself, which made it tough to stay up there every week."

Krak: "He was his own worst enemy because he could not stand to play poorly."

Larry Tomasino: "He was very serious, really."

Rosburg: "I saw Jack play a lot. Jack could really play. I think if he had a better attitude, he would have won a lot more tournaments."

Fleck did win again, and Rosburg was the victim. After a strong defense of his Phoenix Open title—he missed a playoff with Arnold Palmer and Doug Sanders by a stroke—Fleck charged to his third PGA Tour victory at the Bakersfield Open late in the 1961 season. Besides his final-round 67 that tied Hogan at Olympic, he played perhaps his finest tournament round, a closing 65 that made up 6 shots on third-round leader Jon Gustin and tied Rosburg to force a sudden-death playoff. This time, he sank the winning putt, a 10-footer for birdie on the first playoff hole. His final PGA Tour victory earned him $3,500 and a one-year royalty on an active oil well near Bakersfield, which he never received.

.   .   .

Ben Hogan had not played in a U.S. Open since 1961. With the national championship set to return to the Olympic Club in June 1966, the USGA granted Hogan a special exemption to play in its tournament, the first such exemption in the tournament's long history. Working at a Chicago country club, Fleck sent in his entry form for the U.S. Open qualifier. No longer playing regular tournament golf, he wanted to return to the scene of his greatest triumph.

Fleck qualified and made the return trip to San Francisco, where he encountered Hogan in the locker room before the second round. Just like eleven years earlier, their lockers were only a few yards apart. Hogan set down his duffel and shoe bags, extended his hand, and moved in close.

"Sorry that you did not score well yesterday," he said.

"When you are a club pro and cleaning clubs and shining shoes, you are in no condition to play championship golf," Fleck replied in a joking manner.

Hogan held on to Fleck's hand for a long time, perhaps a minute. There was something else he wanted to say, but the words did not form on his lips. Still staring at Fleck, he finally said, "Good luck out there today."

The two men unclasped hands, and Hogan walked to his locker and sat down on the bench. Fleck would never know what Hogan wanted to say, although Fleck believed it had to do with their 1955 locker-room exchange when Fleck said, "You'll know what I mean."

Fleck missed the cut at Olympic. The fifty-three-year-old Hogan finished an impressive twelfth. In a colossal back-9 collapse, Arnold Palmer blew a 7-shot lead on Billy Casper and lost the following day in an 18-hole playoff.

At the Open at Baltusrol the following year, Fleck was practicing on the putting green when he heard someone behind him say, "Hi, Jack!" He turned around and saw Hogan standing nearby. The two players exchanged pleasantries for a short while. When Fleck resumed his putting practice, he noticed several players staring at him. He had no idea why until Ted Kroll explained their surprised looks.

"That's the only time Ben Hogan has addressed anyone's back," Kroll said.

The putting-green scene underscored the paradoxical nature of Fleck's relationship with Hogan. Fleck had denied the golf legend his fifth Open title, the bitterest of losses. The press wasn't for it, as Bolt and others said, and although Hogan came close again in 1956 and 1960, the record eluded him. Even Fleck sometimes had mixed feelings about his victory over his idol.

If writers and fans felt any ill will toward Fleck, there was always at least one person who treated him with special kindness, and that was Hogan himself. "Hogan must hate your guts" was a refrain he would hear from players through the years, but Fleck would tell them no, just the opposite. Known for being distant and brusque, Hogan seemed to go out of his way to be friendly and gracious toward Fleck. Fleck would never know why, but one old-time acquaintance offered an explanation: Hogan knew that Fleck grew up poor and learned the game on his own through hard work and determination—just like Hogan had.

At Baltusrol, Fleck missed the cut. Hogan finished in a tie for thirty-fourth. It was Ben Hogan's final appearance at the U.S. Open.

Four years later after a slip and near fall while hitting a tee shot in the first round of the Houston Open, Hogan said he'd had enough to playing partners Charles Coody and Dick Lotz and rode away in a golf cart. The following week he decided not to enter the hometown Colonial tournament he had won five times. The left knee was too unstable and the pain was too great. At fifty-eight, the tournament golf career of Ben Hogan was over.

•   •   •

Before leaving the tour, Fleck left Iowa, taking a series of club pro jobs in Michigan, Illinois, California, and Wisconsin. At his first post-Davenport job, which began in late 1956, he owned a major stake in a Detroit-area golf course that he and several business partners had purchased at a favorable price. Six months later the auto industry took a deep plunge, and the lingering effects on the region's economy forced Fleck and his partners to sell the course at a loss. He moved to the San Fernando Valley north of Los Angeles and soon after was offered the head pro job at El Caballero Country Club in nearby Tarzana.

Fleck's club pro jobs never lasted long. The boards of directors would often balk at his compensation and cut his salary despite successful golf operations and satisfied members. One club complained about his frequent tournament play, even though the number of tournaments was specified in his contract. The string of club jobs that ended in resignation was a disillusioning experience.

A much tougher personal blow came when his wife, Lynn, died in 1975. Grief stricken, he roamed the Midwest and West for months, visiting family and doing carpentry and cabinet work. "I just sort of hid out and wept a lot," he said.

Jack eventually returned to golf, and in 1979 he won the PGA Seniors' Championship in Orlando, Florida. As usual, his putting gave him problems on the last few holes. He was so disgusted that he threw his clubs into the trunk of his car and was ready to leave when a friend rushed out to the parking lot and said he was in a playoff. Moments later Julius Boros arrived in a golf cart.

"You will win," Boros told Fleck, putting his hand over his heart. "I feel it here."

Boros's prediction came true on the third playoff hole when Fleck sank an 18-foot putt.

Fleck played the Senior Tour (now known as the Champions Tour) for eleven years. Although he won about $700,000, there were no more individual wins. His three PGA Tour victories and one senior title had all come in playoffs. Fleck did win as a "super senior" (players over age sixty) and at the age of seventy-three teamed with Tommy Bolt to win the De-maret Division of the 1995 Liberty Mutual Legends of Golf. In 2002, the eighty-year-old Fleck shot a 77 at Firestone Country Club in the Senior PGA Championship, a remarkable age-beating score.

In 1991, ten years after leaving California to resettle in northwest Ar-kansas with his second wife, Mariann, Fleck began building a golf course near the small town of Magazine. He named the course Lil' Bit A Heaven after an exotic garden located at the Palmer College of Chiropractic near his hometown of Bettendorf. Heavy rains flooded Lil' Bit A Heaven a year after the course opened in 1992, causing extensive damage. A soil study was not promising. Hardpan lay just beneath the ground's surface. Not willing to carry debt and faced with a significant financial outlay if he was going to make repairs and save his golf course, Fleck sold his 1955 U.S. Open gold medal at a golf memorabilia auction for $35,200. He had no re-grets, later saying, "I don't need trophies to remind me of what I did."

•   •   •

Beginning in 1960 with American Machine and Foundry (AMF), owner-ship of the Ben Hogan Company changed hands through the following three decades. By the early 1990s, the company's current owner, Cosmo World, faced financial troubles and sold the Ben Hogan Company once again to AMF, then based in Richmond, Virginia. In June 1993, the Fort Worth factory closed and three hundred workers were laid off. All com-pany assets moved to Richmond. No longer involved in company decisions and likely suffering with Alzheimer's disease, Hogan was dejected and heartbroken.

"Don't ever grow old," he told one of his secretaries.

During that same period, Fleck phoned Hogan to chat about the old days. In particular, the Hogan clubs Fleck used at the Olympic Club. Beforehand he called Hogan's longtime protégé Gardner Dickinson, who told Fleck that Hogan was senile—his memory all but gone. In a friendly conversation with Hogan soon after, Fleck expressed his appreciation for the clubs and how they helped him at Olympic.

"Is that a good course?" Hogan asked.

On July 25, 1997, a few weeks shy of his eighty-fifth birthday, Ben Hogan died at All Saints Hospital in Fort Worth. Among the honorary pallbearers at University Christian Church were Sam Snead, Tommy Bolt, and Shelley Mayfield. Three hundred miles to the northeast in Fort Smith, Fleck chose not to attend the funeral. Jack the Giant Killer didn't want his attendance to detract in any way from the remembrance of his idol, one of golf's greatest champions.

•   •   •

In May of 2010, Fleck, eighty-eight, counted putts with a visitor in the men's lounge area at Hardscrabble Country Club, his home course in Fort Smith. The invisible scars from what had been written and said in the decades since the 1955 U.S. Open playoff were still there. Fleck agreed that his putter came alive during that third week in June, but he also maintained that his accurate shotmaking on Olympic's tight layout had every bit as much to do with his monumental upset of Hogan. Hogan also made putts in the playoff, he explained, including a few from long range. Hole by hole, shot by shot, the 18-hole playoff was recounted that spring day in northwest Arkansas. Many of the details—club selection, lies, pin locations, distances, spectators, and surroundings—were still seared into his memory. It was, after all, the apex of his career, a story he had recalled and told countless times in the five-plus decades since he was congratulated by Ben Hogan on the final green. For the record, the putt totals were 30 for Fleck and 31 or 32 for Hogan, depending on how the 17th hole was counted, on which Hogan 2-putted from the green's fringe. These may seem like trivial points, but not to a man who had heard words like "fluke" and "lucky" too often through the years, especially since few wins followed the U.S. Open upset.

"Was it a fluke?" Arnold Palmer wrote in his autobiography *A Golfer's Life*. "Some called it that. But nobody I know that's played this game on the level we played it that week at Olympic would dare call it that."

"If I would have won the Open," Inman said, "I would have hated to have everybody say, 'He was lucky. He was a flash in the pan.' That talk is for the birds, because if you win one Open I can tell you you're a pretty good player."

"I wasn't real shocked that he beat Hogan in the playoff," Krak said, "because . . . I knew he was a real competitor. So playing Hogan did not scare him."

Others have won a U.S. Open and not much else, including Sam Parks Jr., Orville Moody, Andy North (three wins, two of them Opens), and Lucas Glover. However, save the unheralded amateur Francis Ouimet in 1913, no dark horse had taken down anyone close to Hogan's stature in a head-to-head duel.

"All you got to do is look at the last two rounds Fleck played and they were unbelievable," Rosburg said. "I don't think he ever got credit. . . . Nobody ever said he played great."

"It took courage, great intelligence, and superb shotmaking for Jack Fleck to win the U.S. Open," added Palmer, "knowing that virtually everybody watching was rooting against him."

•　　•　　•

Throughout his eighties, Jack Fleck still played golf on a regular basis, including Great Grand Champions events on the Champions Tour. Many of his peers agreed that he was one of the best among the fifteen or so surviving players, a group that included Gene Littler, Billy Casper, Dow Finsterwald, Doug Ford, Doug Sanders, Bob Goalby, Don January, and Fred Hawkins. After Mariann died from complications following a stroke in 2000, a friend introduced Jack to Carmen, who became his third wife in 2001. The couple moved into a townhome on Fort Smith's south end. A creek visited by Canadian geese can be seen from their rear patio. Sitting at his dining room table two days after the playoff discussion at Hardscrabble, Fleck said he felt proud to be a U.S. Open champion but still wondered if others felt like he had accomplished something.

Nearby were three of the clubs that beat Ben Hogan: the Hogan 3-wood, a 4-iron from the set of Hogan Precision irons, and the Tommy Armour driver that struck so many long and accurate drives at Olympic in '55. That morning Fleck had climbed into his attic to retrieve the three clubs from the famed set to show a visitor. Carefully packed and wrapped in paper, they had not been out of the box in a long time. The wooden and iron heads were small, common during that earlier golf era. All three had burgundy leather grips that still felt slightly tacky to the touch. Considering their age, the clubs were in very good condition—sort of like Jack Fleck—relics of a long-ago season when an unknown club pro wrote a letter to a fledgling Fort Worth golf company.

ACKNOWLEDGMENTS

This book was made possible because of the encouragement and help of many people. It started with George McDowell, a Ben Hogan aficionado who pointed me in the direction of Jack Fleck. Soon after, I picked up the phone and began a surprising journey that culminated in this book.

My special thanks to Jack Fleck, who from our first phone call allowed me unique access to his past and present life. Thanks also to Jack's gracious and lovely wife, Carmen. My relationship with Fleck widened my golf world in numerable ways. At several Champions Tour events where Fleck and other old-time champions appeared, I caddied, entered locker rooms, ate in player dining rooms, and hung out with golf legends who generously shared their remembrances of the 1955 U.S. Open and early days on the PGA Tour.

In addition to Fleck, former tour and club professionals who contributed to this book include Errie Ball, Tommy Bolt, Dow Finsterwald, Doug Ford, Fred Hawkins, Walker Inman Jr., Mike Krak, Gene Littler, Shelley

Mayfield, Arnold Palmer, Bob Rosburg, and Larry Tomasino. Bolt, Mayfield, and Rosburg passed away after granting interviews, another reminder of how fortunate I was to converse with all these interesting and colorful men.

Other pros whose company I enjoyed as a result of writing this book include Al Besselink, Miller Barber, Gay Brewer, Billy Casper, Lee Elder, Jim Ferree, Bob Goalby, Tommy Jacobs, Don January, Howie Johnson, Billy Maxwell, Orville Moody, Johnny Pott, Jimmy Powell, Doug Sanders, Charlie Sifford, and Bob Toski.

The United States Golf Association in Far Hills, New Jersey, was invaluable in my research efforts. Rand Jerris and the entire museum and archives staff are extremely courteous and helpful folks who, indeed, work "for the good of the game." In addition to Rand, special thanks to Patty Moran, Nancy Stulack, and Shannon Doody.

I'm extremely grateful to the Olympic Club, to which I paid a visit in June 2008. In particular, I want to thank club historian Bill Callan, who provided numerous insights, details, and tournament-related materials that greatly aided my effort to reconstruct the 1955 U.S. Open. Among them was Callan's eyewitness account of events. In June 1955, Callan was a thirteen-year-old junior member at Olympic and served as a scorecard runner during the tournament. He was among the thousands in the walking gallery that followed the dramatic 18-hole playoff. Callan reviewed major portions of the manuscript in detail, correcting my mistakes and the reporting errors that have been repeated through the years. He provided perspective and nuances that enhanced my understanding and added depth to the narrative.

Thank you to Jack Giusto Jr., who shared his grandfather's and father's recollections of Jack Fleck's June 1955 visit to their family motel in Daly City.

Thank you to Ben Hogan's biographers, notably Curt Sampson and

James Dodson, whose thorough profiles of the great champion formed a necessary foundation for this story.

Many thanks to the authors and journalists who encouraged me and wrote blurbs for this book long before it was completed, which helped attract a major publisher. They include John Coyne, Bob Harig, Ian O'Connor, Don Van Natta Jr., and Bob Smiley.

I also extend my appreciation to Aly Colón—writing coach, editor, journalism ethics expert, and friend—who reviewed an early manuscript and wisely guided me through a range of reporting and writing issues. Thanks also to Tom Coyne and Ralph Sagebiel, my father, both of whom graciously read the story and provided valuable feedback and suggestions.

I'm deeply indebted to my literary agent, Rick Broadhead, who fell in love with the story and expertly guided me through a rewrite of the proposal that enabled this book to find a publishing home. I'm also grateful to my initial agent, John Silbersack, who saw the project's potential and helped me along the road to publication.

Special thanks to Rob Kirkpatrick, my editor at St. Martin's Press, who took a chance on me and a golf story from the mid-twentieth century. Rob is a supportive and gracious editor who, like a top golfer, had just the right touch with bringing this story to publication. Many thanks as well to editorial assistant Nicole Sohl and the entire team at St. Martin's Press.

Thank you to the readers and supporters of Armchair Golf Blog, the blog I started in 2005 that led to the book you're reading.

Finally, abundant thanks and love to my wife, Sally, and daughters, Beth and Caroline, who supported me throughout the long process and now know far too much about professional golf in the 1950s.

AUTHOR'S NOTE

A lifelong golfer and golf fan, I first came to this story many years ago. I had no idea that I would later have the privilege to meet Jack Fleck and write a book about one of sports' greatest upsets. As I rediscovered this epic upset, two questions drove me.

Who was Jack Fleck?

How did an unheralded club pro beat the legendary Ben Hogan head-to-head in golf's biggest tournament?

Fleck threw his full support behind the project, with one stipulation. He asked that I take great care to write a factual account about him—especially his play during the 1955 U.S. Open, which he felt had been distorted through the years.

In reconstructing the '55 tournament, I had a wealth of material at my disposal: the official program, course descriptions and maps, pairings sheets, hole-by-hole scores, extensive newspaper and magazine coverage, player interviews, the sage input of the Olympic Club historian, and more.

This book's shot-by-shot account of the playoff was based, in part, on a shot-by-shot wire-service recap of the playoff that appeared in the nation's newspapers on June 20, 1955. It was also based on Fleck's memory, which I found to be reliable. I was able to independently substantiate his recollections on many occasions.

In May 2010 at Hardscrabble Country Club in Fort Smith, Arkansas, Fleck recounted the playoff hole by hole, shot by shot. In some cases, he disagreed with the wire-service account, but usually not in a major way. Mostly, the differences had to do with the length of putts. In this book's account, I typically deferred to Fleck, who stood on each of those 18 greens with Hogan. Indeed, Fleck had a better vantage point than other eyewitnesses.

Whether writing about the playoff or other tournament action, as well as in other aspects of the narrative, I have attempted to put forth the most accurate account possible based on all the material available to me.

With a few minor exceptions, I have refrained from fictionalizing any part of the story. Hogan was a chain-smoker, so I included occasional references to his puffing during the 1955 U.S. Open playoff. Based on my knowledge of tournament golf and the movements and mannerisms of tour pros, including such things as Hogan's golf swing and preshot routine, I added small touches to enliven the tournament narrative.

As I immersed myself in the research and writing of this book, an inevitable question arose: Where does Fleck's upset of Hogan rank in the history of golf and sports?

Early on I discovered Jack Fleck made nearly everyone's list. Compiling its list of ten greatest sports upsets, the Page 2 staff at ESPN.com put Fleck's playoff victory over Hogan at number seven, noting it was "still the most shocking upset in golf history."

Was it, as ESPN.com opined, golf's greatest upset? My answer informed the subtitle of this book.

I know a strong argument could be made for Francis Ouimet, the twenty-year-old amateur who defeated the legendary Harry Vardon and Vardon's fellow pro great Ted Ray in an 18-hole playoff at the 1913 U.S. Open. In my mind, Ouimet's and Fleck's upsets eclipsed all others in the history of golf. Y. E. Yang's upset of Tiger Woods at the 2009 PGA Championship was certainly remarkable, but Yang already had multiple pro wins, including titles against world-class fields. Before he shocked Hogan, Fleck had never finished higher than fourth in a PGA Tour event.

Knowing these are subjective debates, I asked a few respected golf authorities to weigh in.

Hogan biographer Curt Sampson put Fleck at the top of his golf upset list. "Golf was such a small game in Ouimet's time," he wrote, "and his home course and home-crowd advantages were considerable. Fleck had no one pulling for him; Hogan had nearly everyone on his side."

Golf World senior editor Bill Fields, who penned an excellent 1995 profile on Jack Fleck titled "A Fleck of History," gave Ouimet a slight edge. Fields cited the U.S. Open upsets of Sam Parks Jr. in 1935 and Orville Moody in 1969 but noted that they didn't have to outduel a golf icon in order to win. Fields summed up: "Not only because of who Fleck beat but how well he played, it puts his feat just behind Francis Ouimet in the pantheon of golf upsets."

John Derr, a veteran sports journalist who knew Ben Hogan as a friend, has a wide historical perspective. The ninety-three-year-old Derr covered sixty-two Masters, including sixteen as an announcer for CBS-TV. Working for CBS Radio in 1953, he walked every step with Hogan at Carnoustie when the golf legend won the British Open on his first and only try. Derr also put Ouimet's upset first, followed by Fleck and amateur Johnny Goodman, the surprise winner at the 1933 U.S. Open.

Another opinion has arrived in my mailbox as I write this in January 2011. Jack Fleck sent me a recent article about his famous victory written by Doug Fernandes of the *Sarasota Herald-Tribune.* The title: GREATEST UPSET IN THE HISTORY OF GOLF. Another vote for Fleck.

So, with a nod to Ouimet, who was a lifelong amateur, I included the word "pro" in the subtitle of this book. The Ouimet and Fleck upsets stand alone in golf history. When it comes to pro against pro, Jack Fleck's upset win over Ben Hogan rises above them all.

BIBLIOGRAPHY

BOOKS

Barkow, Al. *The History of the PGA Tour.* New York: Doubleday, 1989.

Demaret, Jimmy. *My Partner, Ben Hogan.* New York: McGraw-Hill, 1954.

Dickinson, Gardner. *Let 'Er Rip!* Atlanta: Longstreet Press, 1994.

Dodson, James. *Ben Hogan: An American Life.* New York: Broadway Books, 2004.

Fleck, Jack. *The Jack Fleck Story.* Fort Smith, AR: JC Publishing, 2002.

Frost, Mark. *The Greatest Game Ever Played: Harry Vardon, Francis Ouimet, and the Birth of Modern Golf.* New York: Hyperion, 2002.

————. *The Match: The Day the Game of Golf Changed Forever.* New York: Hyperion, 2007.

Gregston, Gene. *Hogan: The Man Who Played for Glory.* Englewood Cliffs, NJ: Prentice-Hall, 1978.

Halberstam, David. *The Fifties.* New York: Fawcett Columbine, 1993.

Hogan, Ben. *Power Golf.* New York: Pocket Books, 1953.

O'Connor, Ian. *Arnie & Jack: Palmer, Nicklaus, and Golf's Greatest Rivalry.* New York: Houghton Mifflin, 2008.

Palmer, Arnold. *A Golfer's Life.* New York: Ballantine Books, 1999.

Sampson, Curt. *The Eternal Summer: Palmer, Nicklaus, and Hogan in 1960, Golf's Golden Year.* New York: Villard, 1992.

————. *Hogan.* New York: Broadway Books, 2001.

Sommers, Robert. *The U.S. Open: Golf's Ultimate Challenge.* New York: Atheneum, 1987.

Wind, Herbert Warren. *The Story of American Golf.* New York: Farrar, Strauss, 1948.

MAGAZINES AND NEWSLETTERS

Arkansas Business
Golf
Golf Digest
Golfer
Golfing
Golf Journal
Golf Monthly
Golf World
Look

Newsweek

New Yorker

Olympian

Professional Golfer

Sports Illustrated

Time

United States Golf Association Journal and Turf Management

NEWSPAPERS

Augusta Chronicle

Chicago Tribune

Des Moines Register

Hartford Courant

New York Times

San Francisco Chronicle

Washington Post and Herald

PROGRAMS

Official Program: USGA 55th Open Championship

The 60th Open Championship of the United States Golf Association

66th USGA Open Championship Official Souvenir Program

VIDEO

Jack Fleck, *Jack Fleck: Playoff of the Century,* undated

USGA, U.S. Open highlight films, 1955, 1960

WEB SITES

ASAPSports.com

Augusta.com

BasketballHistorian.com

Chronicle.Augusta.com

ESPN.com

Golf.About.com

GolfClubAtlas.com

IndianRiverMag.com

IPGA.com

JewishSF.com

LincolnshireCountryClub.com

PGA.com

PGATour.com

PrivateClubs.com

SportsIllustrated.cnn.com

SignOnSanDiego.com

SPTimes.com

USGA.org

Wikipedia.org

WorldGolfHallOfFame.org

INDEX